5

50 *Hikes*

In Washington

Walks, Hikes & Backpacks
in the Evergreen State

KAI HUSCHKE

The Countryman Press
Woodstock, Vermont

AN INVITATION TO THE READER

Over time, trails can be rerouted and signs and landmarks altered. If you find that changes have occurred on the routes described in this book, please let us know so that corrections may be made in future editions. The author and publisher also welcome other comments and suggestions. Address all correspondence to:

Editor, 50 Hikes™ Series
The Countryman Press
P.O. Box 748
Woodstock, VT 05091

LIBRARY OF CONGRESS CATALOGING-IN-PUBLICATION DATA
Data has been applied for.

Book design by Glenn Suokko
Composition by Linda Carey
Cover photograph by James Randklev–A field of wildflowers in Paradise Meadow, Mt. Rainier National Park
Interior photography and maps by the author, maps © The Countryman Press

© 2005 by Kai Huschke

First Edition

The Countryman Press
P.O. Box 748
Woodstock, Vermont 05091
www.countrymanpress.com

Distributed by W. W. Norton & Company, Inc.
500 Fifth Avenue
New York, NY 10110

Printed in the United States of America
10 9 8 7 6 5 4 3 2 1

DEDICATION

To Lhotse

The spirit of your survival exists, not only as a collection of memories, but as a healing energy. This energy is helping those who helped you, as well as others you have never met, to better survive their own degrees of darkness and light. I am sorry that I was the one who led you astray. Thank you for displaying, as you often have, your wild strength.

50 Hikes in Washington at a Glance

HIKE	AREA
1. Shi Shi Beach to Point of the Arches	Olympic National Park
2. Cape Alava to Sand Point Loop	Olympic National Park
3. Hoh River to Hoh Lake	Olympic National Park
4. Klahhane Ridge Loop	Olympic National Park
5. Dungeness Spit	Dungeness Wildlife Refuge
6. Royal Lake/Royal Basin	Olympic National Park
7. Marmot Pass	Buckhorn Wilderness
8. Mount Ellinor	Mount Skokomish Wilderness
9. Mount Constitution	Moran State Park
10. Heather Park/Galena Chain Lakes Loop	Mount Baker Wilderness
11. Mazama Park and Park Butte Lookout	Mount Baker National Recreation Area
12. Thornton Lakes	North Cascades National Park
13. Diablo Lake	North Cascades National Park
14. Cascade Pass	North Cascades National Park
15. Rainy Pass to Maple Pass Loop	Okanogan National Forest
16. Cutthroat Pass	Liberty Bell Roadless Area
17. Horseshoe Basin to Windy Peak Loop	Pasayten Wilderness
18. Green Mountain	Glacier Peak Wilderness
19. Boulder River	Boulder River Wilderness
20. Pilot Ridge to Blue Lakes	Glacier Peak Wilderness
21. Greider Lakes	Greider Ridge Natural Resources Conservation Area
22. Lake Serene	Mount Baker–Snoqualmie National Forest
23. Necklace Valley	Alpine Lakes Wilderness
24. Alpine Lookout via Merritt Lake	Nason Ridge
25. Estes Butte	Entiat Mountains

Type   D=Day   O=Overnight (1 night)   M=Multiday (2 or more nights)
Difficulty   E=Easy   M= Moderate   S=Strenuous

TYPE	DISTANCE (miles)	RATING	DOGS	NOTES
D	8.8	E	No	Amazing wild coastline
D	9.1	E/M	No	Petroglyphs & sea stacks
O/M	29.8	E/M	No	Rain forest & subalpine zones
D	12.4	M/S	No	Unique geology; great vistas
D	9.8	M	No	Lighthouse; wildlife
D/O	12	M	No	Fantastic subalpine setting
D/O	10.6	M	Yes	Wildflowers; vistas
D	3.4	S	Yes	Dynamic short hike
D	8.6	M+	Yes	Unique tower; 360-degree views
D	7.5	M	Yes	Wildflowers; grand mountains
D/O	10.4	M+	Yes	Lookout; subalpine setting; vistas
D/O	10.6	S	No	Subalpine cirque lakes
D	7.4	E/M	No	Rain forest; Ross Lake Dam
D/O	7.4	M	No	Glaciers & mountain vistas
D	6.8	M	Yes	Mountains galore; two lakes
D	10	M	Yes	Stretch of the PCT; great views
O/M	16.8	M/S	Yes	Boreal zone in unique highlands
D	7	M	Yes	Brilliant wildflowers; Glacier Peak view
D	5	E	Yes	Two cascades; lowland river forest
O	20.6	M+	Yes	Open vistas; cirque lakes
D/O	4.8	M/S	Yes	Two subalpine lakes
D	7.6	S	Yes	Waterfall; quaint lake; Mt. Index
O/M	16	S	Yes	Gentle subalpine valley full of lakes
D/O	10	M+	Yes	Lake; lookout; mountain goats
D	9.4	M/S	Yes	Great mountain vistas

50 Hikes in Washington at a Glance

HIKE	AREA
26. The Enchantments	Alpine Lakes Wilderness
27. Bandera Mountain	Mount Baker–Snoqualmie National Forest
28. Waptus Lake to Spade Lake	Alpine Lakes Wilderness
29. Bean Creek Basin	Wenatchee National Forest
30. Spray Park	Mount Rainier National Park
31. Palisades Lake	Mount Rainier National Park
32. Summer Land Meadows	Mount Rainier National Park
33. Pinnacle Peak	Mount Rainier National Park
34. Van Trump Park	Mount Rainier National Park
35. Beacon Rock	Beacon Rock State Park
36. McCoy Peak	Dark Divide Roadless Area
37. Mount Margaret Backcountry Loop	Mount St. Helens NVM
38. Lava Canyon	Mount St. Helens NVM
39. Lily Basin to Heart Lake	Goat Rocks Wilderness
40. Bird Creek Meadows Loop	Mount Adams Yakama Reservation
41. Mount Aix	William O. Douglas Wilderness
42. Eagle Lakes	Sawtooth Roadless Area
43. Columbia Mountain	Colville National Forest
44. Crowell Ridge	Salmo-Priest Wilderness
45. Little Spokane River	Little Spokane River Natural Area
46. Trees of Stone Trail	Gingko Petrified Forest State Park
47. Frog Lake/Marsh Loop	Columbia National Wildlife Refuge
48. Juniper Dunes	Juniper Dunes Wilderness
49. Kamiak Butte Loop	Kamiak Butte County Park
50. Oregon Butte	Wenaha-Tucannon Wilderness

Type   D=Day   O=Overnight (1 night)   M=Multiday (2 or more nights)
Difficulty E=Easy   M= Moderate   S=Strenuous

TYPE	DISTANCE (miles)	RATING	DOGS	NOTES
M	17	S	No	Premier subalpine/alpine hike
D	7	S	Yes	Lake; vista of Mount Rainier
M	17.4; 26	M/S	Yes	Beautiful lakes and mountains
D/O	5	M	Yes	Short hike into a wildflower basin
D/O	8.6	M	No	Wildflower meadows; Mount Rainier
D/O	6.6	D/M	No	Lakes; wildflowers; unique mountains
D/O	8.2	M	No	Fantastic meadows; glaciers; vistas
D	3	M+	No	Views of Mount Rainier; scrambling
D	5.2	S	No	Multiple waterfalls & grand wildflowers
D	2	M	Yes	Old volcano; Columbia River views
D/O	8	S	Yes	Wildflower ridges & mountain vistas
O/M	15	M/S	No	Views of St. Helens; unique environment
D	3	O/S	Yes	Unique geology; multiple waterfalls
O	11.4	M	Yes	Wildflower basins; lakes; vistas
D	5	E/M	Yes	Brilliant wildflowers; Mount Adams
D/O	11	S	Yes	Great vistas; wonderful alpine setting
O	14.6	M	Yes	Lakes; high-mountain pass
D	5.6	M	Yes	Old lookout; wild berry bushes
D/O	15.8	M	Yes	Unique open ridge hike; lake
D	3.4	E	No	Blue heron habitat; multiple life zones
D	1	E	Yes	Rare and unique petrified forest
D	3.8	E	Yes	Lakes; basalt coulees; wildlife
D	E+	E/M	Yes	Sand dunes; juniper trees; wildlife
D	3.3	M	Yes	National natural landmark; great vistas
D	5.6	M	Yes	Lookout; unique setting

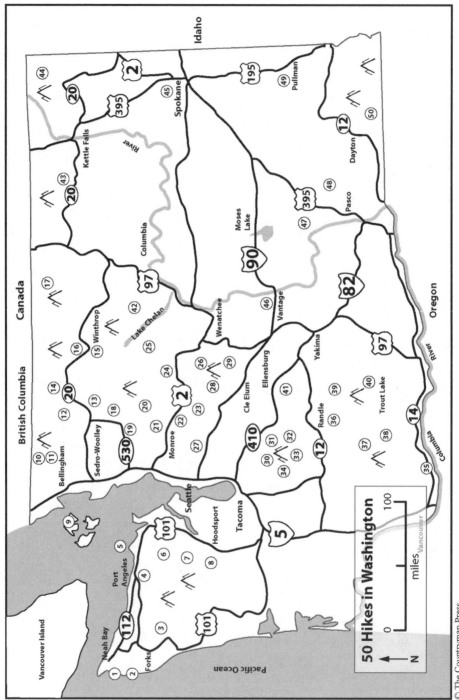

50 Hikes in Washington

N

0   miles   100

CONTENTS

Acknowledgments

Thank you to Kermit Hummel for trusting me with this project. The hard work and guidance of Jess Abston, Jennifer Thompson, Darren Brown, and Clare Innes of the Countryman Press helped bring shape to this book. A big thank you to Atlas, Lhotse, Laura Holyoke, Steve Finch, Kathy Munoz, Klaus Huschke, Lars Huschke, and Eric Christensen for joining me in exploring many of the fantastic places described here.

Thank you to the lady from Whidbey Island for strolling with me along Shi Shi Beach; to the ranger at Ozette for sharing knowledge of the local flora; to John at the Alpine Lookout for helping me identify numerous mountains in the Glacier Peak Wilderness visible from the man-made perch; to Sara for warm, easy conversation on a cool, rainy day near Cutthroat Pass; and to everyone else I came in contact with while assembling this book. Thank you to all my family and friends, especially Laura, my blood source. A special thanks to Joe and Rick from Olympia; the two of you have an incredible depth of compassion not easily revealed or so freely offered in today's society.

Introduction

What we know as Washington, and the fantastically varied regions and destinations discussed here, does not exist. By this I only mean to say that when we talk of the Olympic Peninsula or Palouse Country we mustn't forget that these places are artificially bounded in geographies that do remarkably well naturally bounding themselves.

Washington only became a state—a nearly perfect rectangle—in 1889. Before statehood, all of this acreage was called the Washington Territory, which in its largest stage also included present-day Idaho and parts of Montana and Wyoming. However, the Washington Territory was merely a smaller, segmented piece of a greater expanse known as the Oregon Territory, stretching from northern California through Oregon, Washington, Idaho, and the vast majority of British Columbia. A consortium of countries that included Russia, Spain, England, and the United States took out the political carving knife and, starting in the early 1800s, portioned up these wildlands into what we identify today as several U.S. states and an individual Canadian province.

Despite the so-called discovery of America and centuries of European sailing powers darting along the Pacific coastline in search of the fabled Northwest Passage in waterways like the Columbia River and Strait of Juan de Fuca, the state we know as Washington was already occupied by ancient people who had crossed the former Bering land bridge between present-day Alaska and Siberia some 12,000 years ago, eventually reaching coastal and interior areas.

These tribes of the Pacific Northwest had names for the mountains, rivers, and creatures, many of which were viewed as gods or instruments for sophisticated stories or myths of the geology and geography of the land. But there were no artificial boundaries in the sense of ownership we know today, just natural ones like the Columbia River, the Cascades, the Olympics, the coastline, the Channeled Scablands, the Selkirk Mountains, the Snake River, the rain forest, the ponderosa pine zone, the Palouse prairie, and the subalpine zone. However, even this naturalistic view is still much too small, too constricting.

The Cascade Mountains are actually just a link in the Cordilleran chain of mountain ranges running from Canada to the tip of South America. The Columbia Plateau is only a portion of the Greater Columbia Basin that spreads across an area the size of France (213,000 square miles). The Douglas fir forests of Washington don't just end when you step across the Cascade Divide from west to east; these trees run over through Montana and spread south to Oregon and California and north into southern British Columbia.

This book puts its own artificial boundaries over the state in an attempt to collect samples of the life zones and diametrically opposed geographies that constitute its amazing personality. The Olympic Peninsula and surrounding landmasses of the

The Shi Shi Beach on Washington's coast

Puget Sound represent perhaps the finest single example of the range of what there is to discover while hiking or backpacking.

Lower portions of the Hoh and Quinault Rivers host fantastical rain-forest worlds, ideal for ogres and goblins, with massive trees, hanging moss, and man-sized ferns. And the Olympic coastal wilderness contains Sitka spruce forests, shorelines dotted with rock haystacks, and a galaxy of tide pools. Subalpine meadows are ablaze with a rainbow of colors in places like Sol Duc Park and Mount Ellinor. Glaciers capping Mount Olympus remind us of our past and can predict our future (global warming). And in contrast to the rain- and snow-drenched portions of the peninsula, the San Juans contain islands that are classified as deserts.

Other wild places like the Ginkgo Petrified Forest remind us of a geographic and geologic past. Kamiak Butte, a quartzite is-

land in a sea of basalt, holds onto species like mountain kittentail, having survived the icy prison of the last ice age and more recently witnessing the disappearance of the surrounding prairie grassland, which has been consumed by farms of wheat, bluegrass, canola, and lentils.

To know that Horseshoe Basin in the Pasayten Wilderness holds remnants of a geographic past in a boreal zone normally found in the farther reaches of Canada, that the rocks of the Point of the Arches are older than the core of the Olympic Mountains, or that 10,000 feet of basalt once covered the area near where you'll walk when you visit the Columbia National Wildlife Refuge will without doubt enrich your experiences when you choose to partake in Washington's outdoor wonderland.

However, you don't need complete explanations to know what it's like to see the morning sun glide into the alpine parkland

Mount St. Helens

and glacial moraine beneath the Park Butte Lookout, to watch a herd of elk graze in the Holmstedt Lake basin of the Mount Margaret Backcountry, to count the life-forms in a tide pool near Cape Alava, or to be included in the boundless circle that is nature.

Think small and big at the same time when you're exploring the hiking trails suggested here. Think beyond the roads, parks, wilderness areas, and wildlife refuges. Think about the pure freedom of the geography, plants, and animals that define these various places and you will begin to see the vastness of this multi-lensed world.

Think of the yellow wallflower ever so carefully popping yet another bloom, the spots fading on a whitetail fawn, or the banana slug slipping out from a fern's shadow on its slimy course to break down plant matter on the forest floor. Think of the

glaciers pulling and pushing across the slopes of Mount Rainier, pulverizing rock into dust beneath their icy weight. Think about the runs of rivers and mountain ridges. Think about what you can see, hear, smell, touch, and taste. Think of what used to be and of the natural events that occurred over millions of years or only a few seconds and had a hand in making the things you experience today.

Let the natural surroundings reveal their secrets to you as you roam the trails discussed here and points beyond.

HAZARDS

The majority of hikes described here take you into a wilderness setting. You arrive in a place removed from the ease and luxury of modern-day conveniences and amenities of all kinds. Once you're edging along the Whittier Ridge in the Mount St. Helens Backcountry or have arrived at the

Thornton Lakes in the North Cascades National Park Complex, your ability to leave easily and/or quickly will be hampered by uncultivated terrain. Even though the hazards you may confront in these remote and semiremote places are for the most part relatively harmless or rare, you do need to be prepared for the worst-case scenario.

The key hazards can be thought of in three categories: weather, geography, and animals.

WEATHER

The lowest elevation included in these hiking destinations is sea level; the highest point is the summit of Windy Peak in the Pasayten Wilderness. The difference is over 8,000 feet, and conditions between these two points can vary considerably—separated by two significant mountain ranges, over 200 miles of terrain, six life zones, and 0.5 degree in latitude.

Temperatures vary across the state, with the area west of the Cascade Mountains typically 10 to 15 degrees cooler than the east side from May to October, when hiking conditions are best. The Okanogan, Columbia Basin, and southeast Washington are usually the warmest regions, with July and August temperatures in the 90s or over 100 degrees. Elevation brings cooler temperatures. Keep protected from the sun, especially at higher elevations where there is less UV protection, and remember to stay hydrated.

For the most part, clouds that threaten precipitation, as well as winds, move east from the Pacific and north to south, normally slipping down from the colder zones of Canada. Thunderstorms, and even snow, are possible during the summer months, especially in the mountains. Remember to stay below tree line during a thunderstorm (no need to be a human lightning rod). Heavy rains can cause serious mud- and landslides, as happened recently in the Olympics and across the North Cascades. Be aware that roads, trails, and even bridges can wash out as a result. Creeks and rivers may be difficult or impossible to ford during and after a heavy downpour.

Carry proper rain gear to keep yourself dry, which will ultimately keep you warmer. The National Oceanic and Atmospheric Administration (NOAA) web site (www .noaa.gov) provides accurate weather forecasts for every area in the state. Local ranger stations and information centers are also key sources for obtaining current weather forecasts.

GEOGRAPHY

Most of the hikes in this book follow established trails that have decent surfaces and are well maintained. If you do go off-trail, perhaps on a talus slope along the Sawtooth Ridge or along a stream bank in the Central Cascades, your exposure to hazards increases dramatically. Specific advice pertaining to the plant world would be to avoid touching prickly currant, devil's club, thistle, nettles, or poison ivy. Also, don't eat anything that you're unable to identify with absolute certainty, especially mushrooms.

On the trail the worst you can expect to deal with are boulders, loose rocks, tree roots, downed trees, heavy brush, mud, snow, or washouts. Trails are particularly muddy in the early season, and as attractive as it may seem to detour around the worst areas, this choice harms the environment you came to enjoy. Instead, grit your teeth and head straight down the middle of the trail. Wet socks and feet are much easier to remedy than damaged plant life, some of which, like heather, can take decades to recover.

Perhaps the most dangerous geographical hazard is challenging backcountry terrain. These hikes are all enjoyed via trail systems, but you shouldn't trust the trail alone in any outdoor setting. A map and compass are invaluable allies in keeping you grounded in relation to your environment. Always carry both, and refer to the map periodically, especially at obvious landmarks like creek crossings, trail junctions, lakes, and passes.

ANIMALS

Our separation from wild animals in everyday life has come to mean that many of us have a fear of wilderness inhabitants like rattlesnakes, bears, and cougars. But the reality is that the chance of a violent confrontation with an animal is extremely remote. Watching a black bear feeding in a high meadow is a fantastic experience. If you feel the distance between you and the bear isn't far enough, make some noise to warn it of your presence. A bear will acknowledge you by either moving away or keeping a watchful eye while it continues to feed. If you want to know more about encounters with large wild animals, read *Don't Get Eaten: The Dangers of Animals That Charge or Attack,* by David Smith.

There is at least one situation, however, in which animal encounters are quite likely. The food you bring into the backcountry is a powerful magnet for animals. Along the coast, raccoons and black bears are the most probable visitors. Securing food in trees and/or in bear-proof canisters is a must. In some areas of the mountains, black and grizzly bears are also a concern. But so too are marmots, squirrels, mice, birds, martens, and other smaller, physically less threatening creatures. Here

again, proper preparation and storage of food is key. Keep your edibles well off the ground and in some kind of container not easily penetrable. Cook food away from tents and try not to leave any food unattended inside your tent.

KEYS TO BEING PREPARED

The two most emphasized and hopefully adhered-to credos of the outdoors are the Ten Essentials and Leave No Trace.

TEN ESSENTIALS

1. Maps and trail information
2. Compass
3. Flashlight/headlamp
4. Extra food
5. Extra clothing
6. Sunglasses
7. First-aid kit
8. Knife/multitool
9. Matches/lighter
10. Fire starter

LEAVE NO TRACE

Leave No Trace is the philosophy of minimal impact and the removal of any obvious signs of human presence. Stay on trails, use existing campsites, camp 200 feet from water sources, pack out solid human waste or utilize cat holes, don't remove branches or cut down trees for firewood, don't disturb plants and wildlife, and pack out everything you pack in. The idea is a simple one: leave the wilderness just as you found it or better. More detailed information is available at www.LNT.org.

PLANNING

It's always a good idea to find out the specifics of the area you plan to visit: weather, road access, and trail conditions. Another important element of backcountry travel is to leave your plans with someone

A wildflower meadow

back home in case of an emergency. Provide them with dates, routes, and contact numbers, along with a time frame for notifying the proper agencies if you don't return. Many of the trailheads have sign-in stations, but these usually require minimal contact information and their purpose is more to monitor trail use than for emergencies. Remember, it's better to be safe than sorry.

RULES AND REGULATIONS

The trails discussed here run through national parks, wilderness areas, state parks, county parks, national wildlife refuges, natural areas, and national forests. Each of these areas has its own rules and regulations. For instance, wilderness areas have maximum group sizes of 12, allow a maximum of 14 days at any one campsite, and have a rule against mechanized travel. Trails on U. S. Forest Service land require

a Northwest Forest Service Pass. This parking pass can be purchased from any ranger station, and the majority of that money goes directly to helping with local trail maintenance and facilities upkeep. Annual passes cost $30 and day passes run $5. For more information, visit www.fs.fed .us/r6/feedemo.

National parks have restrictions on horse use, and dogs are generally prohibited on all trails.

All of the national parks, the Mount Margaret Backcountry (Mount St. Helens), and the Enchantments region in the Alpine Lakes Wilderness require permits for camping. You can reserve these permits in the national parks and in the Mount Margaret Backcountry or you can pick them up in person.

To access the Enchantments, Snow Lakes, Colchuck Lake, or Stuart Lake you must submit your permit information by the end of February (after the 21st) to make it into a lottery drawing for access from June 15 to October 15. Walk-up permits are handed out daily but the number of available slots you will be competing for is quite small (25 percent of the total). If you don't try to reserve a permit in February, your best chance of obtaining a walk-up permit is on a weekday from mid-September to mid-October. (For more information on the permit process call the Leavenworth Ranger District at 509-548-6977.)

The wildlife refuges, national forests, and some of the wilderness areas are open to hunting in season. State parks and national parks don't allow hunting or the possession of firearms. Most places have a ban—permanent or temporary—on open campfires at elevations over 3,500 feet—or lower, depending on the level of fire danger.

Always verify the current rules and regulations with local management offices before hitting the trail.

EQUIPMENT

If the clothing feels good, wear it. But try to select items made with synthetic material instead of natural fibers. These materials are more comfortable, dry quickly, usually have better breathability, and retain heat better than wool or cotton. Straight wool isn't bad, but leave your jeans, cotton T-shirts, and tube socks at home. Cotton doesn't dry quickly, can cause hot spots and rashes when it becomes wet with perspiration, and robs you of body heat.

Good hiking socks are well worth the money. Most are made completely of synthetic material or a blend of synthetics and wool. Good socks pad your feet in the proper places, dry fast, and hold their shape, a good characteristic when you're on a long trip.

In rugged terrain, in wet or snowy conditions, or when carrying a backpack on a longer hike, wearing hiking boots provides sound stability and reduces leg fatigue. However, low-cut hiking shoes, trail-running shoes, and even good running shoes are adequate for most of the hikes listed here. These types of footwear are far more comfortable than heavy hiking boots, and when you're carrying a light load or day-hiking they'll make your legs feel much livelier during and after the outing.

PACKS

The price range among packs is vast. A moderately priced backpack should have enough adjustment points to allow a good fit, be constructed of reasonably good material that will last many hiking seasons, and be outfitted with features that make sense considering the demands of backpacking. I don't recommend one kind of equipment store over another, but specialty outdoor stores typically have personnel that actually hike and backpack and that can help you find a pack for your specific body type.

Day packs, fanny packs, and larger hydration packs are great for day hikes. Most are big enough to carry a supply of water, food, clothing, and other provisions. Fit is still important, but it isn't as crucial because of the minimal amount of weight being carried.

HIKING POLES

There was a time when the elderly were the only people you saw hiking or backpacking with walking sticks. But these days all age groups are enjoying the benefits of adjustable hiking poles with ergonomic grips that transform into a monopod for your camera. Whether or not the poles are cluttered with features or

Pothole lakes in eastern Washington

made of the latest lightweight alloy, their use makes sense for hikers and backpackers of any ability.

Day-hiking or backpacking is much more enjoyable and energizing with poles (old ski poles do the job and cost a lot less). The poles keep a portion of your pack's weight off your legs, keep your arms swinging to aid circulation, and help pull you uphill and absorb some of the impact going downhill. And if you stumble, your "artificial legs" will keep you from falling on your face.

WATER PURIFICATION

It's a good idea to bring at least two methods of water purification on long day hikes and backpacking trips. I recommend a good pump-style system and emergency potable water tablets.

INSECT REPELLENT

The higher the percentage of DEET in bug spray, the better it will protect you. However, DEET is a strong chemical and should be used sparingly (more information is available at www.deet.com). The subalpine zones on both sides of the divide have plenty of mosquito activity from mid-June to early September. Whether or not you have this item in your pack can determine the amount of pleasure you have on a hike.

DUCT TAPE

This item should be the 11th essential. Duct tape is perfect for everything from repairing a pack or a hole in a sock to a cracked flashlight case. It also can serve as a substitute for gaiters or cover hot spots or blisters on your heel. You could carry a whole roll (somewhat heavy) or just wrap a decent amount around the shaft of your hiking pole.

HEADLAMPS

Almost all the headlamps on the market today utilize an LED that burns brighter and longer than conventional bulbs. But they still require AA or AAA batteries. When you aren't using your headlamp or are storing it between hiking seasons, it's a good idea to reverse the battery positions. This way, if you accidentally turn on your headlamp while reaching into the top of your pack for candy you won't drain the batteries.

MOUNTAIN FOOD

Buying dehydrated foods can be quite expensive. If you backpack a lot, a food dehydrator and vacuum-sealing machine are well worth the investment. Fruits like apples, pears, plums, strawberries, peaches, and bananas make great trail snacks, and dehydrating them on your own saves money. Vacuum-sealing and freezing the food items will help keep them fresh two to four times longer.

Whole meals also can be dehydrated or just vacuum-sealed and frozen without dehydration. When you're ready to hike just remove the nondehydrated premade meal from the freezer, and keep it frozen in a cooler as long as possible before you step onto the trail. These meals should be fine for a number of days after they've thawed as long as they're stored in a vacuum-sealed bag. To heat your dinner, just drop the package into boiling water. For more information on dehydrating different kinds of foods, check out the *Complete Dehydrator Cookbook*, by Mary Bell and Evie Righter.

TRAIL ETIQUETTE

Your reasons for wanting to hike in the outdoors probably aren't much different from those of other people who may have chosen the same place you did. If you keep this in mind, it'll be much easier to observe proper manners afield.

There are two specific instances where etiquette knowledge is particularly handy. Some of the trails discussed are open to mountain bikes and a decent percentage to horses and other pack animals. Mountain bikers should always yield to the hiker, whether going up or downslope. If you see the cyclists before they see you, let them know you're there.

When you encounter people on horseback or leading a pack line you need to yield the right of way to them. Whether the riders see you first or you see them first, make sure to say "hello," not so much for the rider but so the horse knows that the object in the trail ahead of it is a human (yes, horses can be a little slow in the head).

Give the horse plenty of room to pass; if the trail isn't wide enough, step off on the downslope side. If the horse gets spooked by you or something else while passing it will turn away (upslope) from you, which should make it easier for the rider to gain control.

HIKE ON OFF-DAYS OR IN THE OFF-SEASON

The access window for some of these hikes is incredibly small, which means that you'll likely encounter quite a few other hikers at peak season. The off-season is limited mainly by the weather, specifically an existing or building snowpack. Some destinations aren't completely snow free until the beginning of July, but that doesn't mean trail access isn't open enough for a visit by the end of June. Being early is a great way to avoid people and to witness the flora's transformation at their earliest stages.

By mid-September the summer crowds have gone back to their jobs and schools, leaving the wilderness open for much greater solitude through the end of October, when conditions typically make hiking more difficult. The weather is usually stable and pleasantly warm, and insect activity is nearly nonexistent.

Weekdays are also a good time to venture out into the desert and mountains or along the coast.

If you like to hike or backpack with minimal human contact, then just keep on walking. Basically, the longer and more difficult the hike, the greater the likelihood you'll avoid other people. There is no hard and fast rule, but typically if you hike at least 8 miles (one way) you'll find some space and solitude.

ABOUT THESE HIKES

The 50 hikes detailed here were chosen as the best of what Washington has to offer in its respective regions and life zones. Areas like Olympic National Park, Mount Rainier National Park, and the Alpine Lakes Wilderness Area are represented with many hiking options mainly because each of these places contains a large number of incredible attractions. This doesn't take anything away from hikes in and around places like the Pasayten, Palouse, Columbia Basin, or Mount Baker. Washington is simply blessed with a wide variety of wonderful hikes.

The difficulty rating for each hike—easy, moderate, or strenuous—is based on the "average" hiker. If you're a beginner or an

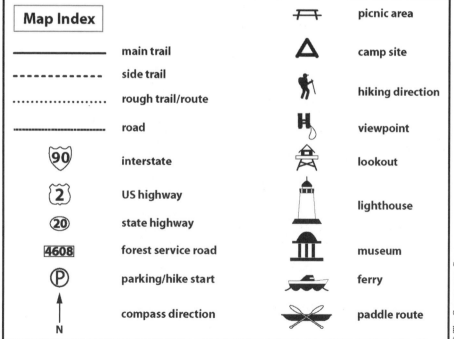

Map Index	
——————	main trail
- - - - - - -	side trail
··············	rough trail/route
▪▪▪▪▪▪▪▪▪▪▪▪	road
(90)	interstate
(2)	US highway
(20)	state highway
4608	forest service road
(P)	parking/hike start
↑ N	compass direction
⛱	picnic area
△	camp site
🥾	hiking direction
⚓	viewpoint
🏛	lookout
🗼	lighthouse
🏛	museum
🚤	ferry
✕	paddle route

© The Countryman Press

expert, you may need to consider this when deciding on the right trails for your conditioning and backcountry skill level.

Location is listed solely to help in finding a particular hike on a state road map or the *Washington Atlas and Gazetteer.* The mileage noted is an approximation taken in a straight line from the nearest, or most popular, town or city in the area to the trailhead. Many driving directions are given from local ranger districts, abbreviated throughout the book as RD.

I purposely didn't suggest hiking time because I believe this can be misleading. For example, you can complete the hike to the Point of the Arches in a couple of hours, but it's more likely that you'll spend half a day to an entire day there. Weather, available time, fitness, seasons, and interest level all play a part in how long a hike will take to complete. The more you hike, the better you'll be able to gauge how many miles you'll usually cover in a given amount of time.

Green Trails maps are suggested for most of the hikes because of their compact size, availability, and wealth of up-to-date, detailed information. Central and eastern Washington are currently not covered by Green Trails so U.S. Geological Survey (USGS) maps are suggested in those areas. If you're considering cross-country travel anywhere in the state, I'd recommend acquiring the appropriate 7.5-minute USGS map, which will have the highest accuracy and detail level.

Hoh Rain Forest

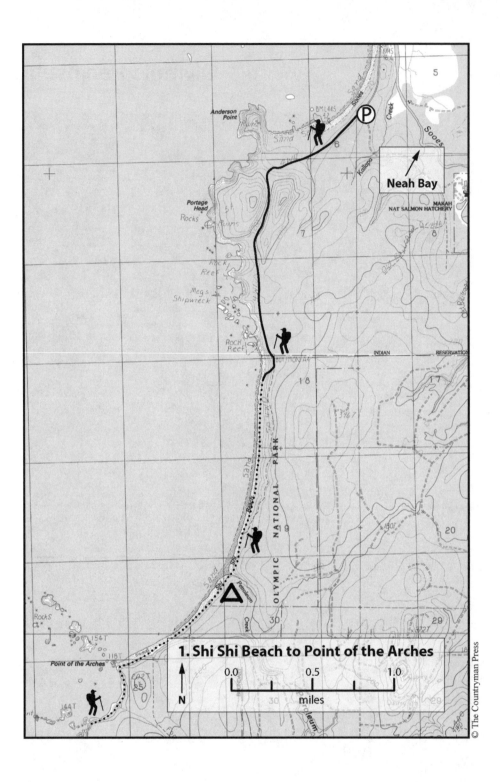

1. Shi Shi Beach to Point of the Arches

1

Shi Shi Beach to Point of the Arches

Type: Day hike

Season: Year-round

Total distance: 8.8 miles

Rating: Easy

Elevation gain: 100 feet

Location: Olympic National Park, 5 miles southwest of Neah Bay

Maps: Green Trails Cape Flattery No. 98S; USGS 15' Rumford; DeLorme map 19

Getting There

The trailhead is on the Makah Reservation, and you must purchase a recreation permit from the tribal nation. These can be obtained at the Makah Museum or Makah Tribal Center ($7 for an annual permit).

Drive west from the Makah Museum (well worth a visit) through the town of Neah Bay, at the end of WA 112 west of Port Angeles. About 0.9 mile from the museum you'll see a sign for Cape Flattery; follow it on Fort Street. Drive a long block and take a right turn, again following the signs for Cape Flattery. Drive less than 100 yards to an intersection where you turn left onto Cape Flattery Road toward the tribal center, Cape Flattery trails, the hatchery, and beaches.

At 2.3 miles turn left on Hobuck Road (signed for the beaches). To reach the Makah Tribal Center, continue straight for less than 0.1 mile. Signs direct you to the building where a permit can be purchased.

Roads split off Hobuck Road at a few points, so just be aware that you need to follow the signs for the fish hatchery. At 4.2 miles, before passing through the gate for the hatchery, you come to the Shi Shi Beach Trail parking area. This is a day-use parking lot only. Recreation permit and trail information can be obtained in advance by calling 360-645-3213 or by visiting www.makah.com.

If you choose to spend the night on the beach you must have a backcountry permit and make arrangements to leave your vehicle somewhere besides the parking lot at

Point of the Arches

the trailhead. Some private residences just short of the trailhead allow you to park a vehicle for a fee. Besides being dropped off at the trailhead, the only other reasonable option would be to hike 8 miles along the coastline from Cape Alava, which is accessed from the Ozette RD to the south.

The Trail

Shi Shi Beach and the Point of the Arches are the crown jewels of the entire 58 miles of Olympic National Park wilderness coastline. The long, elegant, smooth sand crescent of Shi Shi (Makah for "surf beach") is studded on its southern end by the Point of the Arches, a collection of sea stacks and rock formations older than the core of the Olympic Mountains. Rocks here have been hollowed out by the power of the surf to form natural arches. As the tide slips out from these castlelike rocks, tide pools are revealed that hold a dizzying array of sea

life. The whole stretch from beach to arches is awe-inspiring.

The 2-mile forested beach access trail is located on the Makah Reservation. The Makah tribe is historically known as the premier ocean canoeists and whale hunters of all the Northwest coastal Indians. Whales and seals were actively hunted until the late 1920s. In May 1999 a successful whale hunt again took place, reviving the centuries-old heritage and sparking a modern-day controversy. Some activist groups disagree with the killing of whales and protested the Makah's legal and cultural right to do so.

Another important event for the Makah was the discovery and excavation of over 55,000 artifacts at Ozette, a Makah village near the mouth of the Ozette River. Buried and then partially unburied by the ocean, this find of rich historical significance led to the construction of a museum in Neah

Bay so many of these treasures could be displayed.

The Shi Shi Beach Trail has been updated and improved by the Makah tribe with the help of the Washington Department of Natural Resources and the U.S. Forest Service, and nearly a mile of the 2-mile trail is quite nice. It begins in a relatively young stand of cedar trees on an even, wide trail. At 0.1 mile the trail enters an open area that appears to have been part of a burn, either set to create a clearing or as the after-effects of past logging.

The trail is lined with numerous bushes of salal and salmonberry. At 0.3 mile you cross back into the trees and over a series of uniquely designed bridges, starting with the Cantilever Bridge and followed by Beaver Pond, Sunset, and Boardwalk. The trail up through this area is a mix between packed gravel and elevated walkways.

Just past the Boardwalk Bridge the trail makes a hard turn to the left. It crosses over a short mucky section (worse during rainy periods) before reaching another junction of sorts at 0.8 mile. Head right, following an old road that was part of an active Air Force base during World War II.

This section is quite brushy, but the trail remains wide nearly all the way to the short descent onto Shi Shi at its end. A much bigger challenge is the boggy trail surface, which is mucky long after the last rain shower. To make matters worse, no attempts have been made to reduce trail erosion, and hikers are widening the trail as they try to avoid deep mud holes. If it weren't for the incredible splendors at the end of this hike, the poor trail conditions would make it hard to recommend.

After fighting your way straight through the mud, somewhere around 1.3 miles you begin to catch the smells and sounds of the ocean floating through the coastal forest. By this time you'll have gone past Anderson Point and Portage Head, two coastline features (not visible from the trail) that have been host to a portion of the 180 or so shipwrecks along the Olympic coast.

At 1.7 miles the trail edges along coastal cliffs, providing views out toward the ocean and marking the approach into Olympic National Park. The trail down to the beach is somewhat steep, passing over numerous tree roots before reaching the sand and a collection of weathered logs at the 2-mile mark. Take your time descending. It is approximately 2.4 miles to the Point of the Arches from where you hit Shi Shi Beach, which is absolutely gorgeous. The gentle curve of sand serves as a white-gold road to the grand kingdom that is the Point of the Arches.

Be sure to arrive at low or minus tide so you'll be able to walk out to various arches and fully explore the tide pools. Minus tides happen mainly from April to August on various days during the month (tides are affected by the cycles of the moon). Contact the Olympic National Park Visitor Center in Port Angeles for tide information or access the tide tables on the NOAA web site at www.tidesonline.nos.noaa.gov.

Approximately 1.3 miles along the beach (3.3 miles into the hike) you come to a freshwater source cutting across the sand. Upstream, by the edge of the forest, there's a campsite. It's common to see bald eagles along the beach. Mornings and evenings are the most spectacular times to be here, with the play of warm sunlight on the water, sand, and rocks.

Continue on another 1.1 miles to reach the first arm of the Point of the Arches. The shorter second arm is around a cove. Keep an eye on rising tides, as you don't want to be on either arm or along the rocky shoreline of the cove between the two points when high water cuts off access.

At low/minus tide you can walk out to the end of the rocks on both points. The rocks are covered with sea grass, sea lettuce, kelp, sea urchins, sea snails, mussels, barnacles, and other marine life. The pools are filled with ochre sea stars, purple shore crabs, anemones, sunflower sea stars, worms, limpets, and much more. Standing in one of the natural arches you can sense the destructive power and life energy of the ocean. Give yourself plenty of time to explore Shi Shi Beach and the Point of the Arches.

Clown of the Sea

A victim of man's enormous appetite for natural resources over much of the Olympic Peninsula from the early 19th century to the mid-20th century, the sea otter was highly prized for its pelt. By the late 1800s—after barely a hundred years of European and American commercial activity in the area—the lovable clowns were wiped out. But this key creature in the delicate balance of the kelp forest ecosystem was reintroduced in the 1970s and once again lives in healthy numbers all along the Olympic coast.

2

Cape Alava to Sand Point Loop

Type: Day hike

Season: Year-round

Total distance: 9.1-mile loop

Rating: Easy to moderate

Elevation gain: 100 feet

Location: Olympic National Park, 55 miles west of Port Angeles

Map: Green Trails Ozette No. 130S

Getting There

From Port Angeles, travel approximately 44 miles west on US 101 to the town of Sappho and WA 113. Turn right (north) on WA 113, following its 16.5-mile curving route to Clallam Bay. WA 113 is also known as Burnt Mountain Road; approximately 9.5 miles from Sappho it becomes WA 112.

From Clallam Bay, drive approximately 5 miles west on WA 112 to the Hoko-Ozette Road and turn left, continuing 23 miles. A total of 88.5 miles from Port Angeles you arrive at the Ozette RD and parking area.

You must obtain a permit if you plan to camp. These can be reserved or obtained the day of your hike. (Only a limited number of permits are issued.)

The Trail

This beautiful loop hike begins and ends at the Ozette RD, which is staffed from May through September. The friendly rangers are excellent resources for trail conditions, tidal movements, coastal highlights, and identification of the local flora. Interpretative panels at the trailhead highlight some of the historical uses of this area by groups like the Makah tribe and then homesteaders in the late 1800s.

Cross over the Ozette River bridge and walk 0.1 mile to a fork in the trail. The left fork heads to Sand Point and the right to Cape Alava. The hike described here follows the loop toward Cape Alava.

The trail is thickly lined with sword fern, salmonberry, cedar, spruce, and western red alder, along with smaller ground cover

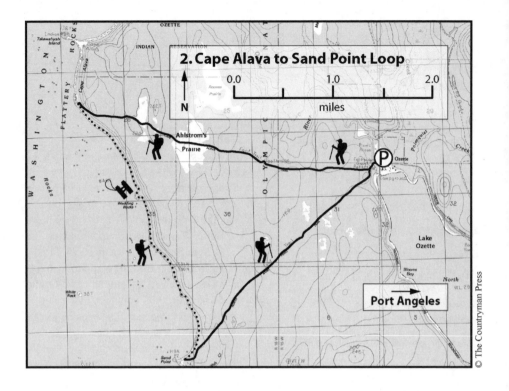

2. Cape Alava to Sand Point Loop

© The Countryman Press

like bunchberry. You'll also discover skunk cabbage, giant-leafed plants that look like something from an Amazonian jungle. In early spring they bear one large corncob-like yellow stalk, decorated with numerous little blooms and hooded by a large yellow bract (leaflike in appearance). The exotic-looking bloom releases an odor that explains this plant's name.

The forested pathways to the coast and back are pleasant, wide, and relatively flat. The trail is a mix of forest floor, boardwalk, and elevated walkways. Because of the number of visitors and the continuously damp ground, the boardwalks and walkways are necessary to help keep trail erosion under control.

At 1 mile a bridge crosses a small creek running through the forest. At 1.5 miles the tree canopy thins a bit, giving the forest en-

vironment a more open feel. And at about 1.7 miles you enter Ahlstrom's Prairie. A 0.4-mile hike to the north would take you to Roose's Prairie, where an old cabin stands in partial ruin.

These prairies were originally cleared by coastal Indians as a means of attracting deer and elk for hunting. The clearings were burned regularly to hold back the coastal rain forest understory and fast-growing spruce and cedar trees (due to 130 inches of precipitation a year). Homesteaders, many of Norwegian descent, settled around Ozette Lake in the 1890s, including two bachelors named Ahlstrom and Roose. The location of Ahlstrom's cabin is marked by a large wooden bench at the western edge of the prairie. Apparently, the two did not take kindly to each other. Relations didn't improve any when Ahlstrom lost control of a

Cape Alava

field burning and torched Roose's house while the latter was away working in a logging camp.

The trail soon reenters the forest, where the trees are noticeably larger and the understory is once again filled with ferns and mosses. At about 2.5 miles you can hear and smell the ocean; and not too much farther along you reach an overview where you can watch the Pacific's waves breaking before the trail heads downhill to the beach at the 3-mile mark.

Cape Alava is the westernmost point in the contiguous 48 states. The large island off Cape Alava is Ozette. This island, along with dozens of other islands, sea stacks, and rock formations, is part of the dual designation of the Washington Islands Wilderness (1970) and the Flattery Rocks National Wildlife Refuge (1940).

The beach near Cape Alava is a combination of sand and small cobble. Timing is everything, so make sure your arrival along the coast coincides with low tide. When the water is out, exposed pools become small aquariums filled with sea urchins, starfish, crabs, and limpets.

You'll see piles and piles of beached trees and driftwood, rubbed smooth and sculpted by the tumbling and pounding surf. Sea kelp and sea grasses, plastic bottles, fishing buoys, and possibly even a stray coconut that's drifted in from the South Pacific may be present.

Beach camps are set near freshwater sources, with cables rigged in nearby trees for storing food. An alternative to hanging food is a bear-proof container that you can borrow (donations encouraged) from the Ozette RD or Olympic National Park

Wilderness Information Center in Port Angeles.

Heading south, approximately 1.3 miles from Cape Alava (4.3 miles in) you arrive at the first headland. It's passable via the beach at low to medium tide, otherwise you need to look out for the red and black circular signs marking the trail over the headland. On the other side you come to a place called Wedding Rocks.

There is a whole series of 300- to 500-year-old petroglyphs here. A map at the Ozette RD tells you their location. Once you've found a few, the others will be easier to spot. Theories of what the petroglyphs mean range from attempts at connecting with the supernatural to simple ancient graffiti.

The stretch between the first and second headland covers about 1.2 miles of very pleasant coastline. The second headland crossing is a bit steeper, and there's a rope system to help you up the slick mud. Past the second headland the beach is more open, alternating between sand and gravel-sized stones. Various seabirds—auklets, gulls, and oystercatchers—are usually present in this area.

At approximately 6 miles the beach meets up with the Sand Point Trail. The large grassy rock outcropping beyond the curve of the shoreline is Sand Point, which offers a fantastic lunch spot and vistas up and down the coast. The entire coastal section of this hike is amazingly scenic.

Keep an eye out for the black and red sign near Sand Point that directs you back to the trailhead. You enter the forest through a boneyard of trees, and the Sand Point Trail makes an easy run back to the Ozette RD. The trail stays under a forest canopy for 0.6 mile before crossing into a more open section with lots of dead standing trees from a forest fire some years back. The trail is again mostly boardwalk and elevated walkways that pass through a coastal rain forest.

At 7.8 miles the trail enters a clearing similar to Ahlstrom's Prairie, but much smaller. At about 8.8 miles Ozette Lake is visible through the trees, and the trail changes to crushed rock. At 9 miles you reach the junction with the Cape Alava Trail, and then take the short spur to the right back to the trailhead.

Hole in the Wall

South of Ozette near La Push is the second of only three official access points into the largest and most remote stretches of the scenic Olympic National Park coastal wilderness. (Oil City near the mouth of the Hoh River marks the third access point.) There is a great day hike from Rialto Beach near La Push. Drive to Forks on US 101 and head west another 13 miles to Rialto Beach via the Mora RD. Heading north from the trailhead, along a cobble shoreline, you can explore the junkyard of washed-up trees, poke around numerous tide pools, walk through a rock monolith known as the Hole in the Wall, and visit a memorial to those lost on the *W. J. Pirrie* in 1920 near Cape Johnson. This 7-mile hike shows a different face from the Cape Alava to Sand Point hike.

3

Hoh River to Hoh Lake

Type: Overnight or multiday

Season: Year-round along the river; mid-June to early October up to Hoh Lake

Total distance: 29.8 miles

Rating: Easy to moderate

Elevation gain: 4,100 feet

Location: Olympic National Park, 30 miles southeast of Forks

Map: Green Trails Mount Tom No. 133

Getting There

From the Olympic National Park Wilderness Information Center in Forks, travel approximately 12 miles south on US 101 and then turn left on the Upper Hoh River Road. Signs are posted for the Hoh Rain Forest and Hoh River Trailhead. At 24.5 miles the road officially enters the park, and there's a fee of $10 per vehicle for a seven-day visit. You reach the trailhead at 30.6 miles. There is an information center (seasonal), short interpretive trails, a picnic area, and a campground here. All backcountry camping requires a permit, obtained in advance or on a walk-in basis from the Olympic National Park Wilderness Information Center in Port Angeles.

The Trail

The word *Hoh* comes from local tribes and carries meanings like "fast white water" or "snow water." The 60-plus-mile river flows down from the Hoh Glacier, one of the largest of eight glaciers that cap the multi-peak summit of Mount Olympus. Its sibling, the Elwha River, originates a short distance to the south off the Bailey Range. The Hoh makes a big, slow, dogleg left turn before following a meandering course to the Pacific Ocean north of the Hoh Reservation.

The Hoh River's reputation comes not from its glacial waters but from the incredibly lush rain forest that grows along its banks in a broad U-shaped valley pounded by 150 inches of precipitation annually. The result is a world of massive trees cloaked in mosses and ferns. The shadowy green

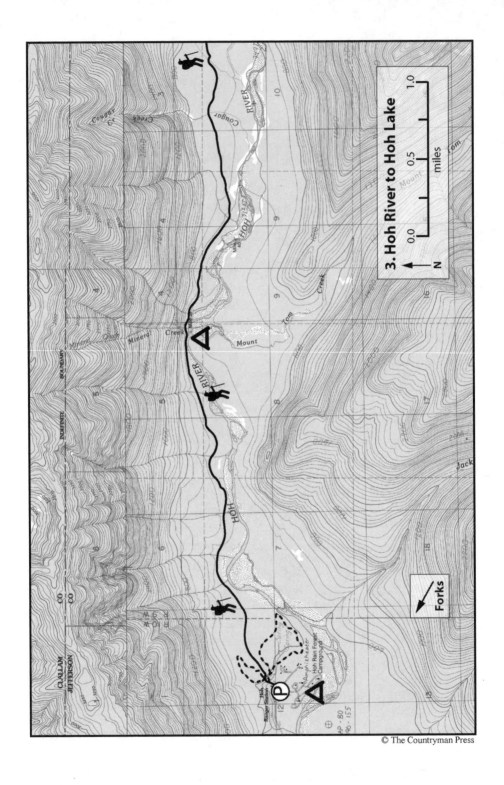

3. Hoh River to Hoh Lake

© The Countryman Press

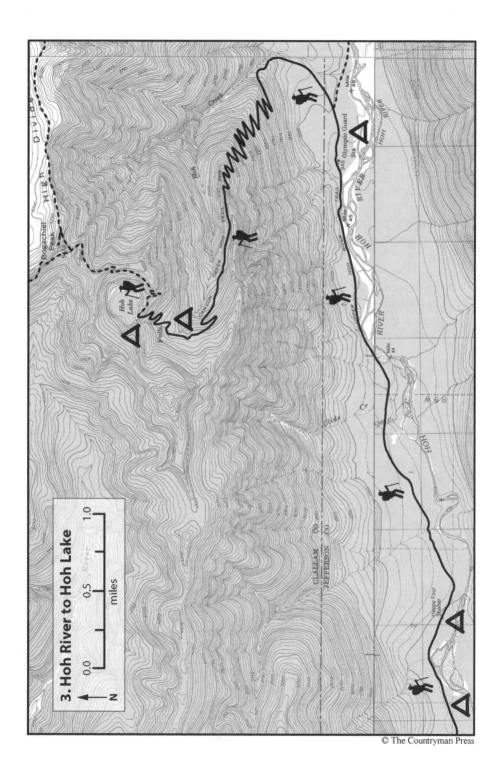

3. Hoh River to Hoh Lake

© The Countryman Press

forest seems even more exotic when you look at the names of local plant and animal life: licorice fern, spike moss, cattail moss, vine maple, and banana slug. Everything is bigger here, especially trees like the western hemlock, which can reach 300 feet with a base circumference of 23 feet.

The Hoh River Trailhead is a major attraction for tourists in Olympic National Park; however, most won't venture farther than the short interpretive trails. The Hoh River Trail starts at less than 600 feet in elevation and gains just 400 feet by the time it reaches the Hoh Lake Trail junction 9.5 miles later. Except for the numerous mud puddles, backpackers will find the long walk very easy. This overall hike is not without some climbing, though, as you gain approximately 3,600 feet on the trail up to Hoh Lake.

The rain forest is lush and alive, but it would be even more intensely thick through the understory if it weren't for the efforts of one creature—the Roosevelt elk. Local residents noticed a dramatic increase in the understory as the number of elk was reduced by heavy hunting pressure into the early 20th century. In fact, Olympic National Park was originally proposed as a sanctuary to protect the Roosevelt elk, which was named in honor of Theodore Roosevelt. It's not uncommon to come across 20 or 30 elk on the trail early in the morning.

At 0.9 mile you pass the first of many designated campsites set between the river and trail. The beauty of the Hoh River Trail is that it moves through this verdant environment the entire way—a rainbow of greens brightened by filtered sunlight and edged by shadow. Branches continue to hold water even days after a rainstorm, sending drops splashing onto the trail below.

The trail swings closer to the river at 1.2 miles, giving you a view of the water's gray hue, which is the result of glacial silt (also called rock flour). There are two more campsites just ahead, one at 1.4 miles and the next at 2 miles.

At 2.5 miles the trail climbs up into the forest slightly, but probably no more than 50 feet above the Hoh River. You reach Tom Creek Meadow at 2.8 miles. This small grassy clearing offers a simple contrast to the world of lichens and moss. The long, thick, black, yellow, or drab-green creatures you see dotting the trail are banana slugs. Natural-born recyclers, these slugs break down plant matter that is ultimately reabsorbed into the soil.

Beyond Tom Creek, the trail moves into the forest but still continues its easy path through the same mix of plants and trees. The calls of chickadee, gray jay, and varied thrush will keep you company, and you may even be startled by the thunderous flush of a blue grouse.

Another creature you may encounter along the trail is a mountain climber. This trail is the most common approach into the heart of the Olympic Mountains and to the various summits of Mount Olympus. Most climbing attempts are made from late June to early September, when weather conditions are typically best. In the world of mountaineering Mount Olympus isn't very tall (under 8,000 feet) or overly technical, but because it's often shrouded in clouds, mishaps and failed summit attempts aren't uncommon.

At 3.3 miles the trail crosses over a short bridge and passes the fifth campsite. At 4.7 miles you enter a large grassy area under a canopy of bigleaf maples and western red alders. A short distance farther on you reach the Five Mile Island campsite area. Once again, tent sites are nicely set along the river.

In the fall of 2003 the trail was washed out about 0.2 mile after Five Mile Island. So

Along the Hoh River Trail

the trail currently drops down into the riverbed of a tributary of the Hoh for about 0.1 mile before climbing back out and eventually connecting up with the original trail.

After passing under a nice tunnel of trees you reach the Happy Four campsite at 5.7 miles. White clover spreads over the forest floor along each side of the trail through here. Something else you'll discover at various points all along the trail is that the uprooted trees keep on living. Their exposed root system holds clumps of forest soil, which play host to licorice fern and other plant and bug species that create an ecosystem out of the toppled tree. The root system acts like the rain forest's version of a coral reef.

At 7.8 miles there is an unavoidable ford of Clide Creek. On the opposite bank is yet another campsite. Don't bother trying to dry out your socks, because in 0.4 mile there is a second creek ford. Water level and flow will determine the difficulty of each ford, but most of the time it's quite easy to get across.

The trail climbs a little beyond the second ford before dropping back down, crossing over a bridge, and arriving at the Olympus Ranger Station and campsite area, which is equipped with a pit toilet (9 miles). The soft, spiky, reedlike plants growing profusely around the ranger station are called horsetail.

Hike a short 0.6 mile to reach the Hoh Lake Trail junction (9.6 miles). If you were to continue straight you'd reach the trail's terminus in about 8 miles at Glacier Meadows, 3,500 feet below Mount Olympus. Instead, head left (north) to follow the trail up a narrow track, slowly gaining elevation as you enter a dense forest understory. The trail eventually works its way along Hoh Creek (10.4 miles) before beginning the first of

nearly two-dozen switchbacks. It's a somewhat steep ascent up a south-facing slope to a ridgeline with a great vista over the Hoh River valley.

As you climb higher there is a noticeable changeover from the rain-forest environment to a mix of salal and thimbleberry, and then fir, huckleberry, and bear grass in the subalpine zone. At 10.9 miles there are clear views up and down the Hoh River valley as well as along the ridgeline south of the river in front of the bulky Olympics.

At 12.3 miles the switchbacks become more frequent, and you pass by a prominent patch of dead standing trees, victims of the August 1978 fire that torched over 1,000 acres. Finally, the trail hits the ridge at 12.7 miles and works its way through newer growth and dead stand before dropping off the ridge onto the northeast slope of the Hoh Creek drainage.

The trail begins to climb again. It's nicely shaded along here, but there are also views of the rocky Bogachiel Peak and saddle above Hoh Lake. A short distance to the right of that rocky peak is the start of the best stretch of the High Divide Trail, which is accessible from Hoh Lake up a steep 1.2-mile trail. The views of the Olympics and the broad and tantalizing Seven Lakes Basin make the extra work worthwhile. And it's possible to take an extended day hike down to the marvelous wild garden of Sol Duc Park.

There is a sign for a camp area downslope at 13.6 miles, which also marks the 3,500-foot level (no open fires beyond this point). In the early season you're bound to pass slopes filled with avalanche lily. At nearly 14.3 miles (4,100 feet) you reach CB Flats, an extremely pleasant open area of spongy ground and tiny tributaries—the main stream splits apart at the base of Hoh

Falls. There are plenty of wildflowers here, like globeflower, alpine white marsh marigold, and shooting star.

The trail winds 0.6 mile above the flats and runs close to the falls. At 14.9 miles, you arrive at Hoh Lake (4,500 feet). The small lake sits in a basin 500 feet below the peak and saddle that were visible earlier along the trail. There are number of great campsites on the south end of Hoh Lake, along with a self-composting pit toilet and bear wires for securing food. The lake is often frozen into late June or early July, and snow lingers around the campsites.

Snow White and the Seven Lakes Basin

A 17.5-mile loop hike begins at the Sol Duc Trailhead, offering everything from waterfalls to subalpine meadows to high-mountain lakes to a stunning vista of the glaciated Olympic Mountains. There are campsites in Sol Duc Park and down in the Seven Lakes Basin. This overnight trip is another of Olympic National Park's premier backcountry outings. Take the Sol Duc entrance off US 101 to reach the parking lot and trailhead (42 miles from Port Angeles). Green Trails maps for the hike include Mount Tom No. 133 and Mount Olympus No. 134.

4

Klahhane Ridge Loop

Type: Day hike

Season: June to October

Total distance: 12.4-mile loop

Rating: Moderate to strenuous

Elevation gain: 4,300 feet

Location: Olympic National Park, 6 miles south of Port Angeles

Maps: Green Trails Port Angeles No. 103, Mt. Angeles No. 135

Getting There

From the Olympic National Park Wilderness Information Center in Port Angeles, drive 5.5 miles south toward the Heart O' the Hills entrance, which leads to Hurricane Ridge. Turn right at a sign for the Lake Angeles Trailhead just before the park entrance, and follow the road past some buildings and into a large parking lot (5.7 miles). The near trailhead is Lake Angeles and the one at the far end of the parking lot is Heather Park.

The Trail

This loop follows the Heather Park Trail up to the dark volcanic rock of Klahhane Ridge, one of the best viewpoints for the north face of the Olympic Mountains, and then descends on the Lake Angeles Trail, where there are brilliant vistas across the Strait of Juan de Fuca. From the parking lot it's 2.5 miles to Halfway Rock, 4.3 miles to the lower end of the spectacular Heather Park, and 6.5 miles to Klahhane Ridge.

The trail climbs under a canopy of cedar and fir trees, alongside bunchberry, vanilla leaf, and dull Oregon grape. It's a moderate climb right from the get-go. If you're lucky you'll spot pinedrops (a tall red-brown stalk with urn-shaped flowers) and the much more prolific western trillium, with its delicate three-petal flower formation.

At 2.2 miles—after a 0.6-mile section of switchbacks followed by a second section with just two switchbacks—the trail bends around a corner and begins a less strenuous course up the east slope above the

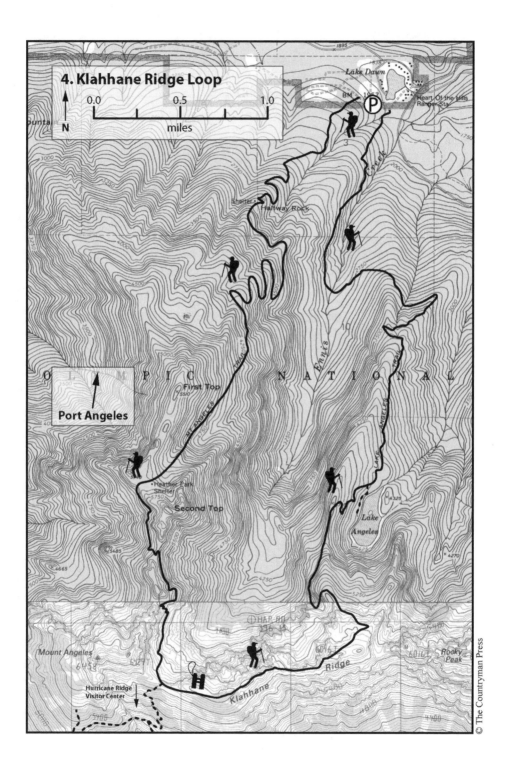

4. Klahhane Ridge Loop

N

0.0   0.5   1.0

miles

Lake Dawn

BM
Heart Of the Hills
Ranger Sta.

Shelter Halfway Rock

O L Y M P I C   N A T I O N A L

Port Angeles

First Top

Heather Park
Shelter

Second Top

*Lake
Angeles*

Mount Angeles

Hurricane Ridge
Visitor Center

Klahhane   Ridge

Rocky
Peak

© The Countryman Press

The Klahhane Ridge Trail

creek drainage. From Halfway Rock at 2.5 miles, there are some nice views of the Strait of Juan de Fuca and the Vancouver Mountains on British Columbia's Vancouver Island. The forest also opens to views of the ridgeline across the drainage, which the Lake Angeles Trail traverses.

At 2.7 miles the trail crosses an open slope with closer views of Klahhane Ridge. Wildflowers like paintbrush, spreading phlox, and western anemone will be blooming in the summer months where the trail turns up a series of switchbacks and on into Heather Park (4.3 miles). As you face the Strait of Juan de Fuca, other notable natural features to look for in the distance include the Dungeness Spit and Mount Baker, Washington's northernmost Cascade volcano.

Heather Park is a gorgeous slope-side park that fills a small cirque with pink blooming heather, sparkling wildflowers, and a cool creek. The trail winds its way through this natural garden and up to a rocky notch.

The rock you will be standing on is the remnant of an ancient seabed made up of volcanic and sedimentary material thrust upward and twisted to form the Olympic mountain range beginning some 50 million years ago. From the notch there are splendid views of the Elwha River Range and the western portion of Klahhane Ridge to the west and southwest. The Elwha River is slated to have two major dams removed starting in 2007, which will allow anadromous fish like steelhead and pink salmon to once again reach upstream spawning beds.

The next 2 miles of trail are somewhat primitive, making it by far the most thrilling section of the hike. The loose-rock trail slides up, down, and around various chutes below the ridgeline leading up to Mount Angeles and Klahhane Ridge. At 5.3 miles, after climbing slightly the entire way, you are below a distinguishable notch, or saddle, off

the northeast flank of Mount Angeles. The trail rises through loose rock for approximately 0.1 mile to the notch. It isn't imperative, but you'll probably want to do this section of the hike when it's free of snow because route-finding can be difficult.

This notch is above a sizable basin and you can see the trail working its way around the upper end of the basin, shadowed by craggy Mount Angeles, toward Klahhane Ridge. The sharply upturned beds of lava and breccia on the ridge and Mount Angeles provide a perfect window into geologic history. Breccia is a coarse, cement-like collection of odd-shaped rock fragments built up over time by sedimentation. The rock ranges in color from black to brown to red, all depending on the materials that compose the various exposed layers.

From the notch, the trail drops down a series of loose-rock (talus) switchbacks before traversing steadily upward across the bowl. Be careful through here, as it's easy to lose your footing or dislodge rocks that could put people below you at risk of injury. You'll be amazed by the vistas as you step onto the dark rock ridge of Klahhane (6.5 miles).

Hurricane Ridge is in the foreground and slightly below you. It's accessible by car and offers views to the Bailey Range and Mount Olympus. Of course, you share this same view from higher up and farther back, and with the added bonus of knowing you worked hard over the last 6 miles to reach this point.

The Klahhane Ridge Trail (*klahhane* means "good times in the mountains") stays mostly on the ridge that rolls along toward the east with views all the way to Mount Rainier. The south slope is wide open, and in the summer it's painted with bronze bells, orange agoseris, and yellow wallflower set between the dark volcanic rocks. The trail is easygoing as you take in the vast surroundings of water, mountains, and valleys.

At 7.4 miles (0.9 mile along the ridge) the trail runs above a beautiful subalpine parkland that's larger and more open than Heather Park. Lake Angeles is also visible from here. After gliding through the park the trail dips over to the west slope of the Ennis Creek drainage and down a few switchbacks before crossing back over approximately 0.5 mile before Lake Angeles. The lake is at 8.9 miles. At the junction, follow the sign for the campsites to reach the lakeshore.

The next 3.5 miles to the Lake Angeles Trailhead drop through tree cover similar to the beginning of the hike, but with far fewer switchbacks. Less than 2 miles from the end (10.6 miles), the trail passes through an old burn and over a bridge. There is a second bridge crossing at 12 miles, where the trees are cloaked in moss and lichen.

Ridge to Ridge to Ridge

It's also possible to access Klahhane Ridge via Hurricane Ridge. From the visitor center, the Sunrise Ridge Trail leaves the west end of Hurricane Ridge in a glorious open subalpine run up to Klahhane Ridge. The biggest elevation gain—approximately 800 feet—comes in the last 0.8 mile of the 3.5-mile trail; otherwise, the hike is more like a grand stroll. It's a 12-mile drive from Heart O' the Hills to the Hurricane Ridge Visitor Center.

5

Dungeness Spit

Type: Day hike

Season: Year-round

Total distance: 9.8 miles

Rating: Moderate

Elevation gain: 60 feet if you climb the lighthouse tower

Location: Dungeness Wildlife Refuge, 5 miles north of Sequim

Map: USGS Dungeness

Getting There

Take US 101 east from Port Angeles, to 4.5 miles west of Sequim to Kitchen-Dick Road, where you turn right. The road makes a 90-degree bend to the right at 7.8 miles. At 8 miles, turn left into the Dungeness Wildlife Refuge. At 8.7 miles you pass a white shack; drive another 0.5 mile to the parking area for the spit (9.2 miles). Parking costs $3 unless you have one of the following annual passes: Federal Duck Stamp, Golden Eagle, Golden Age, or Golden Access. Dogs are not allowed on the trail or on the spit itself.

The Trail

It is estimated that the Dungeness Spit is growing at a rate of 15 to 20 feet every year. As the Dungeness River flows into Dungeness Bay north of Sequim it mixes with the oceanic currents of the Strait of Juan de Fuca, depositing incredible amounts of silt on the 5-mile spit, the longest natural spit in the world. You won't literally be able to see the spit growing, but from the top of the New Dungeness Lighthouse you can see that its terminus has moved over half a mile since the lighthouse was built in 1857. The Dungeness Wildlife Refuge is home to 250 species of birds, 41 species of land mammals, and eight species of marine mammals, so you'll have plenty of company on your stroll to the lighthouse.

The trail from the parking area starts on a wide path in the trees, sloping downhill the whole way. There is a beautiful overlook

---

Dungeness Spit

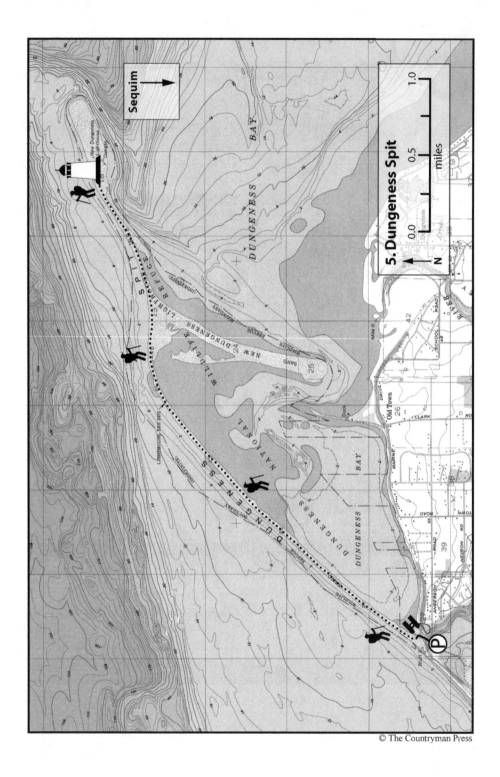

© The Countryman Press

above the bay and the curving sliver of Dungeness Spit. The long tongue hanging off the Dungeness is known as the Graveyard Spit, so named after a band of Tsimshian Indians was massacred by warriors from the S'Klallam tribe. You can also spot the New Dungeness Lighthouse and accompanying buildings out near the end of the spit. It's the oldest operational lighthouse on the West Coast, continuously lit for 147 years.

Signs on the way to the overlook identify various coastal trees and plants, from western red cedar to false lily of the valley, salal, and red huckleberry. The distance to the overlook is 0.3 mile, and it's another 0.1 mile from there down to the spit.

The spit's exposed walking surface varies with the tide level. If you make the hike out to the lighthouse at low tide you can walk on sand and small pebbles. At high tide you're forced higher onto the crown of the spit, which is pretty much a 5-mile-long boneyard of drift trees and stumps. (For tide information, go to www.tidesonline.nos.noaa.gov.) The zone between the ideal and worst case is a slanting surface of cobble, which makes for some slow, and possibly wet, going.

The spit is a narrow strip of land barely exposed above the waters of the Strait of Juan de Fuca. The widest point is a quarter mile and the narrowest 50 feet, leaving various points vulnerable to breaching during high tides or rough seas.

The west, or surf, side is open for walking nearly the entire length of the spit. The only portion closed is the half mile beyond the lighthouse, which is reserved for the birds and animals. The Dungeness Bay, or estuary, side is also reserved entirely for the birds and animals. Common birds include the black brant, seagull, northern shoveler, marbled murrelet, and bald eagle.

If you're walking on the spit at low tide, you'll lose sight of the lighthouse. It doesn't come back into view until the 3-mile mark, where the spit curves enough to the east. From here, it's another 1.5 miles to the lighthouse. There are great views of the Vancouver Mountains, Mount Baker, Mount Shuksan, Mount Rainier, and the Olympics.

The lighthouse, which has been on the National Register of Historic Places since 1993, is maintained by a group of volunteers selected from a waiting list to spend one week there. These volunteers, some of whom wait upward of two years for their chance, are charged with general upkeep of the grounds and with giving tours. The signal light is now fully automated and still performs its original function of warning ships about the shallow waters off the spit.

The original light source in 1857 was a lard oil lamp magnified by a third-order Fresnel lens. This system evolved over the years into its modern form of a six-sided bull's-eye prism lit by a collection of finger-sized lamps that make the lighthouse visible from 17 miles away. The warning system is electronic now, but the original signal device was a half-ton bell cast in Philadelphia and sent on a two-year voyage around Cape Horn.

All sorts of artifacts wash up on the spit, from coconuts to whale bones, glass bottles, and fishing equipment. There is a small museum in the lighthouse with hundreds of items collected by keepers over the years. Seals and sea lions are often seen around the spit, along with deer and coyotes.

A 1,000-foot-long pier once jutted out from Cline Spit near present-day Old Town, the former site of Dungeness. When the bay became too shallow for the larger ships to dock, the town of Dungeness moved to the east and a new pier was constructed that spanned nearly .75 mile.

The Dungeness Lighthouse

Dungeness—the bay and spit were named by Captain Vancouver in 1790—was a key port for sailing ships from the late 1800s through the early 1900s. Deeper, more easily accessible ports like Port Angeles, Port Townsend, and Port Discovery eventually were utilized, leaving nothing of the pier but the few pylons still visible today.

Hooked on Spits

The Ediz Hook curls off the west end of Port Angeles, providing a 3-mile-long natural barrier to the Northwest's deepest harbor. Built by settling silt carried by the Elwha River, the Ediz Hook has been shrinking ever since the damming of the Elwha 95 years ago. A lighthouse was constructed in 1865 and replaced by a schoolhouse-style structure in 1908 that is now a private residence in Port Angeles. Various seabirds and shorebirds, as well as animals like sea lions, can be seen on the spit. The views are magnificent across the Strait of Juan de Fuca and back to the Olympics rising above Port Angeles.

6

Royal Lake/Royal Basin

Type: Day hike or overnight

Season: Mid-June to early October

Total distance: 12 miles

Rating: Moderate

Elevation gain: 2,450 feet

Location: Olympic National Park, 30 miles southeast of Port Angeles

Map: Green Trails Tyler Peak No. 136

Getting There

From Port Angeles, travel east on US 101 approximately 15 miles before turning right (south) on Taylor Cut Off Road. At 17.5 miles the road bends right and becomes Lost Mountain Road. At 20.1 miles, turn left onto Slab Camp Road. Turn left again at 21.1 miles onto FR 2870 in the direction of the Gray Wolf Trailhead.

Drive past the Gray Wolf Trailhead (27.5 miles) and bear right at 30 miles on what will be signed either FR 2860 or 2870 (I've seen this road marked both ways). At 36.6 miles you arrive at a parking area and trailhead before the Dungeness River crossing; a second larger parking area are on the far side of the bridge. A camping permit is required for overnight stays.

The Trail

Mount Deception is one of a handful of 7,000-foot peaks that enclose the two-tiered jewel of Royal Basin. However, there is nothing deceptive about the fantastic subalpine parkland that climbs from Royal Lake in the lower basin to the upper basin, where it touches the sheer slopes below the craggy summits of the Needles (7,300 feet), Mount Deception (7,788 feet), and Mount Fricaba (7,134 feet).

These formidable peaks cradle the headwaters of Royal Creek and form the 4,000-foot west wall of the Dungeness River valley. Heather Creek, one of the two creeks that merge early on their journey to become the Dungeness River, originates from the east side of Mount Mystery (7,631 feet).

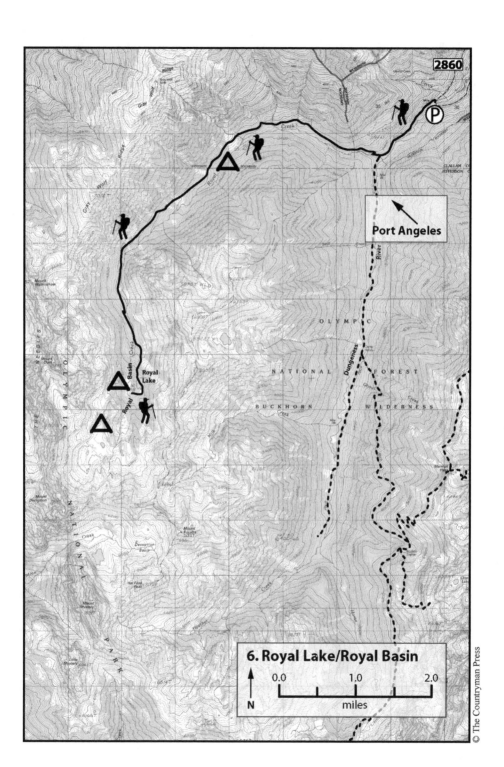

2860

Port Angeles

6. Royal Lake/Royal Basin

0.0   1.0   2.0

miles

N

© The Countryman Press

Mystery is situated south of Royal Basin and holds a subalpine/alpine cirque parkland called Deception Basin.

From the big parking area, walk across the bridge and begin the hike southwest on Dungeness Trail 833. The trail cuts uphill and turns into a pleasant stroll through big fir and cedar trees along the icy, gray Dungeness River. The understory is healthy, with bunchberry, vanilla leaf, sword fern, moss, and white trillium. A scattering of rhododendron bushes along the trail bloom from late June to early July.

You arrive at the junction for the Dungeness River and the Royal Creek Trails at 1 mile. The Dungeness Trail heads left, crossing the river on a log bridge. The trail to Royal Lake/Royal Basin continues straight ahead. Just as the two trails split, so do the Dungeness River and Royal Creek, as this is their confluence. From the junction, the trail climbs a few switchbacks and works its way through the forest above Royal Creek.

At 1.4 miles there is a sign for the Burn Trail/Mount Baldy (the trail cutting back to the right). Keep straight/left to continue moving up the Royal Creek drainage. It's a steady, moderate climb through a beautiful forest, although the incline lessens somewhat in another 2 miles.

At 2.7 miles you break onto an open slope with views of Gray Wolf Ridge to the west. This ridge was formed by upturned lava flows—some of the earliest volcanic outpourings in the Olympics—that were later sharpened to a knife edge by the action of glaciers. Colliding oceanic and continental plates followed by heavy volcanic activity and the ice ages created the Olympic Mountains. But the work isn't finished, as alpine glaciers continue to cut away the soft, outer volcanic rock layers, further defining ridges and peaks, while weather and gravity counter that action by flattening out and disassembling the relatively young and fragile mountains (55 to 15 million years old).

Spruce trees and wildflowers and plants such as paintbrush, valerian, and wild strawberry begin to show up along the open slope. The mountain views are short lived, as you soon slide back into a heavier forest and pass a campsite along Royal Creek. Next, the trail climbs up through five or six small open areas containing salmonberry, buttercup, larkspur, kinnikinnick, shooting star, and cow parsnip. You hike to the constant splash and rumble of the creek, accompanied by the songs of gray jays or chickadees, the squeak of ground squirrels, or the mating calls of grouse. Some-where around the 4-mile mark the trail begins to climb more steeply.

The trail bends south at 5 miles, below the lower slopes of Mount Walkinshaw, to stay close to Royal Creek up into the Royal Lake basin. A short distance after you climb two sets of steps in the trail, the incline becomes less strenuous. At 5.5 miles, after descending through the trees near to the edge of Royal Creek, the trail enters a picturesque wet meadow.

You cross a couple of log bridges over little tributaries that feed Royal Creek. There are tent sites in the short meadow. Beyond the south end of the meadow the trail climbs approximately 0.3 mile to Royal Lake (6 miles).

Technically a tarn—a body of water inside a cirque—Royal Lake shimmers with the reflections of the mighty peaks that surround it. The upper basin previously held more tarns, most likely shallow ones, but over the years they have filled with sediment to form meadows. Heather, with its small, frilly pink and white blooms, is the king

Royal Lake

ruling over a host of other wildflowers and subalpine fir and spruce in the upper basin.

A map posted near the lake shows where the designated campsites are in the lower and upper basins and the location of the ranger station, which is staffed during the summer hiking season. You can explore the basins, scramble up some of the slopes, or just stay put and let the brilliance of the grand surroundings come to you.

Is that Roy or Royal?

One theory about the origin of the name Royal, and the least supported, is that members of Lt. O'Neil's Olympic Expedition named the creek and lake in 1885. How they supposedly came up with the name is not known, which is partly why credit is generally given to two Forest Service employees instead. G. A. Whitehead and Roy Strom followed Milk Creek up to the ridgeline below the north face of Mount Fricaba in 1917 and saw a natural treasure thousands of feet below. The subalpine basin (Royal Basin), according to them, was an untarnished wonder that surely deserved a distinguished name. A third theory, perhaps the most likely but nowhere near as interesting, was that a transcription error by mapmakers converted what was known as Roy Creek and Roy Basin into Royal Creek and Royal Basin.

7

Marmot Pass

Type: Day hike or overnight

Season: Early June to mid-October

Total distance: 10.6 miles

Rating: Moderate

Elevation gain: 3,700 feet

Location: Buckhorn Wilderness, 12 miles west of Quilcene

Map: Green Trails Tyler Peak No. 136

Getting There

From the Hood Canal RD in Quilcene, drive south 1 mile on US 101 to Penny Creek Road and turn right. At 2.4 miles bear left at the fork. The road should be signed for Big Quilcene, eventually becoming FR 27. Bear right at 5.7 miles at the sign for the Big Quilcene Trail. At 7.1 miles turn left onto FR 2750. You reach the parking area and trailhead at 12 miles.

The Trail

The Big Quilcene River Trail is the eastern half of the Dungeness River Trail, which follows the Dungeness River to within 2 miles of its headwaters near the thick, rocky summit of Mount Mystery (7,631 feet), one of many significant peaks visible from Marmot Pass. Less crowded than the hike to the broad slopes of Mount Townsend to the northwest, Marmot Pass is surely its equal in the collection of common and rare wildflowers—both places are recognized as Botanical Areas within the Olympic National Forest—and outperforms Mount Townsend in the mountain-vista category.

Take an easy scramble from Marmot Pass to Buckhorn Mountain at just under 7,000 feet, and you will be among nearly a dozen other peaks like Warrior (7,300 feet), Mount Constance (7,743 feet), the Needles (over 7,300 feet), and Mount Fricaba (7,134 feet), and you'll enjoy grand panoramic views of the Olympics and Puget Sound region. The hike to Marmot Pass encompasses some of the best attributes of the

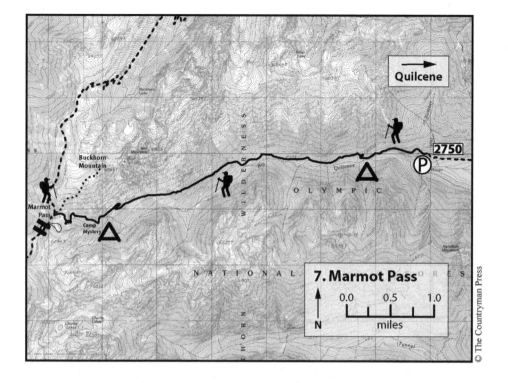

Olympics, perhaps in a better way than any other hike on the entire peninsula.

This hike begins in an unassuming forest above the north bank of the Big Quilcene River. The trail maintains a consistent, moderate inclin10p6.113 from start to finish. There are no muscle-tearing switchbacks, just a straight run up the river valley, gaining 3,700 vertical feet over 5.3 miles.

The early section of the hike is awash in color when the rhododendron bushes lining the trail—some growing to over 20 feet—are in full bloom. The pinkish blooms of the Pacific rhododendron, Washington's state flower, typically show from the end of May through June. They are nothing like the cultivated, spoon-fed varieties you see growing in western Washington gardens—immense, thick with branches, and colored tangerine orange or velvet burgundy. The wild rhodo-

dendron is wiry and holds its blooms more like delicate ornaments than dense bouquets. You'll also find dull Oregon grape, white trillium, and bunchberry growing beneath the fir and cedar forest.

A large Douglas fir tree (4 to 5 feet in diameter) fell across the trail at 0.5 mile some seasons ago, and instead of cutting it the trail crew merely dug out a part of the hillside to allow hikers to pass underneath this natural archway of sorts. At 1.3 miles the trail takes two quick switchbacks uphill, moving farther away from the river.

You pass some campsites at 2.3 miles, and then the trail makes a brief climb before resuming its moderate course across a steep open slope. Something else to identify along the way is red-flowering currant, which produces a bland but edible berry. It

Above Marmot Pass

blooms in late spring and bears fruit in late July.

At 3.7 miles the trail opens up onto a rock slope with views across the Big Quilcene River valley at the rocky ridgeline that connects with Warrior Peak to the south. This section of trail is also the gateway to the vibrant subalpine wildflower world. Get out your wildflower book and begin checking them off: avalanche lily, paintbrush, columbine, lupine, larkspur, pearly everlasting, phlox, and even rare blooms like the chocolate lily. You have hiked about 2,500 feet up by this point and are 1 mile from Camp Mystery.

As the trail climbs you will also find huckleberry bushes, which bear sweet edible berries from the end of July through August. At 4.6 miles the trail bends to the right and enters a compact park in a stand of trees by a small creek, mostly the product of an underground spring. This is Camp Mystery.

The trail edges along the creek beyond the camp, crossing near where the underground spring seeps to the surface. This spring runs year-round, although it loses steam from late summer into fall. The trail follows a lush gully of sorts that is awash with glacier lily early in the hiking season.

Next, you climb up into a shallow basin just below Marmot Pass (5.3 miles). The trail is somewhat steep but has a stable rock surface. The shallow basin below the pass is a blend of tree clusters and open grassy areas, with subalpine fir, spruce, and even whitebark pine joining the mix.

The Tubal Cain Mine valley, Dungeness River valley, Constance Pass, Mount Mystery, Tyler Peak, and other peaks are all visible from Marmot Pass (6,100 feet). The numerous open slopes, rocky ridgelines, and the steep valley of the Dungeness River 3,000 feet below make the pass feel like the top of the world. But don't stop here.

Your best option, although not the only one, is a steep 1.2-mile hike up a faint trail of loose rock to the blocky summit of Buckhorn Mountain (6,988 feet) north-northeast of the pass. Not only will you enjoy the views to Hood Canal, the Olympic peaks, and Mount Rainier, but the grassy and rocky slopes will surely hold your attention with a range of common wildflowers (paintbrush, wallflower, aster, etc.), as well as rare ones like the elegant Jacob's ladder, Flett's violet, and sky pilot.

Graveyards in the Mountains

Much like ships along the rocky Olympic coastline, airplanes and the Olympic Mountains do not have a friendly history. Mount Constance south of Marmot Pass has claimed at least two planes, one in the 1920s, which the two passengers survived, and one in 1975 when all 16 aboard a C-141 died. North of Marmot Pass, in Tull Canyon, where the Tubal Cain Mine is located, a B-17 crashed into a ridge and then slid 2,000 feet in January 1952, killing three of the eight passengers. The fuselage and other parts of the plane are still visible today.

8

Mount Ellinor

Type: Day hike

Season: Mid-June to mid-October

Total distance: 3.4 miles

Rating: Strenuous

Elevation gain: 2,444 feet

Location: Mount Skokomish Wilderness, 35 miles northwest of Olympia

Maps: Green Trails Mt. Steel No. 167, The Brothers No. 168

Getting There

From the Hood Canal RD in Hoodsport on US 101, take WA 119 (Lake Cushman Road) west and then north toward Lake Cushman. At 9.4 miles turn right (east) onto FR 24, following the sign for Mount Ellinor. Drive just over 1.5 miles down FR 24 to FR 2419 (10.9 miles) and turn left, again following the sign for Mount Ellinor. Travel nearly 7 miles, passing the Lower Mount Ellinor Trailhead, to reach FR 2419-014 at 17.6 miles. Turn left and drive 1 mile to the parking area and the Upper Mount Ellinor Trailhead at 18.6 miles.

The Trail

Mount Ellinor is a compact minidynamo set among the vast playgrounds of prominent Olympic peaks and ridgelines. It's quite popular, and like so many subalpine and alpine settings in Washington, this is for good reason. What Mount Ellinor does, perhaps better than any other hike in Washington, is condense what would normally be a 12- to 15-mile hike into less than 3.5 miles. It accomplishes this in two ways. First, it starts fairly high up, relatively speaking, at 3,500 feet; second, the trail to the summit shoots straight up to nearly 6,000 feet in a very short distance. Don't be frightened; like any strenuous climb, the keys are pace, rest, and hydration.

A veinlike system of creeks drain from the steep slopes of Mounts Washington and Ellinor, eventually converging as Big Creek and feeding into popular Lake Cushman. The hike to Ellinor follows a steep forested rib, the southwest wall of the natural funnel for one of the tributaries of this watery network.

A succession of switchbacks slowly works its way up this humped, narrow rib. Stay focused and just keep moving, placing one foot in front of the other. At 0.6 mile you reach a point of temporary relief. This relatively flat stretch lasts less than 0.1 mile before entering the bottom of a steep, rocky slope that leads to a col off the south face of Mount Ellinor.

Relief Flats is an excellent spot to catch your breath and consider that what you just accomplished in a little over 0.6 mile is the vertical equivalent of 5 miles of hiking nearly anywhere else in the state. Next, the trail enters a rocky setting that gives way to a steep, stunning grass and wildflower slope.

The blooms of buttercup, aster, anemone, bluebell, phlox, paintbrush, tiger lily, and columbine bring the slope alive. Add in heather, kinnikinnick, and a whistle or two from a marmot, and surely Mount Ellinor is a natural garden equal to larger Olympic Peninsula settings like Mount Townsend or Sol Duc Park.

The trail angles steeply up a series of rock steps to meet the col on the south ridgeline. The steps were necessary to reduce erosion on the steep grade and to protect the fragile wildflowers from the footfalls of hundreds of visitors each year. At 1.4 miles you arrive at the ridge. The lower ridge trail is lined with subalpine trees and ground juniper, but you soon enter the alpine world of craggy ridgelines and blocky mountaintops.

Mount Ellinor's 5,944-foot summit is reached via a leg-numbing climb of nearly 2,500 vertical feet in 1.7 miles. The payoff is natural vistas far and wide, including Mount Olympus, the high point of the peninsula at nearly 8,000 feet.

All the peaks in the Mount Skokomish Wilderness are visible, from Mount Lincoln to Mounts Skokomish, Pershing, and Washington. Pershing is due north of Ellinor, and the near peak to the northeast is Washington, which you can easily scramble up. To the west is the wide, deep claw mark of the Hood Canal fjord. Eighty miles to the southeast and over 8,000 feet higher than Ellinor is Mount Rainier.

Five Cheers for the Little Guy

With over 900,000 acres, a worldwide reputation, and promotional materials to boot, Olympic National Park grabs the attention of nearly every visitor to the Olympic Peninsula. However, fringe wilderness areas on the park's eastern and southern boundaries have incredibly scenic hikes as well: the Brothers Wilderness, with an earthbound trail to Mount Jupiter; Buckhorn Wilderness, with great trips to Marmot Pass and Silver Lake/Mount Townsend; Colonel Bob Wilderness, with a hike to the summit of the wilderness's namesake via Moonshine Flats; and Wonder Mountain Wilderness, with a trail-less backcountry that's perfect for the true adventurer. Information on all of these hikes, except for Marmot Pass, which is covered in chapter 7 of this book, can be found in *Washington's Wilderness Areas: The Complete Guide.*

Mount Constitution

Type: Day hike

Season: March to November

Total distance: 8.6 miles

Rating: Moderate

Elevation gain: 2,050 feet

Location: Moran State Park, 5 miles northeast of Orcas

Map: USGS Mt. Constitution

Getting There

You must catch the ferry in Anacortes (on WA 20) to reach Orcas Island, which is part of the San Juan Islands, and Moran State Park. There are several options for transportation once you're on the island. You can take your own vehicle over on the ferry or walk on board with a bicycle. Be aware, though, that it is 13.5 miles to the trailhead for the hike to Mount Constitution, and Or'cas Island is quite hilly. Another option would be to rely on island transportation like a taxi or the shuttle bus that leaves from the ferry dock. To find out schedules and fees for the ferry and the island shuttle service, visit these web sites: www.wsdot.wa.gov /ferries and www.orcasislandshuttle.com.

Whether you're driving or riding, the route to Moran State Park follows Orcas Road, also known as the Horseshoe Highway. The road runs up the left leg of the horseshoe of Orcas Island, bending around Fishing Bay and Ship Bay and passing by the Orcas Airport before heading down the right leg to the entrance of Moran State Park (13.2 miles). The Cold Springs Trailhead is on the left, across from a picnic area next to Cascade Lake (13.5 miles).

The Trail

Island mountains or mountain islands—no matter how you wish to call the 700-island San Juan Archipelago, it's interesting to know that landmasses like Orcas are actually the tops of 40-million-year-old mountains formed from twisted ocean sedimentary layers and then subjected to

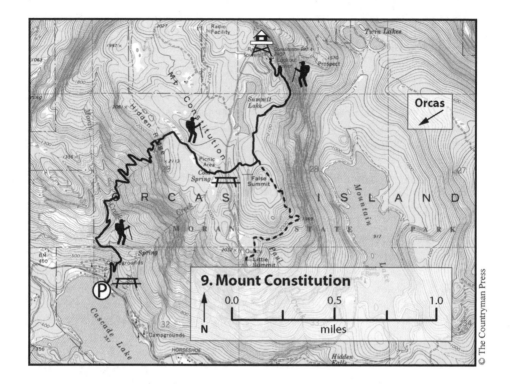

erosion and the actions of various ice ages. What we see today from the area's high-point on Mount Constitution (2,409 feet) is a collection of islands, islets, reefs, and rocks scattered about the Strait of Georgia like green icebergs.

On a clear day Mount Constitution delivers incredible views of the coastal mountain range of British Columbia, Mounts Baker and Shuksan, Mount Rainier, the Olympics, Vancouver Island, and a large portion of the San Juans. The summit of Mount Constitution is certainly the highlight of this hike, but the journey along the Cold Springs Trail also has merit. The sturdy log and stone picnic shelter and outhouses in the grove of western red cedars at the trailhead were built by the Civilian Conservation Corps (CCC) in the 1930s. As you head out on the trail you're immediately immersed in a world of shadows and greens created by the dense tree canopy and the abundance of bracken fern.

The trail follows Moran Creek up to Cold Springs in 3 miles. At 0.1 mile a wide plank bridge crosses the creek and leads to a nice picnic area tucked in the trees on a short rise.

The forest along the lower portion of this hike is made up of Douglas fir, western hemlock, and western red cedar. Since the trail climbs at a decent rate to shortly before Cold Springs, you'll have ample time to investigate the multiple varieties of mushroom and moss growing over the forest floor, on rocks, and on fallen trees. There are at least 80 species of moss and liverworts along the Northwest coast, a small number compared to the 14,000 species worldwide, but confusing enough if you're trying to identify one. (A useful book is *Plants of the Pacific Northwest Coast,* by Pojar and Mackinnon.)

At 1.7 miles the trail slips out onto an open section of grass and rock, which can offer quite a temperature shock after the cool, damp forest setting. The San Juans typically receive very little precipitation because of the rain barrier in the Olympic Mountains. Some of the islands receive as little as 19 inches, although Mount Constitution averages 45 inches, less than the city of Olympia but more than Seattle.

Continue through the open section and back into the trees, climbing a series of switchbacks through a more open forest that now includes lodgepole pine and passing by a rock outcropping before the trail junction at 2.5 miles. Continue straight, in the direction of Cold Springs. The trail dips down to a meadow and then makes an easy half-mile stroll to the Cold Springs Picnic Area (3 miles).

Cross the road (yes, there is vehicle access to the top of Mount Constitution) and hike another 0.3 mile through a lodgepole pine forest to a second trail junction (3.3 miles). Head left at the TOWER sign. You arrive at Summit Lake in another 0.3 mile. Moran State Park (5,252 acres) contains five lakes: Cascade, where this hike started; Summit Lake; Mountain Lake; and the Twin Lakes. The last three lakes are visible from the summit.

A radical transition comes at 3.8 miles, when you depart the sanctuary of the trees and join the open expanse of the greater Puget Sound, with all the visual treats afforded by the 2,000 vertical feet of climbing

you've done so far. Specifically, there are takes on the Coast Mountains north of Vancouver, British Columbia, and Mount Baker (10,781 feet). The slope is much more arid, with shrubs like manzanita and salal dominating.

Continue hiking through the trees up a moderate incline. You pass a few buildings and a parking area before reaching the observation tower at the summit (4.3 miles). The stone tower—outfitted with hemlock posts, rails, doors, and floor in the observation room on the very top—was built by the CCC in 1936. A series of panels explains the history, geology, and geography of Moran State Park and the San Juan Islands.

The views from the tower and picnic area are quite phenomenal. Large signs indicate the locations and names of the landmarks visible from Mount Constitution, including ranges like the Coast Mountains, Cascades, Olympics, and Vancouver Mountains and volcanoes like Baker, Glacier, and Rainier. You can also see the cities of Victoria, Vancouver, and Seattle, as well as San Juan Island, Lopez Island, and the string of smaller islands along the east shoreline of Orcas—Patos, Sucia, Matia, and Clark. All four of these islands are state parks with campsites.

Using the ferry, you can island-hop between Lopez, Orcas, and San Juan. Don't just run out to Orcas for a hike to Mount Constitution; spend time discovering as many of the islands of the San Juans as possible. Two reference books with more information on the San Juan Islands are Moon Handbooks' *San Juan Islands,* by Don Pitcher, and *The Essential San Juan Islands Guide,* by Marge and Ted Mueller.

Architect, Conservationist, Mayor, Philanthropist, and Shipbuilder

Robert Moran was born in 1857 in New York City. He died at the age of 85 in 1943 on

The stone tower atop Mount Constitution

Orcas Island, having lived an extremely rich life. He made his money in ship-building, constructing vessels like the USS *Nebraska*, which was commissioned from 1907 to 1923. He was mayor of Seattle for a year (1888–1889), designed and built his own mansion in 1909 (known today as the Rosario Resort and Spa Hotel), and donated land, resources, and money to preserve what would eventually be called Moran State Park in 1921. His legacy is spread by the visitors who come to play in what he called "a wonderful place in which to forget one's troubles and worries and get back to Nature in her happiest moods."

Western anemone

10

Heather Park/Galena Chain Lakes Loop

Type: Day hike

Season: Late July to early October

Total distance: 7.5 miles

Rating: Moderate

Elevation gain: Moderate

Location: Mount Baker Wilderness, 30 miles east of Bellingham

Map: Green Trails Shuksan No. 14

Getting There

From the Glacier RD along the Mount Baker Highway (WA 542) east of Bellingham, drive 21.5 miles to the Wild Goose/Bagley Lakes Trailhead just past the ski resort.

The Trail

Mount Baker (10,781 feet) and Mount Shuksan (9,131 feet) compete for your attention in a battle of the giants, and there isn't a bad seat in the house. Whether you're enjoying the inspiring views of Mount Baker from Artist Point, meditating on the hulking mass of rock and ice on Shuksan's west face from atop Table Mountain (5,700 feet), or skipping through the wildflowers in Heather Meadows, you'll feel their presence.

A road to Heather Meadows was constructed in 1926 and extended to Artist Point by 1931. (The Mount Baker Lodge opened in 1927 but burned to the ground in 1931.) Amazing as the five-year road-building effort was, it can't compare to the natural splendors of this area.

The hike begins on one of two southbound trails and climbs about 900 vertical feet over 1.5 miles to Artist Point. One is the Heather Meadows Trail, which parallels the road in the climb to Artist Point. The other moves toward the east shoreline of the larger of the Bagley Lakes, where in 0.4 mile it comes to a trail junction. Head left (east) to meet back up with the Heather Meadows Trail.

The meadows look as if they've been meticulously landscaped with lakes,

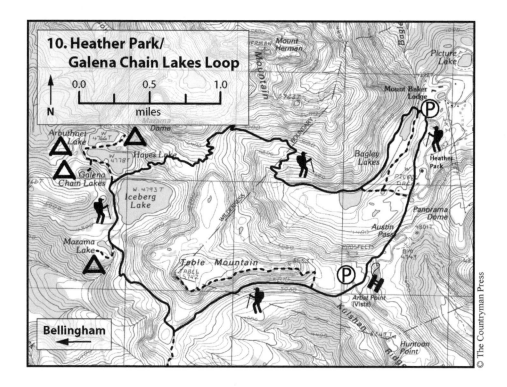

subalpine fir and mountain hemlock, and islands of heather surrounded by glacier lily, buttercup, columbine, subalpine daisy, penstemon, bistort, stream violet, and arnica, all nicely packed against the east flank of Mount Herman (6,285 feet) and the northeast face of Table Mountain.

Beyond the upper parking lot is Artist Point, a prime viewpoint of Mounts Baker and Shuksan. Baker floats in the sky to the south, tethered by Ptarmigan Ridge, a popular access route for climbers. From the point, and along the 1-mile route to the Ptarmigan Trail junction, you can peer down into the 3,000-foot gorge of Swift Creek, which was cut by glaciers.

To the east stands Mount Shuksan, probably one of this country's finest examples of alpine perfection with its multifaced pointed top, sharp arêtes, impressive cirques, hanging glaciers, and regal prominence. It rises 3,000 feet above tree line, a trait more common in Cascade volcanoes.

A quick 0.2 mile down the trail is the junction for Table Mountain. The 2-mile, round-trip hike to the tarn and patchy snow-covered summit plateau offers a "tabletop" view for 360 degrees. To continue the loop, keep moving above the deep gorge to the Ptarmigan Ridge Trail junction (2.5 miles). The trail down to the Galena Chain Lakes moves across an open expanse of loose rock and wildflowers beneath the southwest corner of Table Mountain. The first, and smallest, of the lakes is Mazama (3.5 miles).

The trail winds through stands of trees, heather, and wildflowers over a benched area that holds three more lakes: Iceberg,

Hayes, and Arbuthnet. There are campsites on the south shore of Mazama, Hayes, and Arbuthnet and on the north end between Hayes and Arbuthnet. The main trail cuts between Iceberg and Hayes at 4 miles and climbs—gradually at first, then with more of an incline—for 1 mile to a tiny pass (5 miles) slung between Mazama Dome (5,842 feet) and Table Mountain.

This is a great spot from which to look back down on the parklike setting of the Galena Chain Lakes, as well as over to the smaller of the Bagley Lakes. This is the only point where Mount Shuksan takes center stage over Mount Baker.

You drop down a barren, loose-rock slope to the smaller Bagley Lake at 6.8 miles, pressing hard against Mount Herman as you move along the north shoreline. At 7.1 miles you reach a stone bridge between the two Bagley Lakes. If you hiked along the east shore of the first Bagley Lake at the start of the hike, you can continue straight, working along the west side and around the north end of the lake to reach the trailhead (7.5 miles).

Amazing Race

The Mount Baker Club came into existence in the early 20th century as a business entity focused on promoting the Mount Baker region. The members of this club, specifically Bert Huntoon, were instrumental in pushing for road construction up to Heather Meadows, as well as to the former resort lodge. To gain attention for their mission they organized the Mount Baker Marathon, which utilized a train, automobiles, and foot travel in a race from Bellingham to the summit of Mount Baker and back. The 118-mile race—24 miles on foot—was held from 1911 to 1913. The race was canceled because a hidden crevice on Mount Baker nearly took the life of a competitor in 1913, a chilling (literally and figuratively) reminder to all that mountains aren't a child's playground.

11

Mazama Park and Park Butte Lookout

Type: Day hike or overnight

Season: Early July to mid-October

Total distance: 10.4 miles

Rating: Moderate

Elevation gain: 3,100 feet

Location: Mount Baker National Recreation Area, 35 miles northeast of Sedro-Woolley

Map: Green Trails Hamilton No. 45

Getting There

Start at the North Cascades Forest Service headquarters in Sedro-Woolley, at the corner of WA 20 and WA 9. To reach the trailhead for Mazama Park take WA 9 north 14.7 miles to the town of Acme. Past Acme, the highway crosses the Middle Fork Nooksack River. Turn right onto Mosquito Lake Road just after the bridge. Travel 9.8 miles, crossing a one-lane bridge over the Middle Fork Nooksack, and turn right onto FR 38 (24.5 miles) before a much smaller bridge over Porter Creek. The road is not signed, but there's a gravel pit shortly before the turn.

A half mile up the road a sign for FR 38 confirms you're on the right road. At 29.5 miles, the road forks; follow the uphill fork (left), which is signed for FR 38. The road ends at the trailhead in approximately 35.5 total miles.

The Trail

Glaciated Mount Baker, the blueberry and huckleberry oasis of Mazama Park, and vistas galore from the perch of the Park Butte Lookout—what more could you want? How about a heather and wildflower parkland covered with glacially rounded rock and stippled with tarns, or the orange glow from the impressive Twin Sisters Mountain to the west, or a moraine stacked high like a fortress wall? This hike has all that and more.

A 0.2-mile forested path leads you down to the confluence of the Middle Fork Nooksack River and Ridley Creek. *Nooksack,*

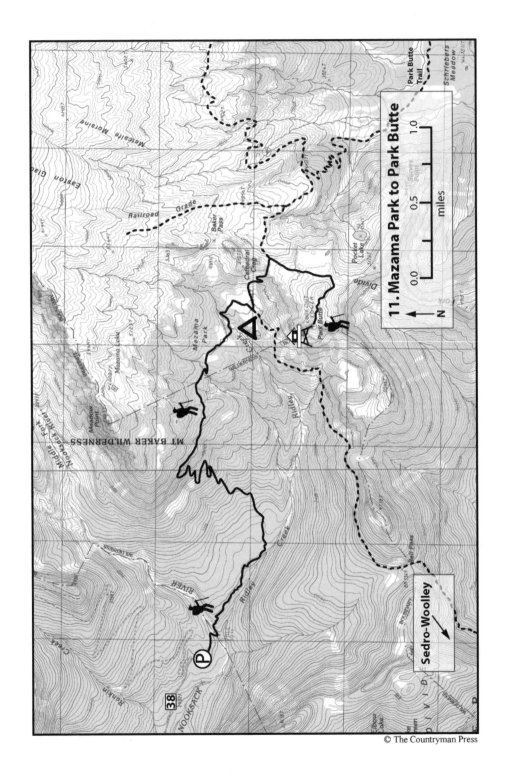

11. Mazama Park to Park Butte

© The Countryman Press

which translates to "mountain men," is the name of a local tribe. The Middle Fork Nooksack originates from the Deming Glacier on Mount Baker, and Ridley Creek from the terminus of Easton Glacier. The swollen streams, creeks, and rivers around Mount Baker—even late into a typical summer hiking season—come in part from these glaciers but more so from the massive amounts of snowfall that bury the mountain. In 1998 Mount Baker set the world record, accumulating 1,124 inches of snow in a single season.

The foot-log across the swift-moving Nooksack was mostly swept away during the heavy rains of fall 2003. There are plans to replace it in 2005, but in the meantime be aware that it's unsafe to ford the river at high water. If you happen to slip into the icy water (below 50 degrees) you risk hypothermia, or worse. However, at low water you'll be able to pick your way across safely at a point near the old log crossing.

Once across, the trail continues up from the left, or north, side of Ridley Creek. It may not seem like it as you scan the cutbank, but there is a well-worn trail through the trees about 35 yards north of Ridley.

You climb a few switchbacks before descending slightly and then taking an easy course parallel to, but back from, the creek. The trail is rough, with tree roots, downed trees, and rocks, and it can be brushed over with deer fern, salmonberry, devil's club, foamflower, and other healthy plant life in the damp, mossy environment.

At 1.3 miles the trail takes a noticeable turn upslope, marking the transition from creek-side to slope-side hiking. As you climb higher, the trail evens out and provides a spongy surface thick with dried needles. Expect a few rugged sections and possible downfall as you gain elevation steadily over a moderate incline.

Switchbacks give way to a long cross-slope contour through sizable cedars at 2.3 miles, where you have filtered views of the red-rock mountain range known as the Twin Sisters (up to 7,000 feet) to the west-southwest, as well the west face of haystack-shaped Park Butte (5,450 feet) straight ahead to the east. After crossing the widest of four creeks—dry creek beds later in the summer—you step into the spectacular Mazama Park (2.8 miles). *Mazama* is Spanish for "mountain goat," which can be seen from time to time along the rocky slopes above the park.

Mazama Park hosts a glorious explosion of wildflowers like paintbrush, lupine, bistort, and tiger lily, along with a profuse amount of mountain blueberry and huckleberry—enough to swell your belly and stain your tongue and fingers for days. The park includes pockets of grass and small tarns before the trail crosses Ridley Creek and moves through the upper portion of the park, still overflowing with berry bushes.

At 3.5 miles there is a sign for Baker Pass (northeast) and Bell Pass (southwest) mounted to a tree beside the trail; go straight ahead toward the sturdy log camp shelter. Draped in faded Nepalese prayer flags, the shelter is perfectly placed for views of the Twin Sisters, Mount Baker to the north, and the Ridley Creek drainage. You can also see the lookout atop Park Butte, tucked in the trees to the left of the summit.

The trail to the Park Butte Lookout, discernable from the shelter, cuts up the rockslide beneath Cathedral Crag. It makes a few switchbacks before topping out in an open park/moraine (4.2 miles), arguably as stunning as any Cascade volcano from British Columbia to California.

Straight ahead, the tall, seemingly man-made rock wall is actually a glacial moraine

Mount Baker looming behind Mazama Park

sculpted by the shrinking Easton Glacier. The Railroad Grade Trail edges along the eastern side of the moraine. If you follow the trail you just climbed from Mazama Park downslope and across the open moonscape expanse, you'll meet up with this trail, which leads to a climber's high camp, complete with amazing views of the glacier below.

It is about 1.5 miles one way from the Park Butte Trail junction up to high camp via the Railroad Grade. Mount Baker looms above you, showing off a few of the 12 glaciers that cover 10,000 acres on this still-active volcano. (Mount Baker last erupted in 1880.) Local tribes aptly refer to the mountain as Koma Kulshan, or "Wounded Mountain."

Head right at the junction for the stroll from here to Park Butte, which runs through a fantastic wildflower and heather parkland. At 4.7 miles the trail begins to bend around the south side of Park Butte, passing by small tarns and above a larger tarn set in a bowl-like indentation downslope. Now on the west side of the butte, the trail passes beneath scattered trees and by two hitching posts suitable for horses (or misbehaving children) before making a short, steep push to the lookout (5.2 miles).

This final approach to the lookout at Park Butte is probably the most mesmerizing of any in the state.

The lookout was constructed in 1932 and operates today as a first-come, first-served overnight shelter. It's equipped with a stove, binoculars, telescope, books (leave one of yours if you wish), and one double bed for the lucky winner. You must pack your own water or pull some from the tarns below, as well as pack in your own stove and gas.

Volunteers from the Skagit Alpine Club help maintain the lookout. For more information, visit www.skagitalpineclub.com. As always, pack out all your trash and leave the lookout in better condition than you found it.

Sunsets and sunrises on the parkland and surrounding peaks are a dessert for the eyes. Some of the visible peaks include Mount Bloom, Hagen Peak, Loomis (directly to the south along the South Fork divide), the Twin Sisters, as well as Mount Baker and Easton and Squak Glaciers.

Shorter and Nearly as Sweet

An alternate, and far more popular, approach to Park Butte originates from the east via Park Butte Trail 603. It's only 2.5 miles from there to the Park Butte junction, which eliminates about 1,000 feet in elevation gain. However, you won't get the added bonus of Mazama Park unless you make an extra side trip.

12

Thornton Lakes

Type: Day hike or overnight

Season: End of June to October

Total distance: 10.6 miles

Rating: Strenuous

Elevation gain: 3,000 to 4,000 feet

Location: North Cascades National Park, 9 miles from Newhalem

Map: Green Trails Marblemount No. 47

Getting There

From the North Cascades National Park Visitor Center in Newhalem, travel west on WA 20 for 3.3 miles to the right turn onto Thornton Lakes Road, which is located just before mile marker 117. The road up to the trailhead is rough and steep at certain points. You reach the small parking area, outhouses, and trailhead at 8.3 miles. If you plan to stay overnight, don't forget to pick up a camping permit.

The Trail

Thornton Lakes is the only hike in North Cascades National Park that can be reached with relative ease while still offering a wonderful, secluded backcountry setting of cirque lakes, intimidating mountains, and rich subalpine flora. The three lakes are clustered together in the shadows of Mount Triumph (7,270 feet) and Trappers Peak (5,964 feet), which can keep their waters frozen well into August.

Don't let the name Mount Triumph fool you; this is still rugged North Cascades country, evidenced by the names of peaks north and southwest of the Thornton Lakes: Mount Despair (7,292 feet) and Damnation Peak (5,635 feet).

The first portion of the hike follows an old roadbed now overgrown with alder, fir, hemlock, fireweed, pearly everlasting, wild strawberry, and ground-covering moss. The road was used for clear-cutting operations until the formation of the North Cascades National Park Complex in 1968. The largest portion—over 634,000 acres—of the 684,600-acre complex was designated the Stephen T. Mather Wilderness in the wave of wilderness area inductions in 1984.

Grab your parasol and get ready to stroll rather than hike for the first 2.1 miles. You pass or cross a half-dozen or so creeklets trickling down the thickly forested slope. There are three large creek crossings, the first (0.5 mile) of which is usually fairly dry later in the summer. The second is at 0.8 mile. Here, and at the next crossing 0.1 mile farther on at Thornton Creek, you can see the destruction of a severe washout from the fall of 2003, which destroyed parts of the trail and moved a tremendous amount of soil and rock.

As of this writing, the Thornton Creek crossing is flagged to make it easy to find your way through the flood debris. The trail initially heads northwest, contouring along the Thornton Creek drainage. At the final creek crossing it turns southeast before making a slow bend to the north. There are views to the east of the Babcock Creek drainage and the much larger Goodell Creek drainage, as well as Mount Ross (6,052 feet).

At 2.3 miles the trail leaves the old roadbed and winds up a forested slope. There is a constant supply of rocks and tree roots on the trail. It's a steady climb, with a couple of short, steep sections thrown in for good measure. You'll feel that 30- or 40-pound pack strapped to your back in this section.

The forest is quite dense through here but is lit by the glow of tufted pipecleaner moss (tubular and caterpillarlike) carpeting the ground. The horizon line beyond the treetops above you says "This is the top!" but it remains elusive until you eventually reach the notch above Thornton Lakes at 4.9 miles.

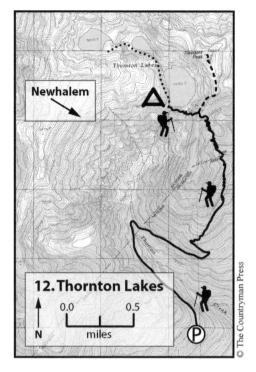

Newhalem

12. Thornton Lakes

0.0   0.5

N   miles

© The Countryman Press

Around 3.3 miles the trail passes over some logs through a damp section overgrown with devil's club, salmonberry, and the tropical-looking skunk cabbage. At 3.7 miles the trail passes under, and then climbs above, a series of large boulders set between the trees.

From here, it's approximately 0.3 mile to a stream-fed meadow decorated with wildflowers, huckleberry, and mountain blueberry. The berry-lined trail then climbs to the Thornton Lakes Trail junction (4.9 miles). A sign indicates Thornton Lakes to the left.

The 0.7-mile, 500-foot drop to the first and largest of the three alpine lakes is steep and can pose a challenge when wet. There are three tent sites near the lake's outlet, and you need a backcountry permit to camp overnight.

The first lake is pressed hard against the western cliff wall of Trappers Peak. The middle and upper lakes are accessible by hiking and scrambling, and they too are magnificent by-products of glacial gouging that ended some 12,000 years ago.

A good short day hike for campers, or as an add-on to the long hike down to the Thornton Lakes, is a scramble to the top of Trappers Peak. At the junction for the lakes, head right (north) to make a 0.9-mile roller-coaster run to the summit. You top out on a few places along the ridgeline before reaching the broad, blocky summit of Trappers. The trail has some steep, scrambling sections, but for the most part it's a strenuous hike up through heather, juniper, and kinnikinnick.

Not only are you rewarded with a superb aerial view of the lakes, but you're also eye-to-eye with Mount Triumph (7,270 feet) a few miles to the northwest, Teebone Ridge (over 6,500 feet) across the Skagit River to the south, and the North Cascades' most formidable collection of peaks: the Picket Range (over 8,000 feet) to the north.

The trail to Thornton Lakes is one of only a few maintained trails that access grand high-alpine lakes within the whole national park complex. So if you want to see other marvelous lakes in North Cascades National Park, bring extra food, an ice ax, and a good sense of direction.

What's This About a Complex?

The "Complex" in the North Cascades National Park Complex includes three separate areas. The northern and southern units (north and south of WA 20, respectively) of North Cascades National Park comprise approximately 505,000 wilderness acres. The Ross Lake National Recreation Area surrounds three man-made lakes—Ross, Diablo, and Gorge—and contains 117,600 acres, with 74,000 acres designated wilderness. The third area, located along the Stehekin River north of the town of Stehekin, is the Lake Chelan National Recreation Area, which covers 62,000 acres (55,800 acres designated wilderness). To make things even more "complex," all of the wilderness acreage is grouped together under the name of Stephen T. Mather, the first director of the national park system.

13

Diablo Lake

Type: Day hike

Season: Early spring to early winter

Total distance: 7.4 miles

Rating: Easy to moderate

Elevation gain: 1,200 feet

Location: North Cascades National Park, 8 miles east of Newhalem

Map: Green Trails Diablo Dam No. 48

Getting There

From the North Cascades National Park Visitor Center in Newhalem, travel 7.8 miles east on WA 20 to the Diablo Dam Road and turn left. The road crosses Diablo Dam. At 9 miles you arrive at the trailhead, where there is plenty of parking.

The Trail

The Diablo Lake Trail takes you low, high, and low again along the north shore of Diablo Lake. The milky-green color of Diablo's water comes from glacial movement—specifically, the grinding of rock down so fine that it becomes glacial flour.

All three lakes in the area—Ross, Diablo, and Gorge—were created by damming on the Skagit River, which changed natural river-bottom habitat all the way into Canada in the quest to feed Seattle with power.

The trail starts along the mouth of Sourdough Creek and then dives into a world of greens, from dull Oregon grape, sword fern, and salal to lichen and moss wrapped around the trees and covering rocks. The dense Douglas fir and western hemlock forest also contains deciduous trees like western red alder and vine maple, with its distinctive green bark in the early years of growth.

The buildings you see below the trail near the 0.3-mile mark are part of the North Cascades Environmental Learning Center, which was due to open in summer 2005. The outdoor education retreat is supported by the National Park Service, Sauk-Suiattle tribe, and Seattle City Light. At 0.4 mile you

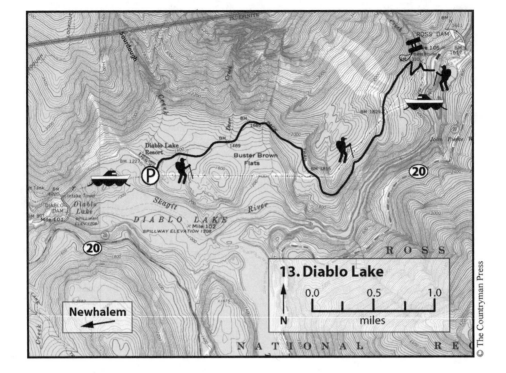

13. Diablo Lake

0.0   0.5   1.0
miles

N

Newhalem

© The Countryman Press

cross a road and arrive at a trail junction. Follow the sign for the Diablo Lake Trail.

The lush Pacific Northwest rain forest continues for the first mile of the hike. The shadowy trail makes a couple of creek crossings, passes through a rocky washout and by a collection of decent-sized cedars, and at slightly over 1.3 miles crosses the bottom of a rockslide. At this point you're about 450 feet above the milky mint-green waters of Diablo Lake. The trail then passes through a boulder field and away from the trees at approximately 2 miles. It makes a catwalklike run beneath and across a tall cliff band that forms the northwest side of the Diablo Lake Gorge.

The 389-foot Diablo Dam was completed in 1930, and Ross Dam, formerly Ruby Dam, was first completed a decade

later. It was eventually increased to its present dimensions of 1,300 feet long and 540 feet high.

The lake is rather constricted through here, resembling the river it once was. There are nice views of Colonial Peak to the southwest and Ruby Mountain to the southeast. This area is quite a bit more arid, with mountain grasses and kinnikinnick thriving instead of mosses and ferns.

The trail begins losing elevation around 2.5 miles, passing under power lines that lead from Ross Dam to the north-northeast. It also slips back into an open forest of tall Douglas firs.

You can hear the churn of the turbines, which are capable of producing 450 megawatts. The Gorge, Diablo, and Ross Dams combine to produce about 780 megawatts, enough power to run 780,000 average homes.

At 3.2 miles you arrive at a junction. A few yards ahead is the best overlook of Ross Lake Dam. Turning down the first of two switchbacks, the trail runs just under 0.5 mile to the wide, sturdy suspension bridge across Diablo Lake (3.7 miles). From the opposite side of the bridge you can see the slot canyon of Riprap Creek feeding into Diablo Lake.

All Aboard!

Tired or pressed for time? Catch a ferry up or down the lake to cut the hiking distance in half. The dock (near Ross Dam) for the Diablo Lake ferry is south of the footbridge. The cost is $5 for adults and $3 for children (age 3–11) one way. The summer-only ferry heads up from Diablo Dam at 8:30 and 3:00, and down from Ross Dam at 9:00 and 3:30.

14

Cascade Pass

Type: Day hike or overnight

Season: Mid-June to mid-October

Total distance: 7.4 miles

Rating: Moderate

Elevation gain: 1,800 feet

Location: North Cascades National Park, 24 miles from Marblemount

Map: Green Trails Cascade Pass No. 80

Getting There

From Marblemount on WA 20 (North Cascades Scenic Highway), cross over the Skagit River and follow the Cascade River Road to its end at the trailhead for Cascade Pass. The road is paved for the first 10 miles and then becomes gravel for the next 13.5 miles, except for intermittent paved portions over the last 2.5 miles. You reach Johannesburg Camp and the parking area at 23.5 miles. Don't forget to pick up a camping permit if you plan to stay overnight.

The Trail

You don't even need to get out of your vehicle at the parking area to enjoy an incredible view. The elevation is only 3,600 feet, but the looming Cascade peaks, dozens of tall waterfalls, and alpine glaciers clinging to rock walls 1,500 feet above all make it feel more like a roost for eagles. These glaciers are the remnants of ice ages spanning millions of years, the last coming 12,000 years ago.

Cascade Pass, your destination, sits between a glacially carved valley and basin. The near basin to the southeast holds the headwaters of the North Fork Cascade River and Pelton Creek, which runs through Pelton Basin to the southeast of Cascade Pass on the way to the Stehekin River. The Stehekin empties into the 50-mile-long, 1,500-foot-deep fjord of Lake Chelan.

So turn the engine off, tie your shoes, and begin hiking, because to really appreciate this wonderful area you need to reach Cascade Pass.

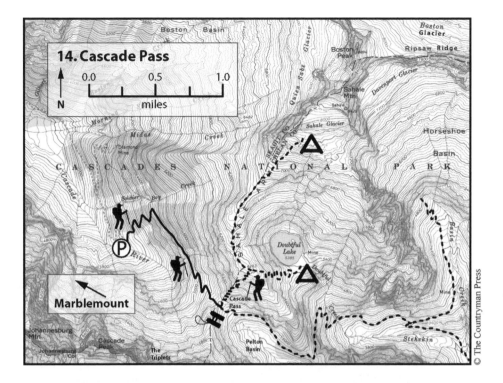

The peaks you see to the south are, from right to left, Johannesburg Mountain (8,200 feet), Cascade Peak (7,428 feet), and the Triplets (7,240 feet). For the first 0.5 to 0.6 mile the trail provides decent views of these peaks. You climb the entire way, but the 30 ramping switchbacks help tame the incline.

The understory is diverse in the beginning and again when you enter the subalpine zone before the pass. The trail is lined with huckleberry, salmonberry, alder, devil's club, foamflower, pearly everlasting, sword fern, and red elderberry. Fir, hemlock, and cedar (higher up) mark the early trail, while subalpine fir and mountain hemlock show up at and above the pass.

The Cascade Pass Trail has a long history, starting as a trade route between coastal and Columbia Basin tribes for nearly 8,000 years. Later, explorers like Alexander Ross utilized the worn pathway during the early 1800s to build the lucrative Northwest fur trade. Later in the 19th century, prospectors used the trail to seek gold and silver. Today, hikers, backpackers, and mountaineers come here to enjoy, rather than exploit, the natural wonders.

The switchbacks are consistent in their grade, coming farther apart early on and then closer together where the tree cover becomes denser. At 1.9 miles a switchback makes a slightly wider swing out onto an open slope, providing views of the top end of Boston Basin and Mount Torment (8,120 feet) and Forbidden Peak (8,815 feet). You can hear Solider Boy Creek running nearby.

Looking over a map of the North Cascades, you'll notice many sinister names for the mountains: Fury, Terror, Despair, Damnation, Desolation, and one that really inspires, Redoubt. But to a mountaineer—and

Deer feeding at Cascade Pass

climbers named most of these mountains—those are words of love and affection.

At 2.1 miles you have a view of the head of the glacial valley and the Triplets perched above. The switchbacks end at 2.5 miles, and the cross-slope contouring begins. The trail moves through huckleberry, mountain blueberry, glacier lily, heather, hellebore, columbine, lupine, tiger lily, and fringed grass of Parnassus. All the major peaks named at the start of the hike are visible now that you're more or less out of the trees. You can see the pass up ahead and a long rockslide that begins 800 feet above you on the southwest slope of Sahale Arm. The trail passes through this slide on the way to Cascade Pass at 3.7 miles.

With just a few steps you're across the tiny pass and looking down into Pelton Basin. You can see Pelton Peak (7,120 feet) and Magic Mountain (7,610 feet) near the basin's southeast end. To your right (south) is Mix-up Peak (7,440 feet).

The same natural forces that created the Cascade Pass vistas continue to shape the valleys and mountains today. The delicate communities of heather and other plant life that sit atop the pass are hammered by ferocious winters, only to appear summer after summer glowing with color. Stay on the trails to avoid damaging the flora. If you happen to arrive early enough you may even see black-tailed deer feeding in the tiny meadow. There is a pit toilet at the pass.

To continue the glorious hike from the subalpine/alpine into a true alpine setting, take a trip up the Sahale Arm. (*Sahale* means "falcon" or "Great Spirit.") From the pass, drop less than 0.1 mile to the junction for the Sahale Arm.

If you were to follow the trail straight ahead for 4.5 miles, you'd reach the sheer-walled amphitheater of Horseshoe Basin and the Black Warrior Mine. But head left

(upslope) for 0.9 mile to follow the Sahale Arm via a beautiful garden of wildflowers, heather, and rock. You eventually reach an overlook and the trail junction for Doubtful Lake (another uplifting name). Ptarmigan, a high-altitude member of the grouse family, are frequently seen along this stretch.

The lake sits about 600 feet below the trail junction, about 0.7 mile farther on. Camping is by permit only. The rocky ridge across and above the lake is part of Horseshoe Basin. The most dominating views are of glaciated Sahale Mountain. Travel another 1.3 miles to the Sahale Glacier Camp at 7,200 feet and even grander panoramas of all the surrounding peaks.

Cascade Pass and the Sahale Arm also offer access for those who enjoy glacial travel and high-mountain adventures. Beyond the Sahale Camp, cross-country travelers follow routes from Sahale to Buckner Mountain via Boston Glacier and the Ripsaw Ridge. South from Cascade Pass adventurers access the Ptarmigan Traverse, a long high-line stretch through the Glacier Peak Wilderness, another region full of mountains with less than sanguine names: Formidable, Sinister, and Disappointment.

Dar's Gold in Dem Dar Hills!

Horseshoe Basin is an amazing, broad, tall-walled cirque capped by Ripsaw Ridge and draped in numerous long cascades. A wet meadow environment at the bottom of the basin hosts a splendid collection of wildflowers, from glacier lily, anemone, and globeflower to paintbrush and fireweed. Higher up in the basin is the entrance to the Black Warrior Mine. Dress warmly and take a headlamp to explore the 4-mile-long tunnel that was once a functioning copper and zinc mine. This side hike covers 9 miles round trip from Cascade Pass.

15

Rainy Pass to Maple Pass Loop

Type: Day hike

Season: Late June to early October

Total distance: 6.8-mile loop

Rating: Moderate

Elevation gain: 2,000 feet

Location: North Cascades National Park, 35 miles west of Winthrop

Maps: Green Trails Mt. Logan No. 49, Washington Pass No. 50

Getting There

From the North Cascades Scenic Highway Visitor Center, also known as the Methow Valley Visitor Center, in Winthrop go west on WA 20 (North Cascades Highway) for 35 miles. Turn left at the sign for the Rainy Pass Picnic Area, and park in the lot a short distance past the trailhead.

The Trail

Don't be surprised if you're possessed by the urge to perform a *Sound of Music*–like twirl from the high point (6,800 feet) of the Rainy Pass to Heather Pass to Maple Pass loop hike. Peaks, arêtes, spires, ridgelines, alpine glaciers, and a volcano overwhelm your senses with dizzying beauty and clarity as you straddle the Lake Ann and Rainy Lake cirques.

Mountain highlights include Black Peak (8,970 feet), Liberty Bell (7,720 feet), and Kangaroo Ridge (over 8,000 feet), as well as Glacier Peak (10,541 feet), Washington's most remote Cascade volcano, to the distant south. No joke, the Rainy Pass to Maple Pass loop is outrageously stunning. Strap on your boots and see for yourself.

You need to exercise some restraint, though, because the mountain spectacles take a little effort to reach. From Rainy Pass the mountains seem far above you, but by the time you reach the passes and the high point (3.8 miles) on top of the narrow arête between Corteo (8,080 feet) and Frisco Mountain (7,760 feet), you are eye-to-eye with dozens of mountains in the Black Peak

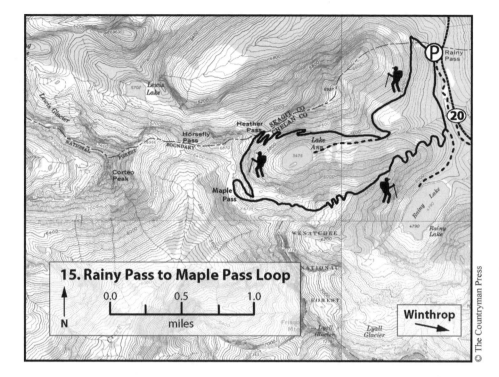

15. Rainy Pass to Maple Pass Loop

0.0   0.5   1.0

N

miles

Winthrop →

and Golden Horn batholiths of the North Cascades.

The first half mile of the Lake Ann Trail runs through a forest of fir, hemlock, and spruce with an understory rich with huckleberry. At the 0.5-mile mark the trail breaks out briefly onto a brushy slope of alder, fireweed, salmon-berry, devil's club, and pearly everlasting. The trail weaves in and out of the trees for a stretch before bending around a small rocky basin (0.8 mile) decorated with various wildflowers. There are views of Whistler Mountain (7,790 feet) and other high points along the ridgelines to the east.

At 1.3 miles you reach the junction for Lake Ann. For access, follow the trail that heads downhill, passing a couple of shallow ponds before reaching Lake Ann in approximately 0.6 mile. The wet, boggy meadow along the lake's outlet is alive with wildflowers from mid-July to early August.

To reach Heather Pass, continue straight through the trees before coming out onto a rocky slope to begin a long curve around the basin and above Lake Ann. You are in a sweet-smelling zone of subalpine spruce. There is much to study along here, like the avalanche chutes and long scree sections on the opposite side of the basin, the small island close to the head of the lake, and wildflowers from lupine, aster, and paintbrush to Sitka valerian, arnica, mountain bog gentian, and columbine.

At 1.9 miles, after gaining approximately 900 feet to this point along a long, ramping, rocky pathway, the trail turns upslope via a few switchbacks to reach Heather Pass (6,000 feet) at 2.2 miles. A trail to the right takes you across the heather-covered pass to an overlook of a basin beneath Corteo Peak and the west-to-north ridgeline with

Early-winter spires

high points like Black and Fisher (8,040 feet) Peaks.

Lewis Lake seems to hang off that ridgeline at 5,700 feet. A beautiful waterfall spills from the lake's outlet, visible from the highway high on the western side of Rainy Pass. An unmarked path slips down to Lewis from Heather Pass. Route-finding skills, a compass, and a map are encouraged for hikers on this mini-adventure.

The trail to Maple Pass rises above the Lake Ann basin, opening up even more vistas to rows of North Cascade peaks to the east and northeast. Heather, wildflowers, huckleberry, and blueberry line the pathway.

At 3 miles you arrive at Maple Pass (6,600 feet). This pass is the first of two high points that provide 360-degree panoramas. Glacier Peak is visible to the south.

The next 0.8 mile of trail is absolutely amazing. You are completely immersed in the grandeur of the alpine zone. Be sure to stick to the main trail (usually the widest and most well traveled). Excited travelers have, over time, created an ant farm–like network of trails along here, needlessly destroying the plant life.

At 3.6 miles the trail climbs 0.2 mile up to the highest point along the hike at approximately 6,800 feet. McGregor Mountain (8,124 feet), Bowan Mountain (7,894 feet), and McAlester Mountain (8,123 feet) are visible to the south and southeast. Okay, now you can twirl like an Austrian au pair.

From here the trail slides down the arête separating Lake Ann and Rainy Lake, zigzagging to a narrow overlook of Ann. In the opposite direction, you can see Rainy Lake some 2,000 feet below, as well as the

Lyall Glacier farther up in the cirque. You descend through rocks decorated with larch to a grass and wildflower section stippled here and there with subalpine trees to a brief rock catwalk before hiking through a forest for the remainder of the trip.

At 4.7 miles there is another view down to Lake Ann and the wet meadow leading away from it. The first mile in the forested section is still open enough for mountain views and intermittent overlooks of Rainy Lake. Numerous huckleberry and white-flower rhododendron bushes line the trail.

You are fully in the trees at 5.8 miles, eventually crossing a total of four elevated walkways before meeting up with the asphalt trail to Rainy Lake at 6.3 miles. The trail to the right takes you to Rainy Lake in approximately 0.4 mile, while the left path leads back to the trailhead in just under 0.5 mile (6.8 miles). The asphalt path (Rainy Lake Trail) has a couple of bridge crossings and educational signs with information ranging from the purpose of lichens to why certain tree species are present.

The Rainy Pass to Maple Pass loop hike is bound to be the highlight of your vacation slideshow.

Climber's Paradise

The area around Washington Pass–Rainy Pass is a magnet for climbers. There are documented routes up nearly every visible peak. The solid granite makes for safe climbing, and routes range from easy scrambles to the highly technical. Fred Beckey's *Cascade Alpine Guide, Climbing and High Routes 3: Rainy Pass to Fraser River* is a must for climbers heading up mountains like Liberty Bell or Cutthroat Peak or making a winter ascent up Silver Star Mountain.

16

Cutthroat Pass

Type: Day hike

Season: Late June to early October

Total distance: 10 miles

Rating: Moderate

Elevation gain: 2,000 feet

Location: Liberty Bell Roadless Area, 35 miles west of Winthrop

Map: Green Trails Washington Pass No. 50

Getting There

From the North Cascades Scenic Highway Visitor Center, also known as the Methow Valley Visitor Center, in Winthrop travel WA 20 (North Cascades Highway) west for 35 miles. Turn right at the sign for the Pacific Crest Trail north to reach the parking area, outhouses, and trailhead. (The turn is before the official sign for Rainy Pass.)

The Trail

You won't find trout at Cutthroat Pass, only waves of North Cascade peaks set in a tranquil environment of rock and heather. Cutthroat is the first of over a dozen passes crossed by the weary feet of Pacific Crest Trail (PCT) through-hikers on the last stretch of their 2,650-mile journey, which began two and a half to three months earlier by the Mexican border and will eventually end at Manning Provincial Park in Canada.

You glide more than hike along the first section of the trail. It makes only two switch-backs before moving ever so gently up a forested slope. A small creek drops from high on the west face of Cutthroat Peak at 1 mile, followed by a foot-log crossing of Porcupine Creek at 2.2 miles.

The rocky, snow-patched basins with waterfalls to the southwest belong to Corteo (8,080 feet) and Black Peak (8,970 feet). These peaks, along with other dramatic mountain formations like Kangaroo Ridge, Early Winter Spires, Silver Star, and Cutthroat Peak are part of the Golden Horn batholith, the young buck of the Cascade granites formed some 50 million years ago.

After crossing Porcupine Creek the trail

climbs more steeply, passing through a stand of trees and lined with huckleberry and heather. At 2.9 miles you break out into a huge basin guarded by an unnamed fang-like peak to the west-northwest and Cutthroat Peak (8,050 feet) to the east-southeast. The basin is heavily treed up through the midsection, but the trail stays out in the open except for the 0.3-mile stretch that comes just after the initial opening of the basin.

The predominantly granite rock you see is a mix of black, gray, tan, and burnt orange, creating a marvelous swirl of color. Above tree line, long scree slopes drop from the rocky ridgelines. The trail rims the lower-middle section of the basin as it moves toward Cutthroat Pass (6,800 feet), the obvious saddle to the northeast that you see when first entering the basin. This part of the basin is quite damp, supporting a variety of wildflowers like valerian, paintbrush, yellow violet, and the ever-so-adaptable lupine, along with blueberries and heather.

At 3.6 miles you pass a small campsite next to a stream. From here the trail climbs more steeply (but not too badly) up a series of switchbacks. Subalpine fir, spruce, and mountain hemlock begin to show up, and you even pass through a nice grove of larch, their needles a golden-sun yellow come autumn. Just before the pass, the terrain changes to a natural garden of rounded boulders and rock outcroppings, green grasses, and heather set among impressive 7,000- to 8,000-foot peaks.

The northeast ridgeline above Cutthroat Lake seemingly rises before your eyes in those last few strides up to Cutthroat Pass (5 miles). The views are stunning, with Cutthroat Peak in full splendor to the south, Vasiliki Ridge running down from the summit of 8,876-foot Silver Star Mountain to the east, and the tightly packed towers of the Needles to the northeast. You can see a variety of

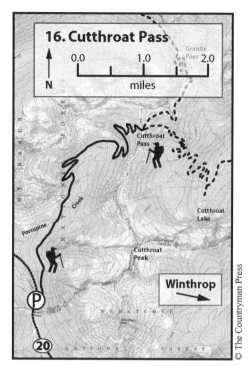

© The Countryman Press

basins, cirques, and creek valleys overshadowed by dramatic peaks, towers, and spires.

Cutthroat Lake is a 4-mile spin that drops some 2,000 feet down to an elevation of 4,800 feet—the exact amount you just gained to reach Cutthroat Pass. Continuing northeast for an easy 1.2 miles on the Pacific Crest Trail brings you to Granite Pass, which has grand takes on a whole new collection of North Cascade peaks. If you're feeling really ambitious, you can hike another 50 miles or so to Canada and the end of the PCT.

The Eastside Approach

Cutthroat Pass is also accessible via the Cutthroat Lake Trail at the end of Cutthroat Lake Road (signed) off WA 20. If you're driving west from Winthrop, look for the turnoff before Washington Pass. The driving distance from Winthrop is approximately 28 miles. The hike covers 6 miles one way and goes by Cutthroat Lake on its way to the pass.

17

Horseshoe Basin to Windy Peak Loop

Type: Overnight multiday

Season: Late June to October

Total distance: 16.8 miles

Rating: Moderate to strenuous

Elevation gain: 4,000 feet

Location: Pasayten Wilderness, 30 miles northwest of Tonasket

Map: Green Trails Horseshoe Basin No. 21

Getting There

From Tonasket, at US 97 and WA 20, cross the Okanogan River and follow signs for the town of Loomis. Turn right on WA 7 (Loomis-Oroville Road) for Loomis, which you reach in 16 miles. At 18.2 miles, turn left onto the Toats Coulee Road, which is also FR 39. The Forest Service road sign is posted 0.8 mile up the road. At 26.2 miles, bear left toward the Iron Gate Trailhead. At 32 miles, turn right onto FR 500. This 6-mile road is quite rough, so it's best to have a vehicle with high clearance. You arrive at the parking area and outhouse at 38 miles.

The Trail

The Pasayten Wilderness has some of the longest hikes in the state, and to really experience the diversity and beauty of the landscape you need to trek 20 miles. However, the Horseshoe Basin to Windy Peak loop puts you in an incredibly unique region of the North Cascades in just under 17 miles.

Horseshoe Basin's magnificent geography is the result of the retreating continental glacier some 12,000 years ago. The glacier left behind open basins, rounded mountaintops, and a boreal ecosystem uncommon this far south. The rolling hills, high elevation, and intense summer thunderstorms have managed to keep 311 species alive in a wetland/meadow environment.

In contrast, the rocky plain and summit of Windy Peak (8,334 feet) are nearly free of any vegetation. It's like another world, with unbelievable vistas of the pointer peaks of

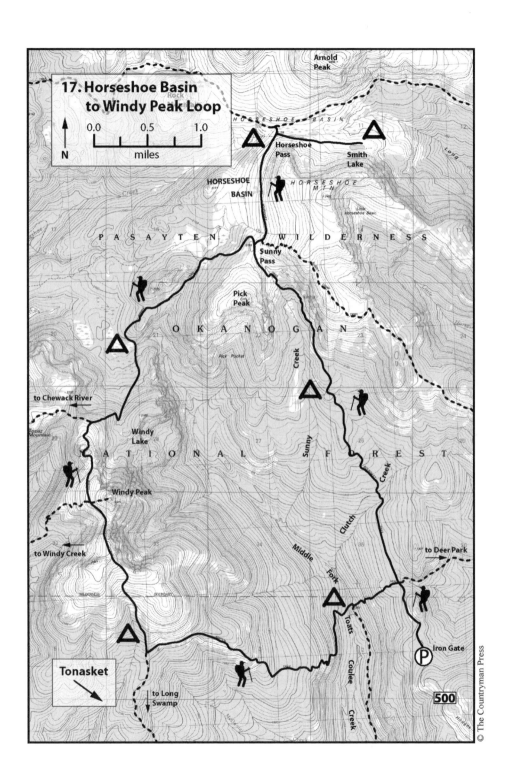

17. Horseshoe Basin to Windy Peak Loop

0.0   0.5   1.0
miles

N

Arnold Peak

Rock

HORSESHOE BASIN

Horseshoe Pass

Smith Lake

11   12

Long

HORSESHOE BASIN

HORSESHOE MTN

Little Horseshoe Basin

PASAYTEN   WILDERNESS

Creek

13

Sunny Pass

Pick Peak

OKANOGAN

Creek

to Chewack River

Pick Pocket

27

Topaz Mountain

Windy Lake

N   A   T   I   O   N   A   L

Sunny

F   O   R   E   S   T

Windy Peak

to Windy Creek

Middle

Clutch

Creek

to Deer Park

Fork

Toats

Iron Gate

Tonasket

to Long Swamp

Coulee

Creek

P

500

© The Countryman Press

the Pasayten to the west and a canyon rim-like overlook of Horseshoe Basin to the north. This loop hike takes you to the summit of one of Washington's 100 tallest mountains via high passes, creek-side trails, lodgepole forests, grassy slopes, and aspen groves.

Due to the great distances and wealth of worthy destinations, the Pasayten Wilderness is popular with horsemen. But at nearly 600,000 acres there is enough terrain to keep hikers and horseback riders spread out, allowing everyone the opportunity for a wonderful, secluded backcountry experience.

Most of Trail 533 into Horseshoe Basin follows an old roadbed with an easy grade. An open, grassy slope at the beginning offers views of Windy Peak to the northwest before you spend most of the next 2.7 miles working through a predominantly lodgepole pine forest along the east side of Sunny Creek.

At 0.7 mile, after a slight elevation loss, you arrive at two trail junctions in a small, open patch in the forest that's slowly being refilled by young trees. The first junction, to your right, is for Deer Park and Fourteen Mile Trailhead on Trail 341. The second junction, 30 feet farther ahead to the left, is for Trail 343, which you'll take on the return trip from Windy Peak. Continue straight on a nearly level trail to reach a crossing of Clutch Creek at 1.4 miles. Beyond the creek the trail climbs moderately, brightened here and there by purple aster and yellow fleabane.

In the latter half of August there is ripe whortleberry to pick. The plants are just 6 to 8 inches high, with numerous oval leaves that hide the BB-sized reddish/purple berries. Though small, they have a big, sweet taste similar to huckleberries. There are also a variety of mushrooms to hunt, especially in early summer, after thunderstorms, and during wet periods in early autumn. David Arora's *All That the Rain Promises and More . . . : A Hip Pocket Guide to Western Mushrooms* will help identify the good, the bad, and the beautifully strange.

Englemann spruce appear as you move farther along, and at 2.7 miles a grass and wildflower slope offers a break from the corridor of trees. Just beyond here the trail begins to climb through the bottom of the fingerlike basin leading to Sunny Pass. The west side is walled in by Pick Peak (7,620 feet) and the east by a long rock band that's part of Horseshoe Mountain (7,300 feet).

Unfortunately, the trees through here have been victimized by disease, which caused the rust-red needles and dry branches on these dead and dying trees. Even so, scientists have noted that the increase in forestation to the area of Sunny Pass and Horseshoe Basin is a fairly recent phenomenon, believed to be the result of drought, overgrazing, and trampling, which all threaten the boreal wetland environment in Horseshoe Basin.

At 3.4 miles the world opens up into the head of a marvelous basin filled with buttercups, paintbrush, cinquefoil, and yarrow. Sunny Creek, quite narrow and overgrown with a thick carpeting of grass, begins at a spring in the middle of the basin. At 3.8 miles is Sunny Pass (7,200 feet), a natural and fantastic viewpoint for nearly the entire Horseshoe Basin.

To the north, from left to right, the high points are Rock Mountain (7,617 feet), Armstrong Mountain (8,106 feet), and Arnold Peak (8,076 feet). Trees cover a portion of the basin, but for the most part you can see in every direction. To the west are dramatic mountain formations like Cathedral Peak (8,601 feet) and Remmel Mountain (8,685 feet).

The wildflower explosion continues throughout this area, which measures at least 5 square miles. This is a special place. Nowhere else in Washington do you find an open, rolling-hill environment at 7,000 feet with a boreal ecosystem.

From the pass, the trail drops gently around the lower slope of Horseshoe Mountain to the junction for Smith Lake and Horseshoe Pass (7,000 feet). You can see Louden Lake near the east slope of Rock Mountain.

You come to two trail junctions at Sunny Pass and shortly beyond. Trail 342 forks left at the pass toward Windy Peak, the return trail for this loop hike. Less than 0.1 mile on the trail toward Horseshoe Pass is Trail 375 (on the right). It originates from the Fourteen Mile Trailhead. Campsites in Horseshoe Basin are located near Horseshoe Pass, Louden Lake, and Smith Lake. Distances for this portion of the hike are measured from Sunny Pass.

At 0.9 mile a trail cuts back hard to the left; continue straight to reach the campsites and lakes. At 1.2 miles Trail 361 leads east to Smith Lake. This area has numerous campsites, most set in or near the small cluster of trees. The trail to Smith runs between the rocky north slope of Horseshoe Mountain and the grassy south slope of Arnold Peak.

A beautiful stroll through a wet meadow with several small creek crossings brings you to the lake (2 miles from Sunny Pass), which is situated at the east end of Horseshoe Basin. Many trail and cross-country day hikes are possible from Smith Lake and/or Horseshoe Pass. I recommend that you carry Green Trails Maps No. 20 and 21 or the USGS map for Horseshoe Basin.

The Pasayten Wilderness is home to the largest lynx population in the Lower 48.

Black bear, gray wolf, and grizzly bear also frequent Horseshoe Basin.

To continue the loop to Windy Peak, return to Sunny Pass and follow Trail 342 down along the southwestern edge of Horseshoe Basin. At 4.4 miles (counting mileage from Sunny Pass) the trail enters a small meadow and crosses a stream. As it drops in beneath the west side of Pick Peak, you enter a dense forest.

By 5.6 miles from Sunny Pass the trail has passed through a lovely forested section decorated with rock boulders, bottoming out in an open meadow with access to a creek. There are a few tent sites here, complete with nearby views of Windy Peak. Across the creek, the trail climbs moderately for the first 0.2 mile before taking a steep course up to the junction with Trail 360 (6.5 miles), which leads down to the Chewuck River.

Unfortunately, the climbing doesn't end at the junction, but your efforts are rewarded with views that lay open the whole Horseshoe Basin and terrain to the north. Windy Lake is below here on a bench to the east-northeast. The trail aims for a gap off the right, or north, shoulder of the barren summit of Windy Peak. Pass through the gap (6.9 miles) and continue climbing into this beautifully stark moonscape.

Vistas now include the heavily treed Chewuck River valley to the west. The prominent features in front of you from 12 o'clock to 3 o'clock are Remmel Mountain, Apex Mountain (8,297 feet), Cathedral Peak, Wolframite Mountain (8,137 feet), and the Bauerman Ridge (over 7,900 feet).

At 7.4 miles you reach a four-way junction. Downslope to the right Trail 362 follows Windy Creek to the Windy Creek/Chewuck Trailhead. To the left (upslope) is the spur trail to the summit of 8,334-foot Windy Peak. The trail straight

ahead completes the loop back to the Iron Gate Trailhead.

The trail continues to climb up to a rock and gravel plateau at 7.9 miles (8,000 feet). A short spur trail on the right leads up to a saddle between two rock formations, but this is merely a viewpoint. It's worth stopping for a moment to reflect on the tremendous contrast in the environments of Windy Peak and Horseshoe Basin a few miles to the north.

Take the wider path dropping off the plateau down a trail that's somewhat difficult to follow. In fact, along most of the journey up and over Windy Peak from the four-way junction the trail is marked with cairns. This route is a little difficult to follow in the snow if you haven't done it before.

Stay more to the left side of the basin you're dropping into. The north side of the ridgeline drops steeply away as the ridge itself runs toward a long grassy slope. The trail remains somewhat high in the beginning and then angles toward that grassy slope.

At 8.2 miles the trail turns toward the center of the basin and becomes much easier to follow. It then cuts into the bottom of the long grassy slope before reaching the trees and making a 90-degree turn to the left at 8.5 miles.

The trail continues to lose elevation, and there's another trail junction at 8.9 miles (6,900 feet). Going straight on Trail 342 would take you to the Long Swamp Trailhead. Instead, head left on Trail 343 to complete your trek back to the Iron Gate Trailhead.

For the next mile the trail runs mainly along open, grassy slopes painted with an array of colors from wildflowers like buttercup, yarrow, paintbrush, showy aster, lupine, and scarlet gilia. You enjoy views across the forested drainage of the Middle Fork Toats Coulee Creek and beyond the wilderness boundary.

At 9.6 miles you pass through a patch of sweet-smelling sagebrush. The trail makes a bend at 9.9 miles and loses more elevation as it sinks into a forest of lodgepole pine. Shortly before the descent to the last low point of the hike—the foot-log crossing on the Middle Fork Toats Coulee Creek (11.3 miles)—you wind down a steep slope of rich green grass decorated by an aspen grove that pops with bright yellow leaves in autumn. The aspen offer a welcome change of pace from the coniferous forest you pass through all along this hike.

There is a campsite at the creek crossing. The junction with Trail 387 is at 11.4 miles.

Trail 343 climbs steeply up the east side of the creek drainage via switchbacks through a similar environment of long grass and aspen. The path tops out and then meets Trail 533 at 12.1 miles. Head right to finish off the last 0.7 mile back to the trailhead (12.8 miles). Including the hike to Horseshoe Pass and into Smith Lake, the total distance covered comes to 16.8 miles.

Pasayten Fan Club

If the Horseshoe Basin to Windy Peak Loop leaves you sold on the Pasayten Wilderness, you might want to try the trip to Buckskin Lake farther to the west. From Harts Pass, the state's highest vehicle-accessible pass at 6,200 feet, this 20-mile hike rolls across two open ridgelines with mountain panoramas and wildflowers galore. In contrast to Horseshoe Basin, this area of the Pasayten has steep slopes, deep V-shaped river valleys, and sharp peaks. But you still have open views at 6,000 feet for nearly the entire hike. The elevation gain is approximately 4,000 feet, and the hike is strenuous. Check out Green Trails Pasayten Peak No. 18 and Washington Pass No. 50 maps.

Central Cascades

The Boulder River

18

Green Mountain

Type: Day hike

Season: Mid-June to early October

Total distance: 7 miles

Rating: Moderate

Elevation gain: 3,000 feet

Location: Glacier Peak Wilderness, 30 miles northeast of Darrington

Map: Green Trails Cascade Pass No. 80

Getting There

From I-5, take WA 530 east to Darrington. Travel north from the Darrington RD on WA 530 for 7.2 miles, and then turn right onto the Suiattle River Road (FR 26). You drive mostly on pavement for 10 miles before the road changes completely to gravel. At mile 26.2, turn left on FR 2680. Look for the sign to Green Mountain. This road is somewhat rough and narrow, so use caution. You come to the trailhead at 32.5 miles. There is one small parking area near the trailhead and more parking available along the road before and after the trailhead.

The Trail

On maps, Green Mountain (6,500 feet) looks small and isolated from the much more imposing mountains in the Glacier Peak Wilderness. The lookout that stood on the summit for nearly 70 years is gone, but hikers can still enjoy the amazing views from this diminutive mountain. Snowking (7,433 feet), Dome Mountain (8,940 feet), and Glacier Peak (10,528 feet) encircle Green Mountain like white pyramids. The short distance and impressive wildflower displays only add to this hike's popularity.

The hike to Green Mountain follows Trail 782. The lookout, originally built in 1933 and now on the National Register of Historic Places, was removed from the mountaintop in the summer of 2002 because the unstable foundation left it liable to collapse. The plan is to eventually restore and reassemble the Green Mountain Lookout in its original location.

Central Cascades

Before you even set foot on the trail you are treated to excellent views of Sulphur Mountain (6,735 feet) to the southwest and Lime Ridge (over 6,500 feet) to the south. The first mile or so takes you through a thick stand of fir and cedar, and little vegetation grows along the forest floor, so there's good visibility between the trees. Soft light sifts through the tree canopy, giving the forest a tranquil feel.

The trail climbs a series of long, ramping switchbacks right from the beginning. Dull Oregon grape, bunchberry, and lichen and moss grow well in the forest. Approximately 0.4 mile into the hike, the trail gains elevation more steeply over a rolling slope. At 1.2 miles the trail breaks out onto a lush green hillside, initially lined with a thick corridor of scrub alder and thimbleberry.

The trail follows a more moderate incline as you wind upslope beneath the southern end of the ridgeline that spawns Green Mountain and Mount Buckindy (7,360 feet).

The wildflower explosion is truly amazing. Paintbrush, tiger lily, valerian, penstemon, columbine, lupine, cow parsnip, and nearly two-dozen other wildflowers, along with shrubs like mountain blueberry and huckleberry, thickly cover the entire slope. This giant wild garden is one of Green Mountain's major attractions. Bears also enjoy the flora here, and spotting sign or even a bear along this open stretch is a real possibility.

From the open slope you have marvelous views back down the Suiattle River valley and across to numerous snow-clad peaks. At 1.9 miles the trail enters a small stand of trees before resuming its garden tour via a collection of longer switchbacks. If you look south along here, you can see prominent Glacier Peak, the remotest of Washington's Cascade volcanoes. Climbers must travel at

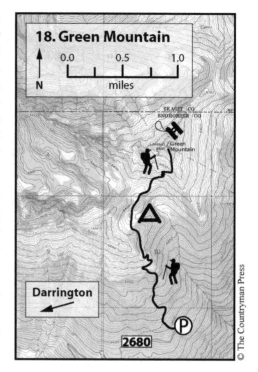

least 10 miles to reach any sort of high camp for a summit attempt.

At 2.2 miles the trail crosses a small bench and climbs somewhat steeply to an overlook of a forested basin with two small tarns. At 2.4 miles you drop into the parkland basin, which offers campsites and another beautiful contrast on this short hike. Be aware that this area can hold snow well into July. The trail runs into a larger, more open basin (2.6 miles) that is thick with wildflowers and heather blooms from July to mid-August.

The trail takes a long, looping path through the basin, which is home to a large community of marmot, to eventually reach a ridgeline off the summit of Green Mountain. The section of trail up the basin is the steepest of the entire hike. Once you gain the ridge it's less than 0.2 mile to the site of the

Green Mountain vistas

former lookout and the summit of Green Mountain (3.5 miles).

Mountain views include nearby Mount Buckindy to the north, Sentinel (8,261 feet), Dome, and Sinister (8,460 feet) to the northeast and east and the beautiful snow- and ice-encrusted Glacier Peak to the south. To the north-northwest you can see Mount Baker (10,781 feet), the state's northernmost Cascade volcano. You may even share your temporary perch with a golden eagle or two, which periodically soar above the nearby ridgelines.

It's easy to see why Green Mountain makes such a good location for fire spotting, but the beauty of the setting doesn't make the job any easier. Green Mountain may seem hospitable in comparison to the larger glaciated peaks surrounding it, but in winter this area is hit hard with winter storms and snowpack averaging 25 feet.

The Iron Highway Race

Before the advent of modern corporate giants, there was the battle for commerce in the Pacific Northwest between the Northern Pacific Railroad and the Great Northern Railroad (GNR). Each sought to link the agricultural products of eastern Washington with the timber-rich products stacked up at key ports around Puget Sound, much of it bound for Asia. The Northern Pacific Railroad found its crossing in Stampede Pass south of Snoqualmie Pass, and trains began running in 1887. The GNR was in operation in 1893 over Stevens Pass, but only after a long struggle through thick vegetation and rugged terrain like the Suiattle River valley. Cady Pass (E. F. Cady), Linsley Pass (D. C. Linsley), and Stevens Pass (John Frank Stevens) pay tribute to the hard-fought battle between the formidable Cascades and the relentless force of industry.

19

Boulder River

Type: Day hike

Season: Year-round

Total distance: 5 miles

Rating: Easy

Elevation gain: 150 feet

Location: Boulder River Wilderness, 12 miles west of Darrington

Map: Green Trails Granite Falls No. 109

Getting There

From I-5, take WA 530 east to Darrington. Head south from the Darrington RD on WA 530 for 0.4 mile to the intersection and turn right, continuing on WA 530 to the west. At 8 miles, turn left onto French Creek Road (FR 2010). The turnoff is difficult to spot, so look for it approximately 0.8 mile past mile marker 40. Drive 3.8 miles on FR 2010 to the trailhead (11.8 miles).

The Trail

The Boulder River Wilderness had a short-lived history of mining and logging before the magnificent, compact, and rugged ridgeline was preserved for nature's sake. Most of the 49,000-acre wilderness is without any trail access, and it's a landscape that combines maddeningly thick undergrowth with extremely challenging mountains like White-horse (6,563 feet), Mount Bullon (5,974 feet), and Three Fingers (6,850 feet).

Equally important was the protection of the lowland environment along the Boulder River. Only Olympic National Park has such lowland forests of grand older-growth trees. Along the Boulder River Trail you see 200-year-old Douglas fir, western hemlock, and western red cedar growing over 200 feet high and 6 feet in diameter. Yes, there are older, taller trees in Washington, but there may be only a handful of intact lowland forests like the one along the Boulder River.

The Boulder River Trail is officially Trail 734. It follows an old railroad grade and logging bed, scars of a fading past. If you want a workout you'll need to hike off-trail because this hike gains less than 200 feet over

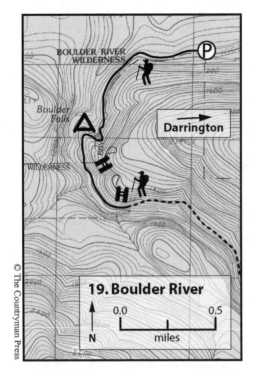

19. Boulder River

0.0   0.5

N   miles

imity with a veil of mist. To gain a different perspective on the falls, walk down an access trail to the rocky river edge.

In spring and early summer, color reaches this green world in the form of white trillium, flashes of yellow violet, and the delicate purple flowers of bleeding heart. Of course, as mushroom hunters know, there are always fungi present, especially in the wetter periods of spring and fall. Continue on from the first trailside falls up a steeper, rockier trail before resuming a more relaxed course along the river through an older-growth forest with thimbleberry (ripe by midsummer).

At 2.5 miles a second waterfall drops 30 feet or so from the canyon wall in a single stream. This makes an ideal turnaround point, although the trail continues 2 more miles to another campsite along the river. The trail once connected to Tupso Pass, which leads up to the wilderness high point of Three Finger Jack and a magnificent lookout.

Despite its lack of mountain vistas, the Boulder River Trail has the benefit of being accessible year-round—try hiking anywhere else in the Central Cascades in January.

You Take the Low Road, I'll Take the High Road

If the Three Fingers Lookout interests you, drive to the opposite side of the wilderness rather than trying to ford Boulder River and bushwhack your way up the overgrown portion of the Boulder River Trail to Tupso Pass. The Three Fingers Trail 641 climbs by small lakes onto the stunning parkland of Goat Flats, complete with fantastic views of Mount Baker, and up to the Three Fingers Lookout. The 1933 lookout is available overnight on a first-come, first-served basis, but it's a strenuous climb and glacial travel skills and equipment are necessary. The rock platform on which the lookout sits was created by blasting away 10 to 15 feet of the summit. Reference maps include Green Trails Granite Falls No. 109 and Silverton No. 110.

5 miles. You stay low along the river bottom, never reaching a prominent high point. The forest of Douglas fir, hemlock, red cedar, and moss-draped bigleaf maple is somewhat open, with an abundance of sword fern and salmonberry growing along the trail.

At 0.6 mile the trail rounds a corner to parallel the river's run out toward the North Fork Stillaguamish River 5 miles to the north. It also gains a touch of elevation before leveling off along more of a hiker's pathway and officially entering the Boulder River Wilderness at 0.9 mile. The trail and river are close together through here, and there are some campsites situated above Boulder Falls, which is hidden in the canyon below.

At 1.3 miles you reach a split cascade that is the highlight of the hike. Stay on the trail or walk a short distance up to enjoy the view of the 60-foot falls pouring in a single stream from the rock wall across from you. The water splits a third of the way down the cliff, lightly coating everything in close prox-

20

Pilot Ridge to Blue Lakes

Type: Overnight

Season: Mid-June to mid-October

Total distance: 20.6 miles

Rating: Moderate

Elevation gain: 4,700 feet

Location: Glacier Peak Wilderness, 18 miles southeast of Darrington

Maps: Green Trails Sloan Peak No. 111, Glacier Peak No. 112, Benchmark Mountain No. 144

Getting There

From I-5, take WA 530 east to Darrington. Drive south from the Darrington RD on WA 530. At 0.4 mile you arrive at an intersection; continue straight on FR 20, also known as the Mountain Loop Highway. At 9.7 miles the road changes from pavement to gravel. At 16.7 miles, turn left onto FR 49 (Sloan Creek Road). Travel 6.8 miles (23.5 miles from the ranger station) and bear left at the sign for the North Fork Sauk Trailhead (23.7 miles), which you reach in another 0.2 mile.

A 6-mile section of the Mountain Loop Highway was washed out in four separate locations during fall 2003 between Barlow Pass and Bedal Creek (not of concern if you're accessing the trailhead from Darrington to the north). Repairs are scheduled to begin in spring 2005, and the road should be open by spring 2006.

The Trail

I have no idea who decided that there should be a trail up the steep-sided drainage of the North Fork Sauk River, but the result is a gem of a backpacking trip. You traverse an open ridgeline with views of Glacier Peak and Mount Rainier, take a wonderful spin through the upper end of the wildflower-carpeted basin beneath Johnson Mountain, and end up at the Blue Lakes, which deserve more-sparkling names to match their beauty.

The hike begins on the North Fork Sauk River Trail 649. There are great stands of old-growth fir and cedar along this section.

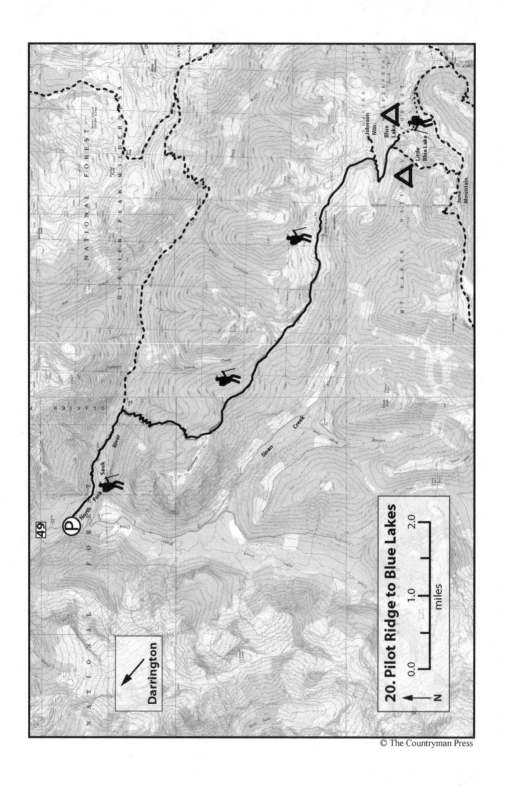

20. Pilot Ridge to Blue Lakes

Darrington

N

miles
0.0   1.0   2.0

49

© The Countryman Press

Take your time and gaze at these trees, but don't trip over any tree roots. The river-bottom vegetation is typical of the west side, with a lush mix of sword fern, devil's club, skunk cabbage, and bunchberry. The river runs nearby, roughly 11 miles from its headwaters below the east slope of Johnson Mountain.

The trail officially enters the Glacier Peak Wilderness slightly over 0.2 mile in, marked by a wooden sign anchored to a tree. The grade up to the junction with the Pilot Ridge Trail is relatively easy, with an occasional moderate stretch thrown in. At 0.7 mile the trail makes a slight detour uphill to bypass a recent washout.

You veer closer to the river shortly before reaching the junction at 1.5 miles. Head right (south) on Pilot Ridge Trail 652, which crosses the North Fork Sauk River within 100 yards. There's no bridge, but numerous logs jammed together typically make for an easy crossing. On the other side, enjoy the very short stretch of moderate hiking before the trail starts climbing up the north slope.

From this point—2,400 feet in elevation—you climb 3,000 feet in just 3 miles. Numerous boulders and tree roots don't make the trail any easier. Enjoy!

At 3.6 miles, right after the 37th switchback (oh yes, there are plenty of switchbacks), the trail eases up ever so slightly and takes a more meandering path upslope for 0.3 mile to another two switchbacks. At 4 miles you enter a brushy area with wildflowers and less tree cover. Top off your water containers at the small creek, as there's little to no other water on the way to the Blue Lakes.

The trail continues climbing from here for 0.2 mile before moving up the ridge. The initial ridge section is still steep until it reaches a magnificent pocket meadow of heather (4.5 miles). You have fantastic views of the southeastern slopes of Glacier Peak (10,541 feet) to the north-northeast and Mount Rainier (14,410 feet) to the south-southwest. The trail soon ducks back into the trees and loses some elevation for the next 0.8 mile.

At 5.3 miles you regain that elevation and then some in a steep 0.5-mile uphill push. The reward is worth it, though, as the trail leaves the trees and crosses a wildflower-choked slope with clear views of the cluster of peaks in the Monte Cristo region to the southwest and the jagged tops of the Stuart Range to the southeast. Rainier, the state's highest peak, once again dominates the horizon to the south. Two words: absolutely gorgeous.

At 6 miles the trail once again falls to the backbone of the ridge, complete with views across the North Fork Sauk River drainage. You reach a small saddle in the ridge around 7.6 miles where the trail makes a short push uphill before crossing onto a slope above a tributary in the Sloan Creek drainage. Down trail, Johnson Mountain (6,721 feet) is the prominent peak visible in the near distance. This slope is covered with glacier lilies in mid-June, which give way to pasque flower, lupine, and paintbrush later in the short growing season. Across the basin/drainage you can see the short finger ridge that takes you on to the Blue Lakes.

The trail junction for Johnson Mountain is at 9.1 miles. If you head straight and climb some 700 feet over 0.5 mile you arrive at the summit of Johnson Mountain. Or stay to the right and drop elevation along the finger ridge to begin the 1.2-mile run to Blue Lake and the 1.4-mile hike to Little Blue Lake.

The latter is visible as you work down the slope to another junction at 10.1 miles. Continue downhill to reach Little Blue Lake at 10.5 total miles. Or go straight to climb to Blue Lake at 10.3 miles.

The trail along Pilot Ridge

Blue Lake, over twice the size of Little Blue Lake, is set in a cirque below the southeast slope of Johnson Mountain, with adequate campsites and possibilities for solitude. There are day hikes to Sauk Pass, Lake Salley Ann, Johnston Mountain and June Mountain and cross-country access to two small unnamed lakes above Blue Lake.

You Won't Find a Count or Any Sandwiches Here

The early 1900s mining town of Monte Cristo received its name from the famous Dumas novel, but perhaps the only thing they have in common is revenge. A major reason for the termination of mining operations was the continuous onslaught of natural events, from floods to avalanches, which eventually shut down efforts to extract natural resources from the incredibly stunning mountains. You can still walk the 4-mile road to the old town, where many buildings remain standing. From Monte Cristo, a trail leads 2.1 miles into wildflower-filled Glacier Basin, set below the splendid Wilmons Peaks (over 6,800 feet), Monte Cristo (7,136 feet), and Cadet Peak (7,186 feet). Or climb up Poodle Dog Pass to Silver Lake and then on to a fantastic rocky ridge to the Twin Lakes (4.8 miles), teetering above the West Fork Troublesome Creek valley. For trail information, contact the Darrington RD (see Resources). The reference map for this hike is Green Trails Monte Cristo No. 143.

Greider Lake

21

Greider Lakes

Type: Day hike or overnight

Season: June to October

Total distance: 4.8 miles

Rating: Moderate to strenuous

Elevation gain: 1,500 feet

Location: Greider Ridge Natural Resources Conservation Area, 18 miles east-northeast of Monroe

Map: Green Trails Index No. 142

Getting There

Travel east on US 2 approximately 11.5 miles from Monroe to reach Kellogg Lake Road, just outside the small town of Startup. Turn left onto Kellogg Lake Road, which forks at 4 miles. Take the right fork toward Spada Lake. At 18.5 miles (7 miles up Kellogg Lake Road) the surface changes from pavement to gravel. There is a sign-in station at 21.5 miles to help monitor recreational activities around man-made Spada Lake.

The road follows the lakeshore to the Greider Lakes Trailhead, a total distance of 28.8 miles. The trailhead has picnic tables and outhouses.

The Trail

The 6,700-acre Greider Ridge Natural Resources Conservation Area established in 1997 is part of the 35,300-acre Ragged Ridge Roadless Area. The trail to the Greider Lakes is one of only a handful making short stabs into an incredibly wild landscape of tall granite peaks and thick underbrush cloaking loose rock slopes and numerous creek drainages. Ragged Ridge is a prime candidate for federal wilder- ness status.

Luckily, hikers can enjoy this raw natural environment via the relatively short but challenging pathway to the Greider Lakes. These lakes sit one above the other in a long and somewhat narrow basin, perfectly illustrating the challenges for anyone considering cross-country travel to the center of the Ragged Ridge wildland.

To begin the hike, walk past a small pond and picnic tables at the trailhead. You immediately climb on a rough trail. Even though

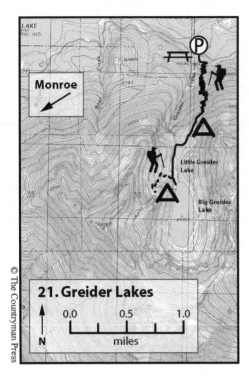

21. Greider Lakes

0.0   0.5   1.0

N   miles

© The Countryman Press

the lake's outlet and continues on along a thick brushy slope of salmonberry, scrub alder, vine maple, and huckleberry. Near the west rim of the basin, the brush covers the entire slope, tall and tangled enough to give you the chills thinking about trying to make your way through such a jungle.

The trail forks just before Big Greider Lake. The right fork heads up 0.7 mile to an overlook along the cliff bands, offering a high perspective of the lakes and vistas to the north along the southern edge of the Henry M. Jackson Wilderness, a collection of chiseled and glaciated peaks like Big Four (6,135 feet), Little Chief (5,280 feet), and Vesper (6,214).

The left fork, at 2.4 miles, after passing a couple of campsites equipped with fire pits, reaches the log-jammed outlet of Big Greider Lake (2,932 feet). The taller peaks up the steep, rocky basin beyond the head of the lake and off the west shoreline are Static (5,100 feet) and Greider (4,829 feet). Rock slides and brush fill the entire basin, interrupted by a few cascades free-falling from the cliff bands.

Big and Little Greider Lakes contain cutthroat and rainbow trout.

Power and Drinking Water

Spada Lake was created 40 years ago as part of the Henry M. Jackson Hydroelectric Project. The first phase was the construction of the Culmback Dam, which backed up the Sultan River to form Spada Lake within a broad section of the Sultan Basin. The dam was made taller 20 years ago, quadrupling the size of Spada Lake and increasing its capacity to provide Snohomish County with drinking water and electricity, enough to service 28,000 homes. Henry M. Jackson was an influential Washington senator who was able to balance economic needs with conservation of wildlands in the state.

the incline isn't too steep, high-stepping onto rocks and over tree roots will definitely get your heart rate up. The hillside is thinly forested in hemlock and cedar, with intermittent views of the east end of Spada Lake.

There are benches along the way for the leg-weary, the first coming at the fourth switchback and the second at 1.1 miles, halfway to Little Greider Lake. If you like to mark your progress, start counting the 39 switchbacks. At 1.8 miles the trail reaches a ridgetop of sorts and begins a much more pleasant stretch through a dense forest to Little Greider.

At 2 miles, two elevated walkways signal your arrival at Little Greider (2,910 feet), its deep green water decorated with lily pads and pressed by forest on the northwest shore. The southeast shoreline combines thick brush and a rocky slope and has a few campsites.

At 2.1 miles the trail crosses a bridge at

Central Cascades

22

Lake Serene

Type: Day hike

Season: Late June to October

Total distance: 7.6 miles

Rating: Strenuous

Elevation gain: 2,000 feet

Location: Mount Baker–Snoqualmie National Forest, 20 miles east of Monroe

Map: Green Trails Index No. 142

Getting There

From the town of Monroe, drive 20 miles east on US 2 to the Mount Index Road at milepost 35 and turn right (your only option). If you cross the Skykomish River you've gone too far. Drive another 0.3 mile to the large parking area, outhouses, and trailhead (20.3 miles). Leave your tent in the car; camping isn't allowed by the lake.

The Trail

An impressive waterfall, a classic Cascade cirque lake, and a Himalayan-style massif that towers above the Skykomish River valley comprise the pilgrimage to Lake Serene. A semisuicidal trail once clawed its way up the steep slope to the lake, but today, after a multiyear improvement project, the pathway is safer and accessible to a greater number of visitors. Avoid peak-season weekends if you want to be alone.

The hike begins on a closed road and then switches to an old roadbed in the first 0.5 mile. Fir, cedar, and western red alder line the path, and the ground is covered by a carpet of moss with mushrooms poking through here and there.

There is a split in the road at 0.1 mile; follow the right fork. The trail is a combination of gravel and small cobble, and the incline is easy to moderate. You cross a small creek at two different points and then pass through a thicker patch of salmonberry and red elderberry bushes at 0.9 mile. At 1.2 miles the trail meets back up with the roadway on which you began and follows it for

0.1 mile before crossing back and dropping down an actual trail (the left fork).

You can hear Bridal Veil Falls as you descend through the trees. There is a trail junction at 1.5 miles. The right path takes you 0.5 mile up to an old mining site and to a spectacular overview of the falls. Stretched thin, the water resembles bejeweled silk lace as it slides hundreds of feet down from a rock slab. Bridal Veil Creek re-forms in a single stream below the falls.

Continuing on the trail to Lake Serene, you cross a small footbridge before reaching a larger, sturdier bridge over Bridal Veil Creek with a bottom-to-top view of the wide ribbon of falls (1.6 miles). Here, the falls make a sheer drop over a craggy rock face in a delicate fan of water. Shortly past the bridge you enter an open area beneath a second spilt of the larger falls above. This is an ideal spot to rest or grab a bite to eat. The real work lies ahead.

You climb steeply from here, beginning a long series of switchbacks. The trail alternates between dirt, rock, and man-made steps set into the slope. It's slow, hard work that may have you wishing they'd built a tramway instead of just improving the trail.

At 2.5 miles views open across the Skykomish River valley to the north of Index Town Wall and Ragged Ridge. Farther north, the pointy hats of the Monte Cristo peaks are visible.

Keep those legs pumping because even though the back-and-forth comes to an end after 21 switchbacks, the climbing continues. The trail keeps on gaining elevation, although it contours cross-slope. Don't miss foraging for huckleberries in late summer. The terrain is much more open here than in the forest you were immersed in for most the climb up from Bridal Veil Falls. You've earned the higher views of the river valley and accompanying peaks and of the sheer

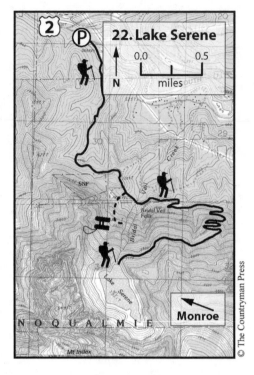

© The Countryman Press

faces of multipeaked Mount Index (5,979 feet).

Finally, at 3.7 miles you reach a sign for Lake Serene. It's less than 0.1 mile down to the lake from here.

The high-mountain setting of Lake Serene (2,521 feet), beneath the 2,000-foot northeast face of Mount Index, makes you feel like you're at 7,000 to 8,000 feet, particularly after the hard climb you just made. But the reality is that the magical site of Lake Serene is no higher in elevation than many open expanses of mountainless eastern Washington.

Regardless of trivial statistics, an outing to Lake Serene can be cathartic whether you're completely alone on a cool autumn day or joined by groups of strangers on a warm July weekend. Please stick to the designated paths around the northwest end of Lake Serene, and pick up all trash.

Central Cascades

Clouds drift above Lake Serene

Wild Sky

Washington is currently close to adding its first wilderness area in 20 years. As with the Alpine Lakes, Glacier Peak, and Henry M. Jackson Wilderness Areas, Wild Sky would help protect pristine alpine meadows and grand Cascade peaks in an area stretching from Gold Bar nearly to Stevens Pass and north to the boundaries of the Henry M. Jackson Wilderness. The 106,000 acres under consideration would be purely for recreational use—hiking, backpacking, climbing, horseback riding, fishing, and non-motorized boating. This proposal includes lowland river valleys of the North Fork Skykomish and Rapid River, along with other significant creek drainages. (Only a small fraction of the river valleys across the state remain unaltered.) Some of these waterways host 700-year-old Douglas fir and provide crucial fish habitat for species like wild steelhead and chinook, coho, and pink salmon.

23

Necklace Valley

Type: Overnight to multiday

Season: July to early October

Total distance: 16 miles

Rating: Strenuous

Elevation gain: 3,300 feet

*Location: Alpine Lakes Wilderness,
4 miles south of Skykomish*

*Maps: Green Trails Skykomish No. 175,
Stevens Pass No. 176*

Getting There

Take US 2 east of Monroe to Skykomish. Drive 0.5 mile west from the Skykomish RD on US 2 to Foss River Road. Turn right and go just under 4 miles to the trailhead (4.2 total miles). The road changes from pavement to gravel a short way off US 2.

The Trail

The countless lakes within the Alpine Lakes Wilderness are typically found teetering from rocky ledges, within glacial cirques, or along river valley bottoms. The Necklace Valley is a rare gem, much like the Enchantments, the premier lake chain in the wilderness. It's a hanging valley with open forests and huckleberry and heather underbrush sectioned by small cliff bands and eight easily accessible lakes. The valley offers a relaxed weekend retreat, ideal for sitting beside a glistening lake or for taking day trips to explore the area. This backcountry destination seems to float among massive mountains and thick slopeside and river-bottom vegetation.

East Fork Foss River Trail 1062 is alive from the beginning with thimbleberry, fern, devil's club, and tiger lily, all under the enchanting light of fir, cedar, and western red alder. The easygoing trail follows an old railroad bed, with a bridge crossing over picturesque Burn Creek at 0.8 mile.

At 2.5 miles, through the trees and devil's club, you can see a marsh area that hosts frogs and many bird species. The trail crosses some elevated walkways set above the boggy ground—perfect for skunk

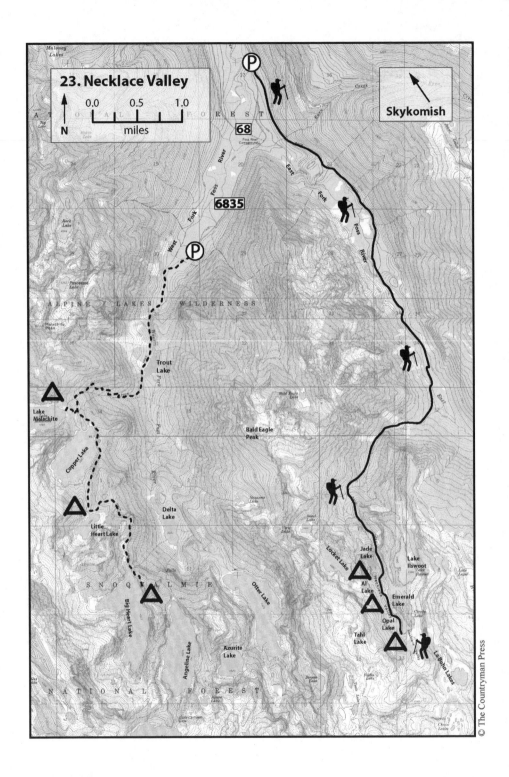

23. Necklace Valley

0.0   0.5   1.0
miles

N

Skykomish

cabbage—before reaching a rise (2.8 miles) with a view down to the East Fork Foss River.

You slide down along the river, never really edging close until the eventual river crossing, but there is also very little up and down in this stretch. You pass in and out of forested areas and into open brushy sections, which, depending on when the trail crew has last been through, can be a little overgrown. You can see the ridgeline across the river and Bald Eagle Peak (6,259 feet), the most prominent visible high point.

At 3.9 miles the trail skirts the bottom edge of a boulder field below a tall rock wall. There is a small campsite near the river at 4.2 miles, perfect if you happen to get a late start or just as a snack stop. The trail meets the river at 4.4 miles.

There are two water crossings. The first brings you to a small sandy beach, another nice location to grab water and a rest. Across the first log, the trail moves into the trees a short distance before turning right onto a large fallen tree that connects to a boulder field across the outlet of a number of the lakes high up in the Necklace Valley. Pick your way up the boulder field, staying straight or a little to the left to get back on the trail. Now the work begins.

The trail makes a very steep run for 1 mile before lessening in grade and then resuming a steep climb up toward Jade Lake, the first of the Necklace Valley lakes. The trail makes a hard push through the trees for 0.5 mile, then meets a natural rock staircase of sorts walled in on each side by scrub alder. This steep section covers about 0.3 mile. At 5.3 miles the trail is again forested and somewhat less steep.

At 5.5 miles the trail crosses a rock slide with views of the creek drainage fed by Jade, Ilswoot, Al, Locket, and Jewel Lakes. After an easy section of trail (5.9 miles), the path climbs a narrow defile filled with boulders

and tree roots set amid mucky ground. Adding to the fun is the fact that the trail can be chocked with brush at times.

A bridge over the outlet for Jewel Lake comes at 6.3 miles. The trail continues to climb, now over more of a trail than a steep, narrow creek bed, to reach the toe of Jade Lake at 7.5 miles. The Necklace Valley string of lakes continues on along the east shoreline of Jade to Emerald at 7.8 miles and Opal at 8 miles.

The log-sided Necklace Valley Cabin sits next to Emerald Lake. It was built in 1951 by a wilderness group called the Trail Blazers and dedicated to Jack Streeter, an area resident killed during WWII. The valley is a gentle ripple of sparse forest, wispy bushes, and a thick, expansive community of pink and white heather.

The trail ends shortly after Opal, at the beginning of the rock- and snow-filled basin leading up to the La Bohn Lakes and La Bohn Gap (5,860 feet). The more snow there is in the basin beneath the gap, the easier the traveling.

There are numerous other high lakes to explore beyond the main portion of the Necklace Valley. An easily reached snowy basin to the west provides access to Tahl Lake, with vistas above Locket and Jewel Lakes, east to the Hinman Glacier and the face of Mount Hinman (7,492 feet) and north to Glacier Peak (10,541 feet).

There is plenty to do and see in the area. Just make sure you have a good map (1:24,000 USGS maps) if you plan to explore areas above and beyond the Necklace Valley. And don't forget the insect repellent or a handful of cigars in the summer months.

West Fork Foss River Trail

An equal number of larger and deeper lakes can be found on a nearby hike that follows the West Fork Foss River. (Drive 2.5 miles past the East Fork Foss River Trailhead on FR 6835). Highlights include a gorgeous waterfall spilling from the outlet of Lake Malachite a third of the way up the trail, as well as the incredible natural spillway that you cross via a logjam at Big Heart Lake, the end of this hike. Like the approach to the Necklace Valley, this trail gains significant elevation–3,200 feet over 7 miles. Five of the lakes are accessible by maintained trail, but to reach lakes like Delta and Otter you must walk through extremely difficult terrain up the river valley above Trout Lake. Remote Chetwoot, Angeline, and Azurite Lakes require detailed maps, orienteering skills, and vast stores of resolve.

24

Alpine Lookout via Merritt Lake

Type: Day hike or overnight

Season: Mid-June to mid-October

Total distance: 10 miles

Rating: Moderate

Elevation gain: 3,300 feet

Location: Nason Ridge, 25 miles north-west of Leavenworth

Map: Green Trails Wenatchee Lake No. 145

Getting There

From the Leavenworth RD, drive 25.5 miles west on US 2 to FR 657, the turnoff for the Merritt Lake Trailhead. The road sign is small and easily missed, so pay attention. Drive another 1.5 miles to the parking area and trailhead (27 miles).

The Trail

Mountain goats frequent the Alpine Lookout so often that perhaps the ridge should be renamed Mountain Goat Ridge. Its given name is Nason Ridge—Nason was one of two Native Americans who killed a couple of white settlers in the area, helping to spark the Yakima Indian War—and it runs approximately 17 miles east-to-west, rising to over 7,000 feet and providing a pleasant hiker's highway into the Cascades. The trail to the Alpine Lookout via Merritt Lake takes you by a quaint subalpine lake and then along an open slope to a blocky, flat ridgetop with broad, sweeping views of Glacier Peak and accompanying peaks from the operational Alpine Lookout.

The square speck of the Alpine Lookout appears slightly over halfway along the visible portion (from the parking area) of Nason Ridge. This gives you a pretty good idea of the approach and destination for the hike. Fir and ponderosa pine dot the lower slopes. Although you're only a few miles east of the divide, the understory is considerably drier and different from trails to the west. However, you still find crossover species like thimbleberry and tiger lily growing along the trail.

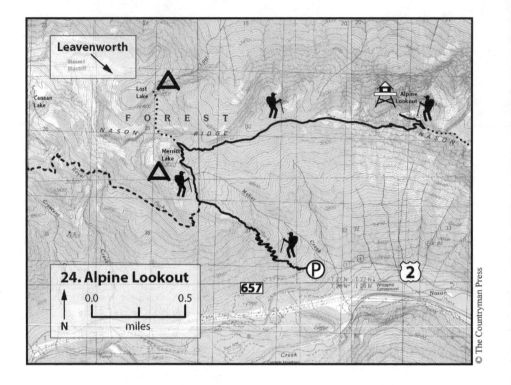

The climb to Merritt Lake and Alpine Lookout is never too severe, but it does hit you right away. You work your way up a slope, or arm of sorts, of the Mahar Creek drainage that eventually wraps itself into tall, steep Nason Ridge. Even though the Nason Ridge area covers less than 20,000 acres, there are 5,000 feet between its low and high points, making it a worthy challenge for any hiker.

At the 1-mile mark, after working up 17 of the switchbacks, the incline becomes more moderate and the distance between switchbacks increases. There are a couple of tent sites approximately 1.5 miles up, ideal if you get a late start or need a place to just hunker down. Keep in mind that there is no water here.

At 1.7 miles there are nice views of Nason Ridge's forested, brushy, rocky sec-

tions and some craggy high points. The rock is schist and gneiss, believed to be 100 to 200 million years old. The trail passes through a boulder field with a small creek and another single tent site.

If you're allergic to switchbacks you'll be happy to know that all 28 of them are behind you when you hit the boulder field. At 2 miles you arrive at a junction. The trail to the left (west) heads towards Crescent and Rock Lakes. Nason Ridge has just a half-dozen lakes, and almost all of them are on the west side.

Heading right takes you to Merritt Lake and onward to the Alpine Lookout. It's an easy 0.5-mile walk to Merritt (2.5 miles) between well-spaced trees, through shadow puddles, and over a crossing of Mahar Creek. The lake is set below tall cliff bands in a nest of trees. There are numerous tent

Mountain goat near the Alpine Lookout

sites just off the east shoreline. Because of the short distance and ease of access, you may have some company if you decide to stay the night.

The trail to the Alpine Lookout climbs above the lake, and in 0.3 mile (2.8 miles) you reach a wide bend to the right. A trail off the outside of that turn takes you 1 mile to Lost Lake. Although not maintained, the trail is traveled enough to make access easy.

Lost Lake is twice the size of Merritt and sits about 100 feet lower in a deep bowl at the foot of Mount Mastiff (6,741 feet). Lost usually offers more solitude than Merritt. You can easily scramble up Mount Mastiff for a high view of the area. Canaan Lake is also in the area, set between Mounts Howard (7,063 feet) and Mastiff. The somewhat rare larch mountain salamander can be found around Lost Lake, but these amphibians shouldn't be disturbed.

The trail onward to the Alpine Lookout drops down onto a forested notch along the ridge before gaining elevation and staying up and out of the subalpine fir and spruce forest. In June, lupine explodes along this portion of trail. You also have good views of the Chiwaukum Mountains south across US 2.

At 3.6 miles you pass through a burn from 1995. The trail loses and gains elevation as it works its way around a collection of rock bands. At 4.3 miles the trail climbs a few steep switchbacks, drops a bit, and then climbs steeply again to a trail junction at just over 4.7 miles.

The spur trail to the left leads 0.3 mile to the Alpine Lookout. The lookout, usually staffed from the Fourth of July through the end of September, has been used for fire detection for the last 85 years. The current building was built in 1975. A herd of mountain goat shares the area with lookout personnel.

The best views (north) encompass a wide swath of row after row of ridgelines containing distinguishable peaks like Mount David (7,420 feet), Sevenfingered Jack (9,100 feet), and Glacier Peak (10,541 feet), what local tribes called DaKobed, or "Great Parent." It is well worth purchasing Green Trails Glacier Peak No. 112, Holden No. 113, and Lucerne No. 114 or a single map of the complete Glacier Peak Wilderness to better study the peaks, ridgelines, and drainages.

You can also see Lake Wenatchee and the Tumwater Canyon leading toward Leavenworth. Besides a few of the steep pushes along the ridge, it won't feel like you've gained over 3,000 vertical feet in 5 miles. Be aware that there are no water sources between Merritt Lake and the Alpine Lookout.

Two Solutions to One Destination

Not too many people hike up to the Alpine Lookout via the Merritt Lake Trail. A more direct hike follows Round Mountain Trail 1529, which leaves from FR 6910 and climbs up the east end of Nason Ridge to reach the lookout in 4.5 miles. This route is slightly shorter but misses worthwhile Merritt and Lost Lakes.

25

Estes Butte

Type: Day hike

Season: Mid-June to mid-October

Total distance: 9.4 miles

Rating: Moderate to strenuous

Elevation gain: 3,500 feet

Location: Entiat Mountains, 30 miles north of Leavenworth

Maps: Green Trails Wenatchee Lake No. 145, Holden No. 113

Getting There

From the Leavenworth RD, drive 15.5 miles west on US 2 to the Lake Wenatchee (WA 207) turnoff. At 21 miles, turn right onto Chiwawa Road. Turn left at 22.2 miles onto Meadow Creek Road (FR 62). The road is paved for the first six of the 11.5 miles to the small parking area and trailhead, located just past Rock Creek (33.5 miles).

The Trail

The hike to Estes Butte (5,942 feet) runs up a subdued ridgeline above the Chiwawa River valley and slightly west of the main bulk of the Entiats, leading to the doorstep of glaciated, alpine peaks. The route is forested until it reaches an old lookout site, where an open ridge begins. Here you'll find arnica, lupine, paintbrush, thick mountain grasses, and plenty of vistas. Beyond the Estes Butte Trailhead to the north, the Entiat Mountains collide with the Chelan Mountains, and the resulting geologic wreckage of granite can be seen in the 9,000-foot-plus summits of Mount Maude, Sevenfingered Jack, and Mount Fernow.

Estes Butte Trail 1527 leaves the small parking area in the direction of the stock ramp approximately 100 yards away. The trail heads into the trees behind the ramp and edges along Rock Creek. At 0.1 mile you reach a junction; head to the right. The trail is wider along here because it follows an old logging road.

The trail can be a little brushy, but at 0.3 mile you pass through a nice patch of thimbleberry, typically ripe toward the end of July. You make a brief upward push across a rockier section before the path flattens out into a more open forest.

At 0.6 mile you arrive at a split. Stay to the left, continuing up the lower end of the Rock Creek drainage on more of a hiker's trail for a short distance before arriving at an obvious switchback to the left.

The first three of the 27 switchbacks are relatively long and moderate. The trail turns more steeply uphill along a creek at the fourth switchback, 1.1 miles into the hike. Be advised that the only reliable water source for the hike to the old lookout site and Estes Butte is found around the 1-mile mark. Like restless ocean waves, the switchbacks arrive one after the other before mellowing to a steady, moderate incline at 1.3 miles. You then return to longer contours before reaching the next switchback. The trail stays mainly in a nicely spaced ponderosa pine and Douglas fir forest for the entire climb up the slope.

At 2.2 miles, where the slope pinches together to funnel toward the ridgeline, the trail becomes slightly steeper and the switchbacks more frequent. You reach a nice benched area at 2.6 miles. Your arrival here marks the end to the switchbacks that helped you gain roughly 2,700 vertical feet.

There is more climbing ahead, but the ridgeline isn't too far off. The trail finally tops out at just over 3 miles, taking a much more relaxed (thankfully!) path toward the old lookout site 0.1 mile beyond. You have some views across the Chiwawa River valley below to the west and to the eastern high points and ridgelines of the Entiat and Chelan Mountains.

The lookout was dismantled in the 1960s, and only cement footings and scrap metal pieces strewn about mark its existence. The clearing offers some fantastic views of Fortress (8,780 feet), Chiwawa (8,459 feet), and Dumbbell (8,421 feet) above the headwaters of Phelps Creek in Spider Meadows. East and northeast of the

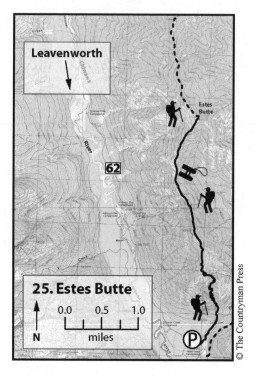

Leavenworth

62

25. Estes Butte

0.0   0.5   1.0

N   miles

© The Countryman Press

Rock Creek drainage you can pick out the rocky points of Garland Peak (7,525 feet) and Fifth of July Mountain (7,695 feet) above the forested ridgeline.

This spot is an ideal turnaround point if you don't feel like adding a bit more elevation to get better views up the valley from Estes Butte. Looking north from the ridgeline you're standing on, Estes Butte is the next closest high point, with a distinctive grass clearing that leads up to the summit. (Mileage from here is measured from the old lookout site.)

Put your roller skates on, because the trail runs steeply downhill for 0.4 mile before making a quick 0.1-mile climb and then dropping another 0.2 mile. This means that you're on a strict climbing-only diet up to Estes Butte.

The trail—officially Trail 1528—is narrower than the one to the old lookout site and may be a little overgrown, but you shouldn't have

The view from Estes Butte

any trouble following it. It's steep, though, and you hit loose rock and dirt in the last stretch to the top of the butte.

At 0.8 mile from the lookout site the trail appears to fork; stay to the left. Here you break from the trees into a short, steep, brushy section. At 1.1 miles you're still climbing, but at a lesser grade and near the lower end of a grassy slope. The grass grows in clumps, leaving patches of rocky soil exposed with plenty of room for a variety of colorful wildflowers.

At 1.4 miles the trail again appears to fork, and again you want to continue climbing on the left branch. The trail reaches the trees and a sign for the Glacier Peak Wilderness boundary. Head left for 40 yards to the top of Estes Butte at 1.6 miles.

From Estes Butte you can gaze at Clark (8,602 feet) and Buck (8,528 feet) Peaks to the west, Carne (7,100 feet) and Seven-fingered Jack (9,100 feet) to the north, and the beefy mass of the Stuart Range (8,400 feet) nearly 50 miles to the south.

Spider Meadows

If you were to continue driving up the Chiwawa River valley (past the Estes Butte Trailhead) you would eventually meet a trail that follows the Phelps Creek drainage into the narrow grass and wildflower oasis of Spider Meadows (4 miles). The meadows are squeezed within a collection of 8,000-foot peaks, and a trail climbs from the tranquil meadows onto the Spider Glacier, which hangs from Spider Gap (7 miles) at 7,100 feet. From the gap you can slip down the Lyman Glacier and travel on to destinations like Lyman Lake, Cloudy Pass, and Image Lake. The distances listed above are one way, and the map reference for the hike is Green Trails Holden No. 113.

26

The Enchantments

Type: Multiday

Season: Mid-July to early October

Total distance: 17 miles

Rating: Strenuous

Elevation gain: 5,400 feet

Location: Alpine Lakes Wilderness, 9 miles southwest of Leavenworth

Map: Green Trails The Enchantments No. 209S

Getting There

From the Leavenworth RD, travel west through the town of Leavenworth on US 2 for 1 mile to Icicle Creek Road. Don't forget to pick up your reserved camping permit or check for a walk-up permit at the ranger district. Turn left and drive 8.5 miles, passing the Snow Creek Trailhead and Eightmile Campground. Turn left onto FR 7601 at the sign for Eightmile Lake, Lake Stuart, and Colchuck Lake (9.5 miles). Continue 3.8 miles up a dirt road to the large parking area and outhouse for the Stuart/Colchuck Lake Trailhead (13.3 miles).

The Trail

The Enchantments is an inspiring zone of rock, water, and ice. Nowhere else in Washington are you able to dance so well between the subalpine and alpine. A sloping granite bench at 7,000 feet sits between the Cashmere Crags of Prusik Peak (8,000 feet), Little Annapurna (8,440 feet), and Dragontail (8,840 feet). Like diamonds against black velvet, the blue and green glacial tarns and magnificent yellow larch stands sparkle against the smooth white granite and glaciers. With lake names like Talisman, Leprechaun, Pixie, and Gnome, you feel like you've entered a fairy-tale setting.

You follow a trail paralleling Mountaineer Creek for the first 2 miles of this hike. Mountaineer is fed directly by snow and glacial melt from the north faces of Mount Stuart (9,415 feet), Sherpa Peak (8,605 feet), and Argonaut Peak (8,453 feet), as

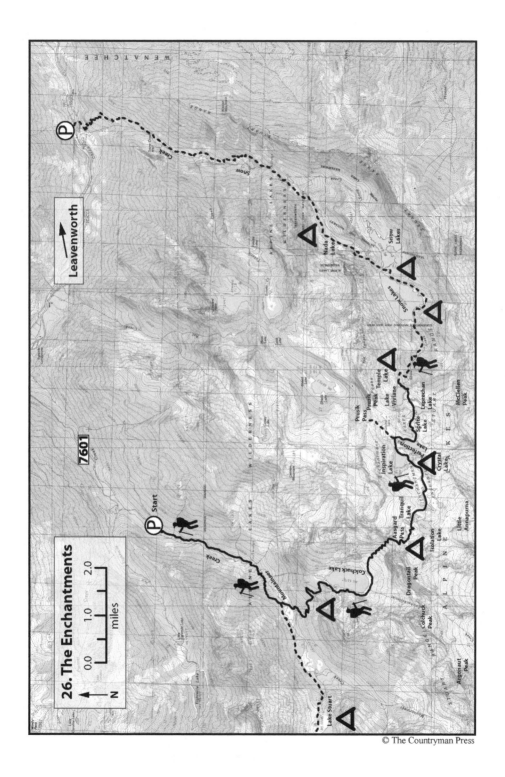

26. The Enchantments

N

0.0   1.0   2.0
        miles

Leavenworth

7601

© The Countryman Press

Hiking beneath jagged Prusik Peak

well as by the outlets of Lake Stuart and Colchuck Lake. Needless to say, the water volume stays fairly constant throughout the hiking season.

The hike begins with an easy climb through a mostly fir and cedar forest sprinkled with devil's club, fern, moss, and huckleberry bushes. This pleasant course lasts until the sturdy footbridge across Mountaineer Creek at 1.7 miles. There are occasional views of the peaks above the headwaters, and you can see Eightmile Mountain (7,996 feet) to the west and Cannon Mountain (8,638 feet) to the east.

Across the creek the meandering trail climbs up to less obstructed views of vari-

ous peaks in the Stuart Range. At 2.3 miles the trail splits, and you need to head left toward Colchuck Lake. You cross Mountaineer Creek again via two log bridges and edge along the bottom of a large boulder slide. The climb to Colchuck is strenuous, so take your time. There is a viewpoint of sorts at 3.3 miles, again with takes on the Stuart Range as well as the multiheaded mass of Cashmere Mountain (8,501 feet) to the north.

White-flower rhododendron bushes pop their blooms here from late July to early August, helping to keep your mind off the rough trail that continues to take huge bites of elevation—2,200 vertical feet from the trailhead to Colchuck Lake.

You finally reach the north end of Colchuck at 4 miles. Keep moving out of the trees to find campsites and various rock outcroppings that are ideal for a scenic lunch. Royal blue to glacial green, Colchuck Lake is like an oval swimming pool with high dives from nearby Colchuck and Dragontail Peaks.

Visible Colchuck Glacier is one of the mountaineering routes to the summit of 8,705-foot Colchuck Peak, while Dragontail's 2,000-foot northwest face holds about a half-dozen established rock-climbing routes. The granite Stuart Range was formed between 80 and 90 million years ago, with final touches added by glaciers advancing and retreating over 2 million years of ice ages.

The steep gully off the left, or east, shoulder of Dragontail is the route up to Aasgard Pass. The harsh formidability of Colchuck is offset by the tranquil waters of the lake, the soothing white granite, and the blaze of yellow larch trees in early fall. Relax, eat, and drink at the lake because even though it's only 2 miles to the pass, the trail offers the most difficult stretch of hiking in this entire book—2,200 vertical feet, most of it in 0.8 mile. Ouch!

It's worth it, though, because what lies on the other side of the pass is truly extraordinary. Start around the west shoreline of Lake Colchuck, where the trail seesaws up and down. You pass a small tarn as you hike/boulder-hop your way around the head (south end) of the lake.

The route along here, as well as to Aasgard Pass and through the entire Enchantment lake basin, is cairned (marked with piles of rocks). A noticeable line of scrub alder grows over the rock and boulder slide, and the trail mostly stays on the edge, making only a few dives into the brush before reaching the bottom of the gully.

Aasgard Pass looks quite distant across the lake. Although it appears closer by the time you reach the gully, you have to tilt your head back to see it—just like you would to look up at a skyscraper—an obvious indication that a serious mental and physical challenge lies ahead. If you set a manageable pace, rest often, and hydrate, you should do just fine.

If there is still considerable snow in the gully and/or strong snowmelt on the cliff walls above, which might dislodge rocks, then you may want to consider accessing the Enchantments by way of the Snow Creek Trailhead described at the end of this chapter.

The route follows the edge of a cool runoff stream until veering toward the left side of the gully to work around a noticeable bulge about halfway up. You continue to stagger higher and higher, pressing along a rock wall until the trail cuts across the runoff beneath some tall boulders. The gully is alive with the constant rush of water, the wind- and snow-stunted larch trees, and a variety of wildflowers.

After 4,400 feet of elevation gain over 5.3 miles you finally reach Aasgard Pass, where you can look down on Isolation and Tranquil Lakes floating beneath Dragontail Peak and Little Annapurna. The pathway slides past these lakes and over to a collection of tiny, stream-connected tarns. Communities of heather and miniature larch trees add to the quaintness and serenity of a place that is locked in a deep covering of snow from November to July.

The trail moves beyond these lakes, with an overlook of Crystal Lake, and in between Inspiration and Perfection Lakes to the trail junction with Prusik Pass (7 miles). The 0.6-mile trail up to the pass leads to a basin holding three other lakes. Prusik Peak looms over the amazing larch-filled cirque, which is alive with yellow fire in autumn.

The Enchantments Trail wraps around the east side of Perfection Lake (the near peak to the south is McClellan at 8,364 feet), passes smaller Sprite Lake, and drops into another basin via a beautiful stair-stepping creek that flows into Leprechaun Lake (8 miles). The last lake in the Enchantments before the brutal descent—if you choose—to the Snow Lakes is Lake Viviane, balanced above the Snow Lakes basin (8.5 miles).

There isn't a bad tent site in the entire Enchantments. The upper basin is more open and exposed than the middle and lower basin, and there are pit toilets at various locations. The Enchantments are ideal for scrambling, mountaineering, and technical climbing. For serious climbing information, find a copy of the *Cascade Alpine Guide: Columbia River to Stevens Pass,* by Fred Beckey.

Snow Creek Approach

The most popular route into the Enchantments is a 9-mile hike of very little aesthetic appeal that tests your resolve—up or down. Starting from the Snow Creek Trailhead on Icicle Creek Road, the trail passes through a 1994 burn and shadows Snow Creek for over 4 miles in a narrow drainage. You reach Nada Lake at 5.3 miles and the man-made rock dam between Upper and Lower Snow Lakes at 6.5 miles. Next, the trail climbs an extremely steep 1.5-mile section wedged between the Temple and McClellan Peak. By the time you reach Lake Viviane in the lower Enchantments you'll have climbed 5,500 feet over 9 miles. Depending on the permit situation, you may have no choice but to secure a Snow Lakes permit. But you need only spend one night here before moving into the Enchantments. If this is the case, and you have two vehicles in your backpacking party, plan on leaving a vehicle at the Stuart/Colchuck Trailhead to make this a one-way hike instead of an out-and-back. Trust me, the 9 miles out can be brutal.

27

Bandera Mountain

Type: Day hike

Season: June to October

Total distance: 7 miles

Rating: Strenuous

Elevation gain: 2,800 feet

Location: Mount Baker–Snoqualmie National Forest, 15 miles east of North Bend

Map: Green Trails Bandera No. 206

Getting There

From the North Bend RD, follow I-90 east for 14 miles. Take Exit 45, crossing back over the interstate and following the road uphill. At 14.4 miles the road changes from pavement to gravel. You come to a fork at approximately 14.8 miles. Head left on FR 9031; a sign indicates Trail 1038 in that direction. Follow this road for 3 miles to the parking area and outhouses (17.8 miles).

The Trail

Bandera sounds like a peak you might find in the Pyrenees instead of along the I-90 corridor. A short commute from Seattle. *Bandera,* Spanish for "banner" or "flag," does indeed provide banner views into the Alpine Lakes Wilderness region, across Puget Sound, and face-to-face with Mount Rainier. The final push to the ridgeline is brilliantly lit with bear grass blooms, paintbrush, and tiger lily.

The Bandera Mountain Trail 1038 is also known as the Ira Spring Trail. Spring photographed Washington's wildlands, advocated conservation for over 50 years, and collaborated on dozens of guidebooks. Ira's hike—he died in 2003 at the age of 84—begins along an old roadbed dotted with foxglove and lined with fern, cedar, fir, and western red alder.

At 0.5 mile the trail passes a brushed-in creek, and at 0.7 mile it runs along a quaint cascade with patches of salmonberry and devil's club. In autumn this section is lined with amber and gold leaves that brighten

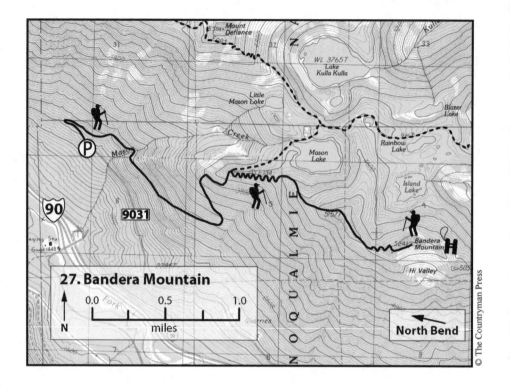

27. Bandera Mountain

the pathway. At 0.8 mile you may notice a trail cutting upslope. This was the former, very steep access trail for Mason Lake, which has now been rerouted to leave the trail to Bandera Mountain just under 2 miles ahead.

The trail leaves the roadbed and follows an old fire line at 1.4 miles. At 1.8 miles you gain elevation more rapidly on the way through a 50-year-old burned area. A couple of switchbacks are thrown in at 2.1 miles before the trail continues contouring up the hillside.

At about 2.4 miles you enter the bottom end of a large rock and boulder slide that is elegantly decorated with thousands of clumps of bear grass. If you time it right—most of the month of June—the long, bushy humps are lit up by a distinctive, tall-stemmed collection of tiny white blooms

that cluster together in the shape of a light bulb.

You arrive at the trail junction for Mason Lake and Bandera Mountain at 2.6 miles. Continuing cross-slope brings you to Mason Lake in .75 mile. The trail upslope catapults you through a colorful galaxy of wildflowers and onto a fantastic perch on Bandera Mountain (5,241 feet).

The rocky slope is carpeted with bear grass, lupine, paintbrush, tiger lily, and other wildflowers. As you gain elevation, slowly because of the steepness, Mount Rainier grows like a pointed white sun above the near ridgeline to the south.

At 3 miles you reach the ridgeline. Mason Lake perches below the other side of the ridge. Kulla Kulla, Blazer, Olallie, Talapus, Rainbow, and Island Lakes are all within a couple miles of Mason—just a small

Bear grass lights up the Bandera Mountain Trail

collection of the 700 lakes within the Alpine Lakes Wilderness. With a few good maps and a compass you could easily explore the Mason Lake region for many days.

To continue to the summit of Bandera, follow the ridgeline through a section of subalpine trees, then up and across a boulder field that requires a bit of scrambling. It's nothing dangerous, but it gives your hands a dose of what your feet have endured for the last 3 miles.

The hike/scramble is just as enchanting as the steep section earlier, full of bear grass, pink heather, and bright wildflowers. If you got an early start the valley below might be steeped in a marine layer, but the climb pulls you into clearer skies that make Mount Rainier (14,410 feet) look like a magnificent painting. You also have vistas south to Mount Adams (12,276 feet) and the Goat Rocks (7,500 feet), as well as north to Glacier Peak (10,541 feet) and Mount Baker (10,781 feet). From the summit of Bandera at 3.5 miles you can study the nearby ridgeline high points of Mount Gardner (4,453 feet), Mount Kent (5,087 feet), and pyramid-shaped McClellan Butte (5,162 feet).

Instead of watching the flow of interstate traffic below, imagine the slow, pulverizing creep of the shrinking Cordilleran ice sheet, thousands of feet thick, which shaped the South Fork Snoqualmie River valley during the Pleistocene era (2 million to 12,000 years ago). Talk about a real traffic jam.

Just Up the Road

For another hike in the area, try Granite Mountain. From the Pratt Lake Trailhead off Exit 47 on I-90, climb a steep slope through an avalanche gully—which should be avoided in the early season—to the ridgeline and a lookout atop Granite Mountain (5,629 feet). You have views here of the Stuart Range, as well as other peaks in the east-central Alpine Lakes Wilderness.

28

Waptus Lake to Spade Lake

Type: Multiday

Season: Late June to October

Total distance: Waptus, 17.4 miles; Spade, 26 miles

Rating: Moderate to strenuous

Elevation gain: Waptus, 800 feet; Spade, 3,000 feet

Location: Alpine Lakes Wilderness, 20 miles north of Cle Elum

Maps: Green Trails Stevens Pass No. 176, Kachess Lake No. 208

Getting There

From the Cle Elum RD off I-90, take WA 903 west toward Roslyn and Cle Elum Lake. After passing through Roslyn and the smaller town of Roland, WA 903 becomes the Salmon La Sac Road as it follows the east shoreline of dam-raised Cle Elum Lake. At 18.5 miles the road arrives at the Salmon La Sac RD and a fork in the road. Take the left fork across the Cle Elum River and go through the Salmon La Sac Campground to the Waptus River Trailhead (Trail 1310) at 19.5 miles. Outhouses are available.

The Trail

Waptus Lake is the largest lake in the Alpine Lakes Wilderness Area and one of the lowest in elevation. Surprisingly, it also has one of the most dramatic backdrops, usually reserved for the hard-to-reach cirque lakes tucked high in the mountains. Forming a long oval at 2,963 feet, Waptus is surrounded by forest and the awe-inspiring peaks of Bears Breast (7,197 feet) and Summit Chief (7,464 feet).

Forget those steep, backbreaking hikes where thousands of feet of elevation are crammed into a couple of miles. The Waptus River Trail is an easy glide through the trees amid dozens upon dozens of tree, plant, and wildflower species. If you want greater seclusion in a classic alpine setting with phenomenal cirque lakes, hike on to Spade Lake.

Right at the beginning of the trail there is an overlook of a gorgeous swimming hole on the Cooper River that you may want to keep in the back of your mind for the return trip, especially if it's a hot summer day. Less than 0.1 mile into the hike, bear right at the junction and then right again approximately 50 yards farther on to begin the 7-plus-mile run along the Waptus River Trail 1310 to Waptus Lake.

The forest remains open for pretty much the entire hike, with very little understory. After the wet season, the trail can be quite dusty, which is typical of most trails east of the Cascade divide, especially those with horse traffic. Various grasses, huckleberry, scrub alder, fern, and vine maple line the trail as it meanders past a few rocky sections. At 1 mile the trail makes one light switchback downhill and passes an unmaintained trail before continuing its gentle rising and falling.

By 2.4 miles, you have crossed two small bridges, past a collection of small ponds in a marsh, and tackled a third bridge near a grassy clearing. You also have had a few views of the ridgeline to the east-northeast over the gentle river valley of the Waptus. Look for Davis Peak (6,426 feet), and Goat Mountain (6,600 feet) farther to the north.

The trail passes through a stand of lodgepole pine before reaching a rerouted section at 2.7 miles. At 3.2 miles you cross the outlet of Diamond Lake, which sits along the Polallie Ridge 2,500 feet above. There are campsites and a pit toilet on the opposite side of the creek. You're close to the Waptus River here, but you won't actually hit it until you're another mile or so down the trail.

Beyond the outlet crossing, the trail climbs above the Hour Creek drainage and alongside some sizable cedars and hemlocks. At 4 miles the forest thins again, allowing views of Cone Mountain (5,295 feet). You come to the west bank of the Waptus River at 4.4 miles. In late spring and early summer the river runs strong and frothy white through here. Believe it or not, kayakers lug their boats up to this point to run the Class II to III+ whitewater during peak flow.

At 4.6 miles there is a great tent site above a couple of natural pools in the river, incredibly inviting on a warm day. Next you pass a tiny cascade between 20-foot-high boulders and a few more tent sites along a broader and calmer stretch of the Waptus before making a small climb to the 5.5-mile mark. This high point provides the best overlook of the glacier-carved river valley and the succession of high points to the east.

The trail briefly splits at 6 miles. The main trail stays to the right. At 6.2 miles you pass through a fairly brushy area, which for the next 0.3 mile is unofficially called "Toad Alley" in homage to the large western toads that live here. Female adults are as big as your fist, and you can see them everywhere, from the middle of the trail to under the brush to soaking in the river.

The greatest collection of flora is also along this stretch, with wild ginger, cow parsnip, bleeding heart, salmonberry, marsh violet, and twinberry all present. It would take some time to list the 180 or so species—not to mention lichen, moss, and fungi—found from the trailhead to Spade Lake.

At 6.7 miles you reach the junction with Trail Creek Trail 1322, which fords the Waptus River and continues on to the Tucquala Meadows Trailhead. The trail to Waptus Lake stays in the trees, crossing a small creek and then descending to another trail junction at 7.7 miles. Turn right to remain on the Waptus River Trail.

At 8 miles there is a wide steel footbridge over the Waptus River. A similar bridge spans Spinola Creek at 8.4 miles. A trail immediately cuts to the left after the bridge, rejoining the main trail in approximately 35 yards. The trail actual circles away from Waptus Lake until the second bridge, where you take a straight course to the south shore.

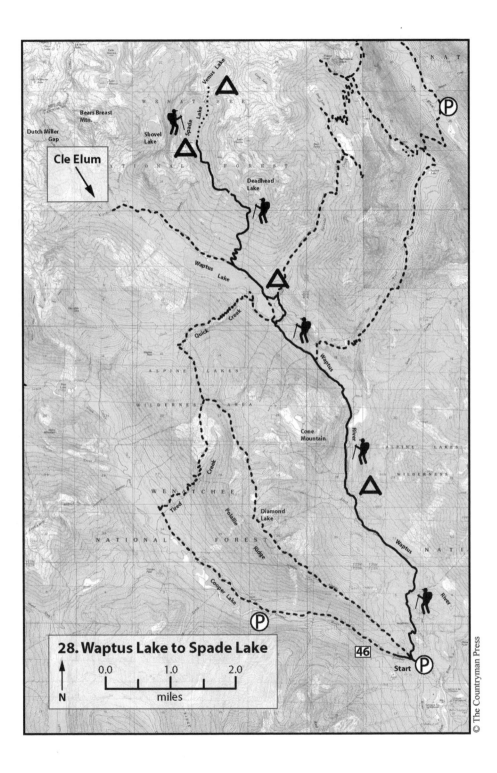

Cle Elum

28. Waptus Lake to Spade Lake

0.0   1.0   2.0

miles

N

46   Start

© The Countryman Press

Waptus Lake

In 0.3 mile you arrive at a camping area (8.7 miles) that can easily accommodate a group of tents. This area is usually occupied by hikers, as horsemen typically stay at the Quick Creek Camp on the opposite side of the lake.

Take your pack off and walk through the trees to the lakeshore for a postcard view. Waptus Lake stretches 1.5 miles toward the Dutch Miller Gap, slung like a hammock between the muscular mountains of Bears Breast and Summit Chief. The fishing isn't bad either.

There is work ahead to reach Spade Lake, but like so many hikes in the Central Cascades the reward far outweighs the effort. (Trail mileage is now listed from Waptus to Spade Lake.) Hike along the northeast shore of Waptus Lake (lined with huckleberry) for 0.6 mile to a junction, passing an alternate campsite. This spot is good for a couple of tents and has more ground cover than the larger site at the south end.

Follow the sign for Spade Lake at the junction. The trail turns upslope on a tight path that climbs steeply over tree roots, rocks, and downed trees to meet the Pacific Crest Trail (PCT) at 1 mile. If it feels like your heart is about to burst from your chest, it's because you've just climbed 450 feet in 0.4 mile. Catch your breath and take it slow because there's more climbing ahead.

Turn right onto the PCT and walk about 20 feet to join the Spade Lake Trail. The next 1.5 miles are a grind up a slightly overgrown trail that follows the outlet for Deadhead Lake before veering cross-slope to the left, or northwest. The key to surviving climbs like this is to find a workable pace, rest often, and drink lots of water.

At 2.5 miles, the trail eases somewhat. At 2.8 miles you cross a small stream and onto an open slope with views over Waptus Lake and the surrounding mountains. You have gained nearly 2,000 feet by this point, and you'll stay near this elevation all the way to Spade Lake, losing and gaining a little along the way. The stream is the only water source before the lake.

Besides the aerial view of Waptus Lake you also have a closer take on the sandstone formations of Bears Breast and an incredibly good view into the cluster of mountains southwest of that peak—Summit Chief, Chimney Rock, and Overcoat Peak, each with visible glaciers.

At 3.7 miles the slope opens up even more to reveal a straight-on view of Bears Breast and the near ridgeline between Shovel and Spade Lakes. You won't see Spade until you're nearly on top of it, but you will notice a waterfall on the cliff to the northwest. This is the Spade outlet creek, which joins the Waptus River in the open area near the head of Waptus Lake below you. The slope has buttercup, lupine, steeplebush, paintbrush, and a variety of other wildflowers.

At 3.9 miles from Waptus Lake the trail turns up a short series of switchbacks and then drops down to a subalpine parkland near the southeast end of Spade Lake. An array of wildflowers bloom here in July and August, along with heather, huckleberry, and blueberry. You pass a couple of small, shallow tarns before reaching a rock bluff overlook of Spade at 4.3 miles.

There are tent sites around the lake outlet and along the bluff. Spade is a deep-blue cirque lake, walled in on three sides. As you follow the trail down to the water you'll notice the tall gray, tan, and red ridgelines running the ength of the northern horizon. These are the south faces of glaciated Mounts Hinman (7,492 feet) and Daniel (7,899 feet). This area resembles the moraine environment high in the Himalayas.

Halfway up Spade there are more campsites on a rounded and forested peninsula that pokes into the lake.

Venus Lake, about half the size of Spade, sits deep in a rocky cirque 400 feet above the lake, but it is accessible. There are a few tent sites near its outlet. To reach Venus, follow the outlet along the east, or right, side, which requires a combination of steep hiking and light scrambling.

So You Wanna Get Looped?

It's possible to make a loop of the hike to Waptus Lake. This entails heading up the Quick Creek drainage—at the trail junction before the two bridge crossings by Waptus Lake—hiking on to the junction with the Tired Creek Trail, then following the long up-and-down run along Polallie Ridge. This route adds 5 miles to the hike, and for the most part the rewards don't quite exceed the effort. A better option would be to day-hike up to the old lookout site just beyond the Tired Creek Trail junction. This is an excellent high viewpoint over Waptus Lake, and out across to Bears Breast, Summit Chief, the Wenatchee Mountains to the northeast, and even south to Mount Rainier.

29

Bean Creek Basin

Type: Day hike

Season: Late June to mid-October

Total distance: 5 miles

Rating: Moderate

Elevation gain: 1,800 feet

Location: Wenatchee National Forest, 15 miles north of Cle Elum

Map: Green Trails Mount Stuart No. 209

Getting There

From I-90 at Cle Elum take WA 970 approximately 11 miles east and turn onto Teanaway River Road. At 7.4 miles you reach an intersection. Go straight on the North Fork Teanaway River Road. You have a great view of Mount Stuart along here.

The pavement ends just past the 13-mile mark. Take the dirt road (FR 9737) to the right. The road forks at 14.4 miles, but you continue up the left fork toward Beverly Campground and Esmeralda Basin. At 16.8 miles, just before Beverly Creek, turn right onto FR 9737–112. Drive another 1.2 miles to the small parking lot for the trailhead (18 miles). Hikes to Bean Creek Basin and other destinations up the Beverly Creek drainage begin here.

The Trail

Bean Creek Basin resembles an illustration from a children's book, with greens, reds, blues, and yellows mixing in an amazing display of color. Just listen to the wild names of some of the flowers and other plants found along the stream in the magical upper basin and up to the ridgeline: dirty socks (alpine buckwheat), monkeyflower, paintbrush, skyrocket (scarlet gilia), elephant head (lousewort), tiger lily, thimbleberry, and cow parsnip. Even the 5-mile trail to the basin is perfect for kids of all ages.

Beverly Creek Trail is aptly nicknamed "the turnpike," because it shuttles a great number of hikers, backpackers, and climbers to various destinations, including Bean Creek Basin. But even with a steady stream of visitors, Bean Creek Basin is extremely inviting and has minimal human impact, especially in the lush and attractive upper basin.

Cross over Beverly Creek via a bridge and follow Beverly Turnpike Trail 1391—an old roadbed paralleling the creek—for 0.5 mile. At the junction, turn right onto Bean Creek Basin Trail 1391.1. (If you've crossed Bean Creek you've gone too far.) The lower creek drainage is thick with brush, yet the trail stays in the open for about 0.4 mile. Mountain thistle, columbine, paintbrush, thimbleberry, wild rose bushes, and other wildflowers and blooming shrubs splash color along the stream.

At about 1 mile you ford the creek (more difficult in the early season) and work up the northwest side of the drainage through a promenade of scarlet gilia, tiny red trumpet-like flowers blaring from a single stem. Shortly beyond the crossing you come to a sparsely forested stretch where the ground is carpeted in grass. At 1.2 miles two quick switchbacks move upslope before the trail resumes a moderate incline along the Bean Creek drainage.

At 2 miles there is a junction at the lower end of Bean Creek Basin. The trail heading to the right is the official Bean Creek Trail, which climbs about 700 to 800 feet over 1.5 miles to a notch south of Earl Peak. Earl is a worthy scramble, and if you want to stay in a high campsite you'll find one here with views of the river valley and the Cascade volcanoes Rainier and Adams.

Continue straight along a well-worn trail to enter the playland of the upper basin, with scramble access to the ridgeline for Bean and Earl Peaks. Here you come face-to-face with giant Mount Stuart (9,415 feet). This granite massif is perhaps the finest example of its kind, here in the Central Cascades or anywhere in the country.

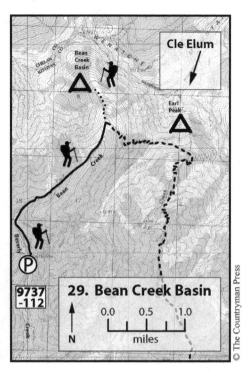

The trail parallels a small creek lined with tufts of lush grass before crossing over and climbing a little higher to reach the beginning of the upper basin at 2.5 miles. The ground is wet and spongy, with a wonderful covering of grasses. Wildflowers like shooting star, phlox, purple aster, monkeyflower, and paintbrush provide plenty of color. Trees grow in small groups throughout the basin, marching up to the craggy reddish ridgeline.

In another 0.3 to 0.5 mile you can be up on the ridge (aim to the right of Bean Peak) with a superior view of the Ingalls Creek drainage and the mesmerizing vistas of Colchuck Peak, Argonaut Peak, and Mount Stuart in the Stuart Range. Even though you get to Bean Creek Basin quickly, you won't have any trouble whiling away an entire day here.

Bean Creek Basin

Baggin' Basins

Esmeralda Basin and points beyond are easily reached via a 7-mile hike that edges along the Esmeralda Peaks (over 6,700 feet), then runs through a tantalizing kingdom of plants and wildflowers up to Fortune Creek Pass. As with Bean Creek Basin, the flora names are fantastical: maidenhair fern, sharp-tooth angelica, goatsbeard, queen's cup, sticky currant, squirreltail, goosefoot violet. A high point north of the pass at 6,600 feet opens up views of the Stuart Range and surrounding mountains. The trailhead is at the end of the North Fork Teanaway River Road (FR 9737). It's Trail 1394, and the reference map is Green Trails Mount Stuart No. 209.

Spray Falls

30

Spray Park

Type: Day hike

Season: Mid-July to October

Total distance: 8.6 miles

Rating: Moderate

Elevation gain: 1,500 feet

Location: Mount Rainier National Park, 20 miles south of Enumclaw

Map: Green Trails Mount Rainier West No. 269

Getting There

From I-5 between Seattle and Tacoma, take WA 161 or WA 167 to WA 410, follow it to WA 165, and continue to Wilkeson. From the Wilkeson Wilderness Center for Mount Rainier National Park in the town of Wilkeson, drive south on WA 165 for approximately 6.5 miles. The road forks at this point; follow the right branch uphill toward Mowich Lake. The pavement continues for about 3.5 miles before turning to gravel. At 17.5 miles you reach the park boundary and a self-registration station for entrance into the park. The fee for a seven-day visit is $10 per vehicle. Travel another 5 miles to the Mowich Lake parking area and outhouses (22.5 miles). This section of road often has a washboard surface. A camping permit is required for Eagle's Roost or other nearby backcountry sites.

The Trail

Spray Park, along with neighbors Mist and Seattle Parks, is one of only a few subalpine/ alpine parklands not officially along the 90-mile Wonderland Trail loop around Mount Rainier (14,410 feet). But like other parks situated just below the icy fingers of Rainier's 26 glaciers, Spray Park is spectacular in its collection of wildflowers and vistas. Bonuses like the Eagle Cliff viewpoint and tropically lush streamside vegetation beneath the impressive Spray Falls only add to the pleasure of a day hike around the park.

From the walk-in campground by Mowich Lake you have the only view of

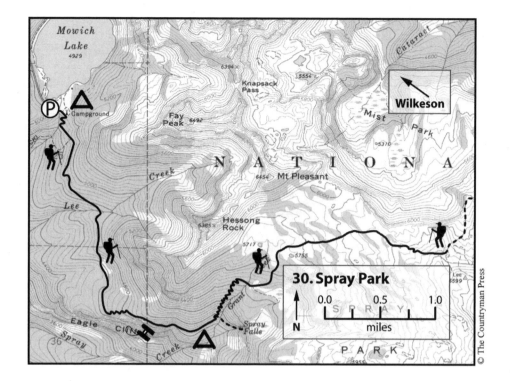

Mount Rainier for a while. Follow the Wonderland Trail—and it's nearly impossible not to take a portion of this trail to other destinations within Mount Rainier National Park—for a quick downhill run of 0.4 mile before the junction with the Spray Park Trail, which stays to the left.

At approximately 1 mile the trail passes through an open area at the bottom of an avalanche chute. This area is thick with vegetation, like Sitka valerian and false Solomon's seal, fed by the life-giving waters of Crater Lee Creek. The wall to the east is 6,454-foot Mount Pleasant.

You pass the bottom of a rock slide at 1.6 miles and then climb a set of dirt and log steps for about 0.2 mile. At 1.9 miles you come to a short spur trail that leads down to a viewpoint on Eagle Cliff. There

you have a front-row seat of North Mowich Glacier on Mount Rainier. But the big mountain remains somewhat obscured until you arrive in Spray Park.

Hike another easy 0.2 mile or so to the junction for the Eagle's Roost Camp. The campsite is below the Spray Park Trail, perched along the eastern edge of Eagle Cliff. At 2.2 miles, after a creek crossing, there is a second junction. Spray Park is to the left and Spray Falls to the right. Don't forgo the 0.2-mile round-trip trail along Spray Creek below the falls, which takes you over Grant Creek on a log bridge.

Spray Falls spills some 200+ feet in a wide swath of paper-thin water, sending a stiff mist downstream. You can scramble up along the creek, and if you're careful but

Paintbrush blooming in Spray Park

adventurous enough it's possible to slide into a large hollow behind the falls. There is an abundance of streamside blooms to photograph, including pink monkeyflower.

The trail to Spray Park climbs up a dozen switchbacks, squeezed by Grant Creek and a smaller, unnamed creek. At 2.7 miles the switchbacks end, but the trail continues to climb along the slope. You move in and out of the trees, cross Grant Creek for the last time, and arrive at the entrance of Spray Park at 3.3 miles.

The park has a mix of subalpine trees, meadows, and tarns, and a brilliant wildflower collection that includes bear grass, glacier lily, buttercup, lupine, paintbrush, pink heather, and tiger lily. Hessong Rock (6,385 feet) borders Spray Park to the

northwest, as does a different face of Mount Pleasant. Oh yeah, there is also Mount Rainier, the tallest volcano in the contiguous United States.

The pleasant scenery continues for the next mile or so as you climb toward the 6,400-foot high point (4.3 miles) in a boulder field at the eastern edge of the park. Looking north you see Mist Park nearly 1,000 feet below. Seattle Park is a short distance to the east. The long, blocky rock formation to the north-northwest above Mist Park is Mother Mountain (6,300 feet).

The high point can be hard to reach if the snow hasn't completely retreated; however, there is a good chance the route will be marked with cairns. The long, dark finger of rock extending over 3,000 feet above you on Mount Rainier is known as Ptarmigan Ridge, and the tall formation nearly 2,000 feet directly upslope is Observation Rock, its foot blanketed by the Flett Glacier. The two largest visible glaciers on Rainier are Russell and Carbon.

But there's more to see than just Rainier: Mount Baker (10,781 feet) is discernable in the distance to the north, Glacier Peak (10,541 feet) closer in to the right of Baker, and the Stuart Range (over 8,300 feet) to the northeast. To catch the peak wildflower season, plan your trip sometime between mid-July and early August. And don't forget the mosquito repellent.

Just Take a Little Off the Top

Mount Rainier is old and dull and shiny and new all at the same time. Its foundation is some 20 to 60 million years old, formed at the same time as the Cascade Range. Volcanic activity reshaped it around 500,000 to 700,000 years ago. The theory today—more aggressive than past estimations—is that 5,700 years ago Mount Rainier lost approximately 1,600 feet off the top in an eruption that sent mud flows streaming toward Puget Sound. So its shape probably once resembled that of Glacier Peak and pre-1980 Mount St. Helens, and its height stretched to 16,000 feet.

31

Palisades Lake

Type: Day hike or overnight

Season: July to October

Total distance: 6.6 miles

Rating: Moderate

Elevation gain: 500 feet

Location: Mount Rainier National Park, 35 miles southeast of Enumclaw

Map: Green Trails Mount Rainier East No. 270

Getting There

From I-5, take WA 161 or WA 167 to WA 410. Take WA 410 south from Enumclaw to the Mount Rainier National Park entrance at White River, and then follow the road for 13 miles to the large parking lot at Sunrise Point. The trailhead is across the road. The seven-day park entrance fee runs $10. Keep in mind that a permit is required for backcountry camping in the park.

The Trail

The hike to Palisades Lake offers a completely different perspective from the vast majority of outings within the park, all of which seem to feed off Rainier's energy. This hike follows a long, gently rolling valley dotted with lakes and set along the ridgeline of the Sourdough Mountains. It's a setting you'd typically expect to find in Idaho or Montana, not in Washington—especially not next to Mount Rainier. Upper Palisades Lake is tucked neatly beneath a cliff wall.

An added bonus of this hike is that you end up at almost the same elevation you started from, dropping and rising in relatively small doses over 3.3 miles each way. And Mount Rainier is nowhere in sight—almost.

The trail starts at 6,100-foot Sunrise Point, a marvelous place from which to set out. There are amazingly clear views up the northeast slopes of Rainier, across to the ridgeline and high points on the western edge of the Norse Peak Wilderness, and southeast to bell-shaped 12,000-foot Mount Adams.

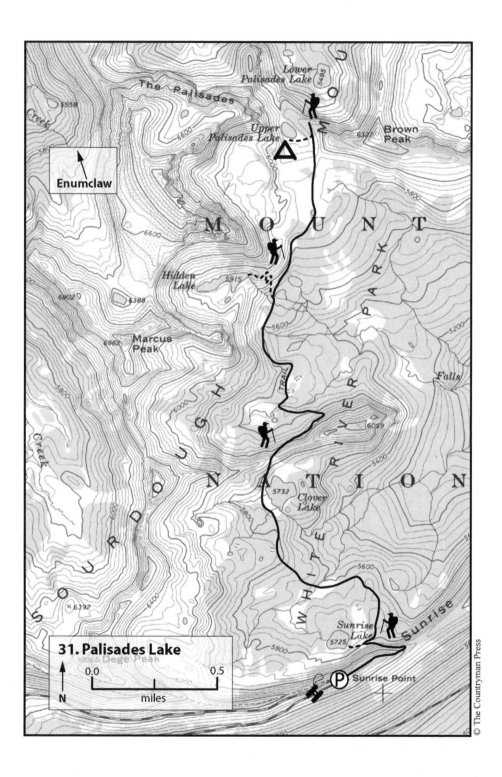

Enumclaw

The Palisades

Lower
Palisades Lake

Upper
Palisades Lake

Brown
Peak

MOUNT

Hidden
Lake

Marcus
Peak

Falls

WHITE RIVER PARK

Clover
Lake

Sunrise
Lake

Sunrise

Sunrise Point

31. Palisades Lake

0.0   0.5

miles

N

Dege Peak

© The Countryman Press

The Sourdough Mountains

The trail to Upper Palisades Lake slides down the open Sunrise Ridge—decorated with paintbrush, Indian hellebore, and lupine in the summer months—before switchbacking downhill to the west to the trail junction with Sunrise Lake in a small rock slide at 0.4 mile. From the ridge, as well as along the descent to the junction, you can see the long, broad valley the trail passes through. Peaks like Marcus (6,932 feet) and Brown (6,322 feet) stand out along the prominent ridgeline of the Sourdough Mountains.

The first section, the upper valley, combines small pockets of green grass and wildflower meadows set between stands of subalpine fir and spruce. The trail loses elevation as it gently winds past small tarns and over Sunrise Creek in this parklike setting. After the creek crossing (1 mile), the trail climbs slightly by dead stand, victims of a small spot fire some time ago.

At 1.3 miles the trail drops down to Clover Lake, which is nicely ringed by grass and wildflowers backed by trees. The trail climbs above the lake through columbine and tiger lily to a notch with views down into an open U-shaped meadow beneath Marcus Peak.

The slopes of the Sourdough Mountains typically resemble those found in southwest Montana, with stands of trees on the lower slopes and patches of vegetation mixed with talus slopes beneath rocky ridgelines. The heather-lined trail continues down to the meadow. You cross a creek and move on to a rise in a more heavily forested section above a small lake at 2.3 miles.

The trail contours around this slope and out into an open area beneath a rock band. You cross another small creek and then arrive at a junction at 2.5 miles. One trail heads left, up to Hidden Lake (0.6 mile one way), well worth a side trip. The largest rock glacier deposit in the Mount Rainier area—100 acres and up to 300 feet thick—is located between Hidden Lake and Upper Palisades.

The other path continues on past Dicks Lake Camp to Upper Palisades. You pass through a heavier forest and by a couple more small lakes. At 2.9 miles the trail opens up into a fantastic, broad wildflower meadow, bordered by the craggy rock of the Sourdoughs to the west and dropping sharply toward the Sunrise Creek drainage to the east.

You pass through a small stand of trees before reaching an overlook of Upper Palisades Lake (3.1 miles). The spur trail to the camping area is located here. Travel another 0.2 mile to the end of the trail, wedged between the Upper Palisades rock formation and Brown Peak.

Below, you can see Lower Palisades and other smaller lakes at the upper end of the glacial valley that runs for a number of miles to the north. A path drops to Lower Palisades, and you can take a crosscountry swing up to Brown Peak and into Bear Park, home of a few more small lakes. There are plenty of exploratory day hikes to be done from camp at Upper Palisades.

Nearby, as the Crow Flies

If you stand on Brown Peak (6,322 feet) and look almost dead east you can see Norse Peak (6,856 feet) about 6 miles off. The peak itself isn't as significant as the mind-boggling views it provides. A 4.5-mile trail climbs up from Silver Creek, running along the Crystal Mountain Resort Road (access is from WA 410) to gain views of hundreds of Cascade peaks, from Mount Stuart to the Goat Rocks and Mounts Adams, Baker, and larger-than-life Rainier. This is a great day hike or overnighter, especially for the amazing sunrises and sunsets.

32

Summer Land Meadows

Type: Day hike or overnight

Season: Mid-July to October

Total distance: 8.2 miles

Rating: Moderate

Elevation gain: 2,000 feet

Location: Mount Rainier National Park, 35 miles southwest of Enumclaw

Map: Green Trails Mount Rainier East No. 270

Getting There

From I-5, take WA 161 or WA 167 to WA 410. Take WA 410 south from Enumclaw to the White River entrance of Mount Rainier National Park. Drive 3 miles to the parking area for Summer Land Meadows, which is on the right just beyond Fryingpan Creek. The trailhead is across the road. A park entrance fee of $10 allows you access for seven days, and a backcountry permit is required for camping in the park.

The Trail

In July and August delicate wildflowers show their strength in the small area of Summer Land Meadows, which is accessible via a short stretch of the Wonderland Trail. Heather, avalanche lily, monkeyflower, and paintbrush blend with the green grass and gray rock in a short-lived visual symphony. The runoff creeks fed by the Fryingpan Glacier above are full of cold, turbulent gray water, and Summer Land is in active transition. Campsites are set in small stands of trees to protect the sensitive meadow and to shield tents from mountain winds. Summer Land is a special place in these brief, warm months.

A short spur trail takes you to Wonderland, Mount Rainier's premier trail, sought out by wilderness adventurers the world over. The hike to Summer Land Meadows gives you a small taste of the highlights that await on the 90-mile loop around Rainier (14,410 feet).

Follow the trail sign to the left for Summer Land, taking the pleasant route through a tall forest of fir and cedar. The trail follows

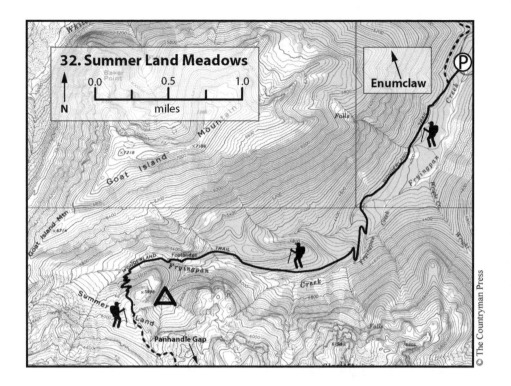

the north bank of Fryingpan Creek before crossing at 2.8 miles. The forest understory is sparse due to the closeness of the trees and the shading effect of the canopy. Old-growth trees here have base diameters of 4, 5, and even 6 feet. The churning rush of the creek in this early stretch is offset by the stillness among the large and small trees.

At 0.5 mile you cross a small creek and enter a brushy section of thimbleberry and cow parsnip. And at 0.9 mile the trail angles up through a longer brushy section of salmonberry, a naturally sweet trail snack. The nice stroll continues with a slow, winding climb starting at 1.2 miles. Just before the trail switchbacks to the right at 1.3 miles you can walk out onto a rocky overlook of Fryingpan Creek to view a small waterfall.

Past a couple of switchbacks, the trail takes a straighter course above the creek. At 2.4 miles you cross two small creeks and leave the cover of the trees to enter an avalanche chute with brush and young cedar, spruce, and fir.

Cross Fryingpan Creek on a foot-log at 2.8 miles. The underside of the log is only a foot or so above the creek around the end of July, and it's completely submerged during the height of runoff. Just past the crossing there is an overview of the creek pouring down a rock wall on the way to its confluence with the White River east of the trailhead. Take a moment to notice all the debris left behind as the water level drops.

Up the drainage you can see portions of the upper slopes of Mount Rainier. The trail stays in the drainage for a distance, gaining nice views of Rainier, Little Tahoma (11,138 feet), and the moraine beneath the Emmons Glacier. Check out the glaciers clinging to the rock faces of Little Tahoma.

Mount Rainier

In autumn the leaves of various shrubs molt into red, yellow, and pale orange. At 3.3 miles you begin a moderately steep climb of switchbacks up to Summer Land Meadows. Approximately 700 of the 2,000 feet of elevation gain for this hike come in this section.

Tree cover thins as you move up, replaced by heather, bistort, mountain buttercup, and paintbrush. Expansive views of the ridgeline of Goat Island Mountain (7,288 feet) open to the north. At 4.1 miles you enter Summer Land Meadows.

This compact, open bench provides spectacular views of Rainier, Little Tahoma, and Goat Island Mountain, but you'll have trouble looking up from the marvelous subalpine/alpine parkland full of wildflowers. The trail passes by a tent area and pit toilet before meeting a cool creek draining from the Fryingpan Glacier 2,000 feet above. The nearby rock band is a perfect place to spot mountain goats.

I highly recommend that you continue on through the meadows and up to the Panhandle Gap in 1.4 miles. The gap—the highest point along the Wonderland Trail, at 6,800 feet—is a great place to scramble around, take a lunch break, and peer down onto Ohanapecosh Park.

If I Had a Nickel for Every Time . . .

To further immerse yourself in the spectacles along the Wonderland Trail, extend your Summer Land Meadows hike on over Panhandle Gap to enjoy the amazing glaciers, moraines, wildflowers, creeks, and waterfalls of Ohanapecosh Park, Indian Bar, and points beyond, crossing the Cowlitz Divide and Nickel Creek and ending at the Box Canyon Trailhead. To do this you'll need to leave a vehicle on each end. The best camp option along here is at Indian Bar. After covering the 16 miles between Summer Land and Box Canyon you only have 75 or so miles left to finish circling Rainier on the Wonderland Trail.

33

Pinnacle Peak

Type: Day hike

Season: Mid-July to October

Total distance: 3 miles

Rating: Moderate

Elevation gain: Pinnacle Saddle, 1,050 feet; Pinnacle Peak, 1,700 feet

Location: Mount Rainier National Park, 1.5 miles south of Paradise Lodge

Map: Green Trails Paradise No. 270S

Getting There

Take WA 7 to Elbe and take WA 706 east to the Nisqually entrance in the southeast corner of Mount Rainier National Park. There is a $10 per vehicle park fee, which is good for 7 days. Drive approximately 16 miles to reach the junction for Paradise and Stevens Canyon Road, the route for the Stevens Canyon entrance. Stay to the right, following the road toward the Reflection Lakes and Stevens Canyon. It is 1.5 miles from the junction to the long parking area next to the first, and largest, of the Reflection Lakes (17.5 miles). The Pinnacle Peak Trailhead is across the road.

The Trail

The scramble to the summit of Pinnacle Peak—dubbed the "Matterhorn of the Cascades" in 1897 by the Oregon-based mountaineering group the Mazamas—is a brilliant outing that shines as brightly as any short hike in the park. From the Pinnacle Saddle between Pinnacle (6,562 feet) and Plummer Peaks (6,370 feet) you can marvel at a southern panorama of Cascade giants like Adams, St. Helens, and Hood.

Hiking in the Tatoosh Range, where Pinnacle Peak is the second highest of 11 prominent peaks, is like being in the front row of the show that is Mount Rainier. From the summit and saddle you can look down on Paradise Park, across to the Muir Snowfield, and up to the icy summit of Rainier.

The trail begins across from the Reflection Lakes, which sit some 500 feet below Paradise Park, Mount Rainier's most popular destination. Many people stop at the largest Reflection Lake to snap photos, have a quick bite to eat, look at the road map, or stretch their legs on the lakeshore trail. Pinnacle's towerlike peak is clear and distinctive from the parking area and even more so from Paradise.

Across the road from the Reflection Lakes the 1.5-mile Pinnacle Peak Trail leads to wonders not available to the masses who never venture more than a few feet from their vehicles. The trail begins along a lush slope of heather, lupine, and mountain blueberry bushes. It climbs for 0.4 mile to the south before swinging west-northwest by a pocket meadow and then climbing once again.

At 0.8 mile you cross a creek, and a short distance farther on the trail passes under a beautiful, thin cascade slipping from a rock band above. It's a somewhat steep climb through the trees before you move across a rock slide.

At 1.1 miles the trail begins to contour around the top of the rocky basin above Tatoosh Creek. You are hiking below the west side of Pinnacle Peak, home of the mountain goat. Rainier and expansive views of Paradise Park are behind you.

You climb a few switchbacks at 1.3 miles before arriving at the Pinnacle Saddle (1.5 miles). The views to the south are absolutely stunning. The broad, green glacial valley is walled in to the east by the Castle (6,440 feet) and Unicorn Peak (6,971 feet), the highest Tatoosh summit.

The slopes appear manicured, with grass, wildflowers, and patches of talus laid out like a championship golf course. In the distance to the southeast you can see the Goat Rocks (over 7,000 feet), which lead your eyes toward 12,276-foot Mount Adams, the state's second-tallest Cascade volcano.

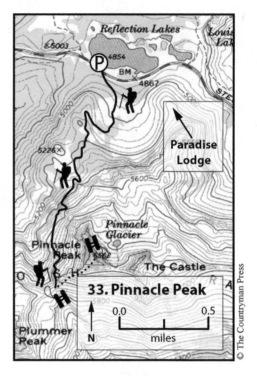

Easy-to-follow trails from the saddle lead to the summits of Plummer and Pinnacle Peaks, to the rim above the basin toward the Castle, and along the backbone of the Tatoosh Range to the east. Of course, there are also grand views of Mount Rainier to the north, with recognizable features like Paradise Park, Muir Snowfield, Nisqually Glacier, and Cathedral Rocks. With views like this, the saddle is an ideal turnaround point for the hike back to the Reflection Lakes. However, it's well worth your time to continue on, no matter what direction you choose.

Although the route is easy enough to follow, keep three things in mind before starting off to the summit of Pinnacle Peak: (1) when the rocks are wet they become incredibly slick and dangerous; (2) don't attempt the summit unless you're comfortable scrambling and unafraid of exposure; and (3) young children should not attempt the summit.

Mountain goats on the slope of Pinnacle Peak

Go approximately 40 yards east from the saddle to a trail that turns upslope. A couple of noticeable paths rise through the scree. Stay on the most defined trail for the climb along a narrow ridgeline running from the summit to the southwest. The trail passes through a small clump of trees before beginning a high-stepping route up to the bottom of a short, steep gully. Don't drift too far to the left or onto the sharp arête (ridgeline). Hike/scramble up the easiest route instead of moving cross-slope.

You scramble the most at the bottom of the 30-foot gully. Take your time and be careful to find good hand and foot placements. Once above this section, take the path through a tightly packed clump of trees to the blocky summit of Pinnacle.

Below the peak to the northeast you can see a small glacial lake and Pinnacle Glac-ier. But grand vistas abound in all directions. You can even spot the tourists pulling in and out of the parking lot back at the Reflection Lakes, like boats docking and departing.

Tatoosh Treat

The southern portion of the Tatoosh Range is enclosed within the Tatoosh Wilderness Area, and Tatoosh Peak (6,310 feet) marks its end. The old lookout location can be approached from the Hinkle Tinkle Trailhead to the east or the Butter Creek Trailhead to the west. Each requires over 3,400 vertical feet of tough hiking, and each moves across giant, grassy, wildflower-filled slopes to Tatoosh Peak. From the Butter Creek side, you get the added bonus of a side hike to the Tatoosh Lakes. The map reference is Green Trails Packwood No. 302.

34

Van Trump Park

Type: Day hike

Season: Mid-July to October

Total distance: 5.2 miles

Rating: Strenuous

Elevation gain: 2,000 feet

Location: Mount Rainier National Park, 70 miles southeast of Olympia

Map: Green Trails Mount Rainier West No. 269

Getting There

Take WA 7 to Elbe and take WA 706 east to the Nisqually entrance to Mount Rainier National Park. It is 10.5 miles to the parking area for the Van Trump Park Trail from the Nisqually entrance. The fee for a seven-day entrance pass is $10. The parking area isn't signed, but if you cross a short bridge with views of Christine Falls you've gone too far.

The Trail

Van Trump Park is named for Philemon Van Trump, who, along with General Hazard Stevens, is credited with making the first successful climb to the summit of Mount Rainier, in 1870. They actually climbed from a camp by Sluiskin Falls above Paradise to the northeast, but wedge-shaped Van Trump Park is a fitting tribute to their achievement. The parkland is full of wild-flowers like buttercups, anemone, and paintbrush on its rise up to cliff bands beneath Kautz and Van Trump Glaciers. (August Valentine Kautz nearly reached the summit of Rainier 13 years before Van Trump, in 1857.)

The Van Trump Park Trail passes by one of the park's most spectacular cascades: Comet Falls. Said to resemble the tail of a comet, the falls plummet 320 feet to a rocky creek bottom, sending a constant wave of mist through the air. It's also worth over-shooting the parking area before the hike to see the face of Christine Falls.

From the small parking area, the trail climbs into the trees—the typical west-side mix of hemlock, fir, and cedar—above the road and soon reaches a view of the head of Christine Falls.

Salal is noticeable near the beginning of the trail. It's quite prolific along the state's coastal region, and its dark, somewhat spicy berries were a staple for numerous Pacific Northwest tribes. The shrub flowers from late June to early July and berries are ripe through most of late summer.

You cross two short bridges or elevated walkways before arriving at a sturdy log bridge over Van Trump Creek at 0.3 mile. From the bridge you can just see the water drop 35 feet over Christine Falls. The pounding water continually carves the smooth, scalloped slot canyon of the creek bed.

Once across, the trail parallels the creek through treed and open sections over a fairly wide but rough trail with rocks and tree roots. At 0.5 mile you work up some switchbacks through the trees, and the incline is a solid moderate. Breaking from the trees, you enter a brushed slope of salmonberry, Sitka valerian, and bluebells about 80 feet above Van Trump Creek at the 1-mile mark.

This section provides your only view of Rainier before Van Trump Park. The trail narrows through here and becomes noticeably rocky and rugged. You pass small stands of trees as you climb up through a boulder field that will leave your quads burning.

At 1.4 miles the trail skirts some trees on the way to Van Trump's wide creek bed, or washout, at 1.5 miles. A nice two-stage waterfall dumps into this rocky drainage. The water eventually joins with the flow off the Van Trump Glacier thousands of vertical feet above.

Over the hump of the creek bed, you can see impressive Comet Falls. The water hugs the rock for 100 feet before free-falling in a silky cascade for another 200 feet. It then gathers itself for another 18-foot drop. Adding to the beauty of the scene is a half-

amphitheater backdrop of tall rock bands capped by trees.

Wildflowers and plants along the trail include monkeyflower, purple aster, fern, and Sitka valerian. You next climb a short series of switchbacks, the first few tightly packed together. At the sixth one, the trail makes a run cross-slope, and at the seventh you are nearly under Comet Falls (1.6 miles).

Take the beaten path to get a closer look at the falls. The air is constantly filled with mist through here, and you can feel and hear the wind created by the falls. Surprisingly, Comet Falls doesn't drop into a deep, green pool but merely crashes against a bed of rounded stones, splashing out in all directions before jumping down the last short drop.

Continue up to Van Trump Park, climbing another three switchbacks and then go

Mount Adams

north and west to get above the rock band over which spills Comet Falls. At 2.1 miles more switchbacks take you up through an open slope of wildflowers and heather, finally offering views that open up to the south.

There is a trail junction at 2.3 miles. Go right to reach Van Trump Park. The trail straight ahead takes you to the Van Trump Ridge, or Rampart Ridge, Trail, which connects with the Wonderland Trail in approximately 3 miles.

The trail into Van Trump Park heads up a compact dirt and log stairway of sorts, giving you ample time to see why this area is considered so beautiful. The open, slanting slopes are packed with bear grass, heather, and wildflowers like glacier lily, mountain buttercup, paintbrush, lupine, and western anemone, whose distinctive seedheads of wavy-looking fur seem straight out of a Dr. Seuss book. The natural garden slopes run into stands of subalpine trees, rock bands, and gouges left by the Kautz and Van Trump Glaciers. In early morning, before sunlight fills the whole park, the bear grass blooms look as if they're lit from within.

The maintained trail ends at 2.6 miles, but an easy-to-follow path continues up into the park. You can see a handful of waterfalls dropping from the rocks a few thousand feet above the park, and there are wonderful views to the south of the Tatoosh Range, Mount Adams, Mount St. Helens, and points beyond. The 2,000 vertical feet you climbed are well worth it.

Indian Henry and a Devils Dream

Just north of the Longmire Museum, the Wonderland Trail crosses the Nisqually-

Paradise Road on its loop around the mountain. A long 12-mile day hike or overnighter follows the Wonderland across Kautz Creek and up a steep trail to Devils Dream Camp. This is a perfect spot to camp, but a permit is required. Beyond the camp you pass Squaw Lake and then enter the broad, nearly level wildflower meadow of Indian Henrys Hunting Ground. Indian Henry, a black sheep of sorts from the Yakama tribe, kept this place secret to take advantage of the numerous huckleberry bushes and easy deer hunting. This meadow and its views of Rainier are certainly one of the highlights of the Wonderland Trail.

35

Beacon Rock

Type: Day hike

Season: Year-round

Total distance: 2 miles

Rating: Moderate

Elevation gain: 600 feet

Location: Beacon Rock State Park,
35 miles east of Vancouver

Map: USGS Beacon Rock

Getting There

From Vancouver, Washington, travel approximately 35 miles east along the Columbia River on WA 14 to Beacon Rock State Park. The entrance to the park is on your left, while Beacon Rock and the parking area for the hike are on the right. There is a $5 parking fee, or you may use your Washington State Parks annual pass ($50 per year). Park hours are 8:00 AM to 10:00 PM in summer; 8:00 AM to 5:00 PM in winter.

The Trail

Beacon Rock is an 848-foot basalt monolith, the eroded core of an ancient volcano. The 1-mile trail rises on catwalks through what looks like a train wreck of sharp switchbacks along the south face.

Dubbed Beacon Rock by the Lewis & Clark Expedition of 1804–1805, the towering rock was renamed Inoshoack Castle (eventually morphing into Castle Rock) by Alexander Ross and Jacob Astor in 1811. Henry Biddle purchased the rock in 1915 and constructed a trail to the top. Finally, in 1916 the U.S. Board of Geographic Names restored Lewis and Clark's original appellation.

From the top of Beacon Rock you have fantastic views of the Columbia Gorge in both directions. The gorge was formed over millions of years, from the uplifting during the rise of the Cascade Mountains to glacial retreat and colossal floods 15,000 years ago to the river's ongoing erosion of the soft volcanic rock layers today or, imagine the motley crew of explorers 200 years ago

The Columbia River from Beacon Rock

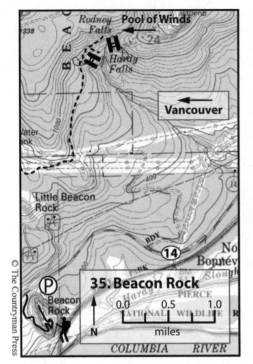

© The Countryman Press

paddling their dugouts along the broad, choppy Columbia River, finally feeling the tidal pull of the Pacific Ocean at a point close to Beacon Rock.

There are rock-climbing routes on Beacon Rock, but the south face is closed from February 1 to mid-July and the east face year-round to protect peregrine falcon nesting areas.

The trailhead is west of the main parking area and begins through a forested area along a wide pathway of crushed rock. At 0.2 mile you pass through a gate, which is locked when the park is closed.

The trail more or less hugs the rock from here, with clumps of grass and an occa-

sional wildflower or patch of thimbleberry or blackberry growing out from pockets along the wall. The trail originally begun by Henry Biddle in 1915 was completed in 1918. There have been improvements over the years to keep the trail safe for visitors, but in essence the route has been the same for the last 86 years. Beacon Rock was donated to the Washington State Parks system by the Biddle family in 1935.

At 0.6 mile the trail becomes even more like a spiral staircase. You face and about-face like a robot in your dizzying climb upward. At 0.7 mile the trail crosses onto the east side in the shade of some trees. It then works its way back to the south and west before reaching the summit.

The 10-square-foot summit area again provides a great overlook of the surrounding Columbia Gorge region. To truly appreciate the size and uniqueness of Beacon Rock, view it from the river or along I-84, which runs along the Oregon side of the Columbia River.

Pool of Winds

Take time while you're in the area to drive into the campground across from Beacon Rock, where you'll find the trailhead for the Pool of Winds hike. This easy 2-mile hike through a shadowy forest delivers you to two waterfalls, Hardy and Rodney Falls, and to a Japanese garden–like collection of pools on Hardy Creek. The upper pool, set inside a natural chamber beneath Rodney Falls, constantly pushes cool, misty air through a tall, narrow slot. The Pool of Winds is a unique spectacle worth the short hike in.

South Cascades

36

McCoy Peak

Type: Day hike

Season: Mid-June to October

Total distance: 8 miles

Rating: Strenuous

Elevation gain: 3,650 feet

Location: Dark Divide, 20 miles south of Randle

Map: Green Trails McCoy Peak No. 333

Getting There

From the Cowlitz Valley RD in Randle, travel west on WA 12 for 1.2 miles to the junction of WA 131 and turn left (south). There are signs for Mount St. Helens as well as the Cispus Center/Trout Lake. FR 25 leads to St. Helens, but you want FR 23 toward the Cispus Center and the trail for McCoy Peak. At 2.1 miles, or 0.9 mile up from the junction, the road splits; the left fork heads toward the Cispus Center and Trout Lake. Travel 8.3 miles (10.4 miles) and then turn right on FR 28.

After crossing the Cispus River and driving a mile from the junction, take FR 29 to the left. This gravel road is signed as the access road for the Boundary Trail and can have numerous potholes if ungraded. Approximately 10 miles up (21.4 miles), after crossing Jumbo Creek, turn right onto FR 115. At 21.9 miles a sign indicates Rough Trail 283 to the left. Turn here to reach the small parking area across from the trailhead.

The Trail

With over 60,000 acres, the Dark Divide hosts many diverse groups. This area is rumored to be the home of the elusive Sasquatch, made famous by home-movie footage shot in the 1970s. Weekend miners—the Dark Divide is named after John Dark, early settler and miner—make camp on their registered claims and pan for glinting minerals in creeks that run from the steep slopes of two major north-to-south ridgelines: Langille and Juniper. Off-road-vehicle (ORV) enthusiasts enjoy many of the trails, mainly in the fall and

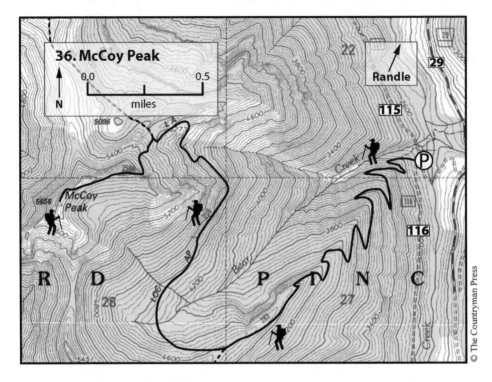

over holiday weekends. And, of course, hikers and backpackers venture off to discover areas like McCoy Peak, with its wildflower slopes and views of Rainier, Adams, and St. Helens.

Conservationists have been working many years now to give the Dark Divide wilderness status to protect the fragile subalpine meadows that line the open ridgelines, which would eliminate motorized and nonmotorized vehicles and mining.

Don't be fooled by the somewhat leisurely beginning of this hike; it isn't named the Rough Trail for nothing. Along Bear Creek, you pass some large old-growth firs before reaching the first switchback. The forest above here is younger and quite dense, allowing for a sparse understory of dull Oregon grape, vanilla leaf, buttercup, and occasionally pinedrops. Reddish-purple in color, pinedrops resemble asparagus when they first push themselves from the ground. They

can grow upward of 3 feet tall and produce numerous little yellow to pink urn-shaped blooms that hang like pompoms from the top of an arrow-straight stem.

The trail does its best over the next 1.2 miles to wear you out. It's extremely steep, cut into the hillside by trail builders who must have enjoyed climbing like mountain goats. Take it slow and rest often; the switchbacks come slowly. At the seventh switchback (0.8 mile) the trail turns onto a finger ridge over the top of a collection of larger rocks, although still in the trees.

Make sure to keep those legs pumping, because the 0.4 mile of climbing still remaining doesn't get any easier. Finally, the trail reaches a scenic overlook of sorts with a view across the Bear Creek drainage to a couple of rocky high points along Langille Ridge.

Not visible behind these high points is McCoy Peak (5,856 feet). Your legs and

The Goat Rocks

lungs can rest easy along the next 0.4 mile, as you pass through a corridor of trees and alongside bear grass, bunchberry, tiger lily, and lupine. At nearly 1.6 miles you reach a trail junction. A sign posted on a tree confirms that you're on the Rough Trail 283, with mileage back to the trailhead and FR 115. Take Langille Ridge Trail 259 to the right, which heads downhill immediately. If you were to continue straight you would reach a ridgeline in about 1.5 miles and then the junction with the Boundary Trail at about 4 miles.

The trail drops through the trees and across a benched slope, losing some elevation on its 0.4-mile run down to Bear Creek. The crossing, through an open damp area, is not too far down from the headwaters. This creek is the only reliable water source up to McCoy Peak, so drink up—after treating the water, of course.

You climb gradually for the first quarter mile or so, coming out onto a brushy slope at 2.1 miles with views of the ridgeline you just hiked up and of Juniper Ridge, far to the east. Look for high points like Tongue Mountain (4,838 feet), Juniper Peak (5,611 feet), and Sunrise Peak (5,892 feet). There are plenty of huckleberries to snack on by the end of July.

At 2.3 miles the work begins again as the trail climbs up to two quick switchbacks at 2.5 miles and then onto an extremely brushy slope (2.7 miles), where the trail is lined with salmonberry, alder, and cow parsnip. Next you climb more switchbacks through more huckleberry bushes and wildflowers like lupine, paintbrush, and yellow wallflower. The hulking cone of Mount Adams (12,276 feet) grows larger to the east.

The trail passes a large, craggy boulder and angles upslope to reach the ridge at 3.2 miles. Right where you set foot on the ridge a brushed-over trail heads left toward the blocky rock face you've just been hiking

under. The trail that continues straight drops down to a small shallow pond in 0.2 mile and moves along Langille Ridge to Langille Peak (5,372 feet) and the trailhead in 2.5 miles. A couple of large fires ripped through the Dark Divide roughly a century ago, leaving behind the wonderful open ridgelines that so many of us seek out today for the views and wildflowers.

Instead, follow the overgrown, unmaintained trail to the left, moving toward a rock slide to reach McCoy Peak. The trail is a little difficult to follow but shouldn't cause you any trouble. You climb a few switchbacks through the rock slide before curving around onto a ridge behind and above the rock face. The trail is somewhat narrow and loose at various points. You reach the ridge 0.7 mile up from the Langille Ridge Trail.

Head right for approximately 0.1 mile to reach McCoy Peak, the small high point (4 miles) along this ridgeline. The ridge continues along in a slow curve to the southsouthwest. McCoy isn't visible on this hike until you're nearly on the summit.

Clockwise from the north, you have fantastic views of Rainier, the Goat Rocks, Adams, and St. Helens. You can also see nearby Langille Peak to the north and the peaks of Juniper, Sunrise, and Jumbo to the east along Juniper Ridge.

What's on the Other Side?

Two excellent hikes access Juniper Ridge to the east: Tongue Mountain and Sunrise Peak. You access Tongue Mountain off FR 29. The steep 4-mile hike leads to an old lookout site on an extinct volcano at the very north end of the ridge, complete with wildflowers and views. To reach Sunrise Peak, pass through old-growth forest and onto a beautiful meadow environment in a 4.5-mile hike. Trailhead access is via FR 23 and FR 2324. Green Trails McCoy Peak No. 333 provides good detail for both hikes.

37

Mount Margaret Backcountry Loop

Type: Overnight or multiday

Season:

Total distance: 15 miles

Rating: Moderate to strenuous

Elevation gain: 2,400 feet

Location: Mount St. Helens National Volcanic Monument, 15 miles south of Randle

Map: Green Trails Spirit Lake No. 332

Getting There

Although it's easiest to reach this hike from Randle on WA 12, the headquarters where you pick up the required backcountry camping permit is located in Amboy. If you reserve a permit in advance, be advised that the process can take up to three weeks.

From I-5 north of Vancouver, take WA 503 east to Amboy. From the monument headquarters outside of Amboy, travel 6 miles north on WA 503. Turn east on the 503 spur toward Cougar. WA 503 changes to FR 90 at 14.6 miles, just above Swift Creek Reservoir. At 30.2 miles, just past the Pine Creek Information Center, turn left onto FR 25, heading north toward Windy Ridge. The route is paved the entire way, but the winding road makes for slow going. At 55.6 miles, turn left onto FR 99, again signed for Windy Ridge. At 64.7 miles, turn right onto FR 26 to the Norway Pass Trailhead (65.7 miles).

The Trail

Like so many places within the blast zone of the 1980 eruption of Mount St. Helens, the parking area and trailhead for this hike are highly exposed. They appear somewhat out of place in the open, mountainous landscape. Trees toppled like children's pickup sticks lie across the slopes, bleached and brittle from nearly 25 years of sun and weather. However, new life is actively growing among these fallen victims. Conifers, berry bushes, and fireweed and other wildflowers are rebuilding the soil and, ultimately, the landscape, which one day may

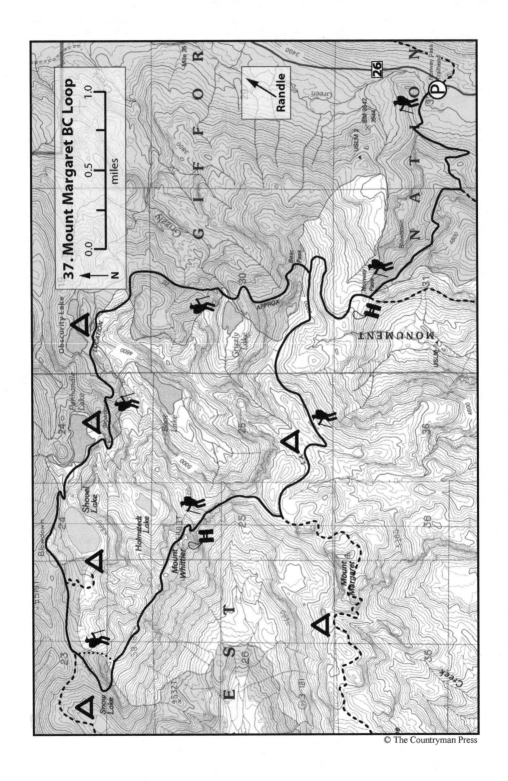

again resemble the thick forest it was prior to that morning in May.

The Mount Margaret Backcountry Loop takes you across thousands of acres of devastated landscape via a ridgeline pathway with views into the shotgun blast of Mount St. Helens's north face, across a spectacular knife-edge trail along Whittier Ridge, and into a string of secluded lakes. This is a unique and inspiring outing.

The trailhead is set in a small valley between two ridgelines—the one to the west running along the shoreline of Spirit Lake and the one to the east showing the blocky high point of Bismark Mountain (4,626 feet). Meta Lake is a short distance to the south in the same valley, visible as you climb up to the first trail junction. The trail surface for nearly the entire hike is a mix of ash and pumice. Pick up some of the large rocks through here and feel how light they are. Look and touch, but make sure these rocks don't end up on your bookshelf at home.

Typical of forests that have been logged or have suffered extreme fire damage, the initial plant mix includes fireweed and foxglove, which thrive in direct sunlight.

At 0.9 mile Boundary Trail 1 meets Trail 227A, which hooks into 227 to reach Independence Pass around 2.5 miles south of the junction. The trail to the right, Boundary Trail 1, cuts upslope and then slides around the north side of this ridgeline onto Norway Pass (2.1 miles).

From Norway Pass, miles of great vistas open into the mangled, drooping mouth (crater) of Mount St. Helens. You also overlook Spirit Lake, whose bottom was raised by 300 feet and water level by 200 feet in the eruption. An incredible logjam covers nearly a third of the 2,200-acre lake. And you can see other Cascade volcanoes like Rainier, Adams, and Hood. The abrupt break between the leveled and standing forests marks the edge of the blast zone.

Continue on the Boundary Trail, looping around a small, open basin beneath a white rock wall and then climbing up to the Trail 211 junction (3 miles), which leads to Bear Pass. Stay on the Boundary Trail, but note that you'll finish the loop on the Bear Pass Trail. The Boundary Trail angles up and across the surreal landscape that currently defines this region of the volcanic monument.

There is plenty of life through here, from huckleberry, paintbrush, lupine, and wild strawberries to steeplebush and Roosevelt elk. Keep your eyes open for elk in the draws and benched areas below this stretch and throughout the hike. Their numbers have come back almost threefold after being nearly wiped out by the 1980 eruption.

Even though elk and other members of the deer family aren't keen on being so exposed, they have flourished here because of the abundance of food, lack of predators (wiped out in the eruption), restrictions on hunting, and ease of travel. If you're out early enough it's not unusual to see over a hundred elk on this hike.

The trail curls around to the north and reaches a saddle at 3.6 miles, nicely framing a view of Mount Rainier. At 4.4 miles you arrive at Bear Camp, which has designated tent sites, a pit toilet, and a natural spring. The camp sits beneath vistas of Rainier (14,410 feet) and Mount St. Helens (8,364 feet). You continue from here above a quaint, rolling basin toward Mount Margaret (5,858 feet).

At 5 miles you reach a small, barren saddle with some dead stand and the Whittier Ridge Trail 214 junction. The Boundary Trail to the left continues along this front-ridge view of St. Helens, passing Mount Margaret and eventually St. Helens Lake and crossing

Whittier Ridge

over Johnston Ridge. It ends near the southwest edge of 5-mile-long Coldwater Lake, formed by the natural damming of Coldwater Creek after the eruption.

Take the Whittier Ridge Trail to the right, more thrill ride than hike. There are points of high exposure, loose and narrow rocky sections, and brief areas where the trail disappears. The crossing can be dangerous when wet, but otherwise this portion of the hike shouldn't be missed. With backcountry experience and caution, you'll be fine.

The trail cuts across a slope of grass and heather before reaching a rocky path at 5.3 miles. The big, open plain below to the west is fed by a dozen small creeks that eventually join Coldwater Creek in its run to Coldwater Lake, visible 4.5 miles to the west-southwest. In the two basins to the north and northeast you can see portions of Boot and Grizzly Lakes.

At 5.4 miles you hike/climb onto the rocks and work your way around an obvious impasse to a rock shelf. This is one of two places with high exposure. The trail drops onto two small notches and then stair-steps along the east side of the ridgeline.

There is a good view down to Boot Lake at 5.7 miles. Topping out above a grassy slope, the trail crosses another exposed stretch before dropping onto a small notch and moving along a shelflike walkway, this time on the west side of the ridge.

At 6 miles you reach Mount Whittier (5,883 feet), with great views of all the nearby Cascade volcanoes and an overlook of Holmstedt Lake. It's an exhilarating hike around and on top of this narrow ridgeline, as the surrounding landscape drops steeply for hundreds of feet. Use binoculars, if you have them, to check below for elk.

The trail runs along the east side of the ridge from Whittier out onto the ridge itself (6.2 miles). You top one small rise, then another, before arriving at the tallest of the three high points beyond Whittier. The trail climbs up a zigzagging path. Once you're near the top you will spot a distinctive trail edging along the west side. It leads to the backbone of the ridge.

This section is round, broad, and grassy, sometimes making the trail difficult to follow. At 6.8 miles—just before the trail drops off the ridge toward Snow Lake (not visible from here)—you must make a decision. One option is to head west and downslope to an overlook of Snow Lake before cutting back to the right (northeast). A short way down the narrow, loose trail you come to a washout in a dirt gully beneath a tall rock band. It is passable, but you'll need the caution, skill, and fitness of a climber. Believe it or not, this is the official route, and beyond this short difficult piece the trail is perfectly hikable over the final stretch to the Lakes Trail 211 junction.

A second and easier option, but one that takes a bit of route-finding, is to drop down the steep slope to the north via some game trails. Keep a northeast bearing in the direction of the clearly visible Lakes Trail 211 about 0.3 mile away. The lake below and to the east is Shovel Lake.

It may look like heading straight is an option, but it isn't. There are tall, impassable rock bands beyond the open ridgetop. Both routes suggested above are manageable, but I recommend the off-trail route rather than the dirt gully.

From the Lakes Trail 211 junction (7.1 miles), head east above Shovel Lake and below scattered rock bands. At 7.5 miles a spur trail leads down to Shovel Lake and campsites just before the main trail ducks behind the long cliff above the lake. You have views of Mount Rainier along here, as well as northeast across the Green River valley to the ridgeline of Goat Mountain.

Once past the cliff band, more views open from the northeast end of Shovel Lake and below the open ridge of Panhandle Lake to the east. The trail crosses the ridge and winds down to the lake, crossing the outlet at 8.6 miles. Climb slightly above and around the lake to reach the spur trail down to the designated tent sites at 8.8 miles.

A little farther on, the trail crosses the outlet for Holmstedt Lake. Even though the total hike covers 15 miles, the geographic area it traverses is quite compact, allowing for different takes on the same features. At 9.1 miles you have climbed out of the Panhandle Lake basin and are looking down on Obscurity Lake. The area is still very open, with barely a tree standing. The ground cover is made up of berry bushes, alder, and wildflowers.

At 9.6 miles, shortly before the lake, you pass a waterfall fed by the Boot Lake outlet. A log takes you across Obscurity's inlet, moving above and along the south shore past two signs for designated campsites and a pit toilet. At 9.8 miles you've left Obscurity Lake and are contouring along a slope with a nice waterfall visible to the east.

The trail then makes a long, somewhat laborious run in and out of various drainages with views across to Bismark Mountain, which stands near the trailhead of this hike. Nice patches of sunflowers and salmonberry show up here and there. Around a corner on the north side of Grizzly Creek you can see Grizzly Lake (11 miles).

The trail climbs steeply above Grizzly. At 11.3 miles there is a nice overlook down to the lake and some large downed trees lined up like ships ready to be launched. From here, the trail bends to the left under a tall rock band and aims for a saddle to the southeast. It's 0.8 mile up to Bear Pass, with an elevation gain of over 700 feet. Sorry, there's no shade to escape the hot summer sun here or anywhere else along this hike.

From Bear Pass you once again have views of Mount St. Helens as you drop about 0.1 mile to meet up with the Boundary Trail (12 miles). Turn left to return to Norway Pass and onward to the trailhead (15 miles). The elevation gain and loss isn't overly severe, but the lack of tree cover, especially when it's hot or during rain or snowstorms, can make this hike strenuous.

It's in the Name

Local tribes like the Yakama long referred to Mount St. Helens—named in 1792 by Captain George Vancouver—as *Loo-Wit,* meaning "Smoking Mountain." That name was quite appropriate as the mountain had erupted or showed signs of eruption numerous times over hundreds of years before May 18, 1980. Even though preceded by a sizable earthquake, steam and ash explosions, the tearing open of a 250-foot crater near the summit, and the release of several avalanches, the big eruption still managed to surprise the world. This history prompted close scrutiny by vulcanologists and the public during Mount St. Helens's most recent threats in the fall of 2004.

The following list of statistics explains how the world around Mount St. Helens came to be: a landslide reached speeds of 180 mph and covered 24 square miles; massive trees were plucked from the ground by superheated air and volcanic debris reaching speeds of 670 mph; a 12-mile-high ash column deposited up to 2 feet of ash nearly 200 miles away; and pyroclastic flow temperatures reached 1,100 degrees Fahrenheit, sterilizing the open plain beyond the Breach (the lower end of the crater). In no more than a few short hours, hundreds of square miles were drastically transformed.

38

Lava Canyon

Type: Day hike

Season: June to October

Total distance: 3 miles

Rating: Easy (top) to strenuous (bottom)

Elevation gain: 1,000 feet

Location: Mount St. Helens National
Volcanic Monument, 45 miles east of
Longview

Map: Green Trails Mount St. Helens
No. 364

Getting There

From I-5 north of Vancouver, take WA 503
east to Amboy. From the Mount St. Helens
National Volcanic Monument Headquarters
outside of Amboy, travel 6 miles north on
WA 503. Follow the 503 spur east toward
Cougar, which at 14.6 miles becomes FR
90. At 18.2 miles, turn left onto FR 83 toward Ape Cave and Lava Canyon. It is
slightly over 11 miles to the paved parking
lot and trailhead for Lava Canyon (29.2
miles). Outhouses are available.

The Trail

Twenty-five years have passed since Mount
St. Helens' eruption in 1980, killing 57 people and tens of thousands of animals, as
well as obliterating hundreds of square
miles of forest. The top 1,300 feet of the
volcano disappeared, and the landscape
around it was dramatically reshaped, including the gorge of the Muddy River. Lava
Canyon, prior to May 18, 1980, was hidden
in thick stands of Douglas fir, western hemlock, and western red cedar.

In a matter of hours, by the cataclysmic
force of a lahar (mud flow), the canyon was
pulverized by millions of cubic yards of rock
and other debris swept up in the 60-mph
flow originating from glaciers high up on the
slopes of Mount St. Helens. This mud flow
stripped away vast amounts of vegetation
and scoured away rock and dirt to expose
sections of columnar basalt, layers of ancient lava flows, and even the yellow
rock foundation of the 35-million-year-old
Ohanapecosh formation.

Today the area is wide open, with beautiful rock formations, the winding Muddy River, and dramatic and powerful waterfalls. This hike through Lava Canyon puts you into a landscape in recovery and deep into the geologic history of a mountain that has yet to have its last word.

Lava Canyon Trail 184 starts from the parking area on a wide asphalt pathway (wheelchair accessible). Interpretive signs along the first 0.3 mile highlight the amazing formation and unearthing of this canyon. The path changes from asphalt to wood boardwalk to asphalt, passing more interpretive signs and an overlook of the water-sculpted lava flow that is now part of the upper canyon.

At 0.3 mile you come to a trail junction. The 0.7-mile Lava Loop Trail heads right, across the Muddy River and back on a 100-foot swinging suspension bridge. Continuing on the trail straight ahead, you have fantastic views of the river and lava formations. The river makes an S-turn before dropping over the first of a number of waterfalls visible from the trail into the lower canyon. The long columnar basalt wall along this upper portion of the canyon was created 11,000 years ago.

You're now on a narrow, steep, dirt and rock trail with some dramatic exposures to the river below. However, from the junction the trail first drops into a section of cedar trees, shadowy, damp, and lined with fern and moss. At 0.5 mile you reach the swinging suspension bridge.

Continuing straight, the trail drops steeply into an open stretch with high exposure. Be extra cautious when the trail is wet or if you have small children with you. The tightrope walk of a trail rewards you with more takes on the shape of the lava flow.

The river drops over another waterfall through here, plunging some 60 feet in a

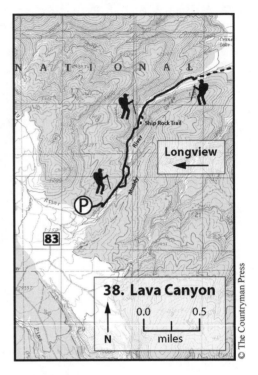

© The Countryman Press

thick stream of frothy water. At 0.8 mile the trail passes a layered lava flow and along a small side stream that you cross. The pathway takes a waterfall-like drop of its own at 0.9 mile, 30 feet straight down. Ladder steps provide the only safe way down to the rocky hollow below to continue the hike. Anyone with small children or dogs should turn around here.

From the bottom of the ladder, the trail passes along another lava outcropping before winding through a small meadow into a boggy enchanted forest shadowed by the canopy of red alders. At 1.3 miles you reach a junction for Ship Rock Trail 184b.

A short distance up the Ship Rock Trail you climb an 11-foot ladder up to a steep section of moss- and lichen-covered ground. The trail then passes through a patch of huckleberry and dead-ends at an overlook of the canyon. Here you have

Lava Canyon Bridge

views of the tall lava wall next to the first ladder descent and of the Muddy River waterfalls stepping down the gorge.

At 1.5 miles, after alternating from treed sections of Douglas fir to open sections of kinnikinnick, you arrive at Smith Creek Trail 225. The bridge over the creek leads you to FR 8322 in just under a mile. Turn around and retrace your steps to the trailhead.

What's This about Apes in a Cave?

On your way to Lava Canyon you will see signs for Ape Cave. There are not, and never have been, apes in this region of the world—unless you count the St. Helens Apes, a youth group credited with extensive explorations of the cave shortly after its discovery by Lawrence Johnson in 1946. The cave isn't actually a cave, but a lava tube (an air pocket in a lava flow) from an eruption nearly 2,000 years ago. It's well worth putting on a fleecetop—the average temperature is 42 degrees—grabbing a flashlight or headlamp, and exploring the lower and upper cave. The total distance is about 4 miles.

39

Lily Basin to Heart Lake

Type: Overnight

Season: Late June to October

Total distance: 11.4 miles

Rating: Moderate

Elevation gain: 2,200 feet

Location: Goat Rocks Wilderness, 5 miles southeast of Packwood

Map: Green Trails Packwood No. 302

Getting There

From the town of Packwood (east of Randle), drive 1.4 miles west on WA 12 and turn left onto Blakely Road (FR 48). The surface is dirt and gravel all the way to the trailhead. Nine miles up Blakely Road (10.4 miles) you come to an obvious fork; stay to the left. Travel another 2.1 miles (12.5 miles) to reach the Lily Basin Trail 86, and park in one of the three small turnouts past the trailhead.

The Trail

The Goat Rocks Wilderness is full of deep, broad, spectacular basins linked by highline trails under dramatic 7,000-foot-tall mountains. Cispus, Lily, Jordan, Goat Creek Basin—each contains a vibrant collection of flora and snow patches that linger into late summer, all beneath the craggy summits of Johnson, Old Snowy, or Gilbert. This hike to Heart Lake through Lily Basin will make you believe you've magically stepped into Montana's Glacier National Park.

The trail ducks into the trees above the road, setting the tone for the incline you can expect throughout the hike. The Douglas fir forest remains quite open, with a sparse understory of small shrubs and bear grass. At 0.6 mile the trail is joined by the feeder trail for Lily Basin. At 1 mile you enter a more open area of young trees. A sizable community of sword fern soon gives way to mounds of bear grass, huckleberry bushes, and an occasional tiger lily. There are filtered views across the lower end of

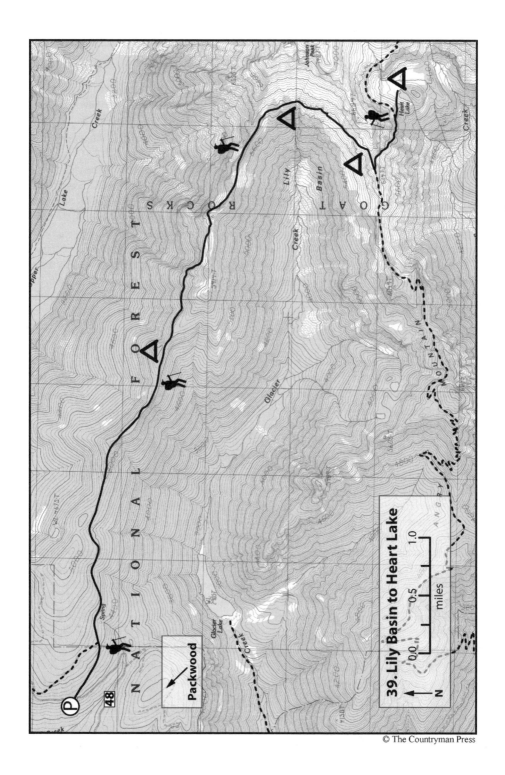

the Glacier Creek drainage, which feeds Glacier Lake some 1,400 feet below.

At 1.4 miles you reenter a mature forested area but maintain the ease of travel and the nearly imperceptible elevation gain you have grown accustomed to. At 1.8 miles, after a pleasant stroll through the trees, the trail finally hits the ridgeline between Glacier Creek and Upper Lake Creek to the north.

The trail eventually drops down along the southwest aspect of the ridge before returning to a narrower portion of the ridgetop. For the next quarter mile or so you take a pleasant ride along the backbone of the ridge before making another dip along the southwest slope at 2.7 miles, once again thick with bear grass and huckleberry bushes.

At 2.9 miles the trail crosses a much broader section of the ridge onto its northeast aspect. Look downslope and back to the north for a glimpse of Packwood Lake. The trail loses a bit of elevation to enter a 0.8-mile stretch above small benched areas, beneath blocky boulders, and across gorgeous slopes of bear grass and pink and white heather. This section also has one of the most abundant and spectacular collections of avalanche lily you will come across in the Cascades. Avalanche lily, like glacier lily, shows itself shortly after the snows have melted, which for this area means sometime between late June and mid-July.

At 3.4 miles you have fantastic views down to Packwood Lake, as well as distant but clear views of Mount Rainier. There are also some nice views of the ridgeline south of Coal Creek Mountain, outfitted with boulder fields and pocket meadows. Downslope on a benched area is a campsite. Be aware that after the snow has melted there is no water source there.

Past the camp, the trail contours across a wonderful green grassy slope and underneath a short band of rock. On the other side of the rock band, just where the trail crosses the ridge, there is a small emergency bivouac site. This is also where you begin the rim trail around the head of Lily Basin, and at 3.8 miles you have your first take on the spectacular basin.

This broad, steep basin hosts sections of brush, wildflowers, stands of trees, rockslides, and avalanche chutes—all beneath the dark, craggy ridgeline of Johnson Peak (7,487 feet). The trail makes a grand contour through the upper end of the basin, with very little elevation gain or difficulty.

The trail overflows with lupine, heather, magenta paintbrush, columbine, tiger lily, monkeyflower, bear grass, phlox, valerian, purple aster, and huckleberry. Across the basin you can see Angry Mountain and the junction you'll arrive at in 2.4 miles.

At 4.2 miles you cross a rocky gully with a feeder stream for Glacier Creek. There is a nice single tent site on the opposite side. As the trail bends around the basin (around 4.4 miles), there is a spectacular view of Mount Rainier.

There are a variety of attractions in the basin, from the wealth of wildflowers to mountain goats on the cliffs below Johnson Peak to cascades sliding over rock outcroppings just above the trail. The Goat Rocks—Johnson is the northernmost of the dozen or so prominent peaks—is really a small collection of volcanoes that went through cycles of violent eruptions and rapid cooling to form their distinctive craggy faces.

At 4.9 miles the trail runs through a rock slide and up a few short switchbacks that top out by another great campsite (room for two tents) at 5.1 miles. This site doesn't have easily accessible water (i.e., patches of snow) after mid- to late July. The junction with Angry Mountain Trail 90 is around the corner (5.2 miles); stay left.

Below the junction is a fantastic spire-like rock formation with a small arch,

Hiking Lily Basin

situated at the top of another lush basin. The trail drops a bit on its way to Heart Lake. The flower mix is slightly different here, with more red paintbrush, mountain daisy, aster, lupine, and penstemon.

To the southwest you have a great view of Mount St. Helens. There is a fork in the trail 0.3 mile from the junction (5.5 miles). The left fork continues up the basin to meet the Goat Ridge Trail in 2.5 miles; the right fork drops down to Heart Lake. It is less than 0.2 mile down to the lake (5.7 miles), which is set in a small basin thick with grass, anemone, monkeyflower, and many other wildflowers. You can see a vigorous little waterfall higher up in the basin and a serpentine creek rushing toward its confluence with Middle Fork Johnson Creek to the south of the lake.

There is an obvious camping area on the northeast, or inlet, side of the lake. In addition to meeting other hikers around the lake, you may be joined by black bear, which have been known to frequent this area.

Stay Awhile

There are numerous worthy day trips within a reasonable distance of Heart Lake. Hawk-eye Point (2 miles), off the Lily Basin Trail shortly before the junction with Goat Ridge, is an amazing viewpoint for all the big South Cascades volcanoes and the Goat Rocks. Keep traveling along the Lily Basin Trail to the cirque of Goat Lake (2.7 miles), which has a straight-down-the-bowling-alley view of Mount Adams. Or slip down the Goat Ridge Trail into the top of stunning Jordan Basin (3.5 miles). The mileage above is one way from Heart Lake, and you may want to purchase a map of the entire Goat Rocks Wilderness or at least invest in Green Trails maps White Pass No. 303, Blue Lake No. 334, and Walupt Lake No. 335.

40

Bird Creek Meadows Loop

Type: Day hike

Season: Late June to October

Total distance: 5 miles

Rating: Easy to moderate

Elevation gain: 1,000 feet

Location: Mount Adams Yakama Reservation, 15 miles north of Trout Lake

Maps: Green Trails Mount Adams No. 367S

Getting There

From WA 14 in White Salmon, take WA 141 north to Trout Lake. From the Trout Lake RD in Trout Lake, take the Mount Adams Recreation Highway north. The road splits at 1.3 miles; follow signs to the right for Bird Creek Meadows. The road surface changes from pavement to gravel at 4.6 miles, where you bear right onto FR 82, again toward Bird Creek Meadows. At mile 11.5 miles, go left onto Bird Creek Road (FR 8290). The road soon forks again; stay to the left.

The road from here is very rough. It is passable for passenger cars but more suited for high-clearance vehicles with rugged suspensions. At 15.1 miles you reach Mirror Lake. A member of the Yakama Nation will probably be stationed beyond the lake to collect a $5 day-use recreation fee for access to Bird Lake and Bird Creek Meadows. Bird Lake and the parking area (16.1 miles) for this hike are 1 mile farther on. Dogs must be leashed for hikes in Bird Creek Meadows.

The Trail

In under 6 miles this dynamo of a hike to Bird Creek Meadows packs in over 60 wildflower species, including cinquefoil, lupine, paintbrush, penstemon, valerian, aster, and monkeyflower. Other highlights include parklands landscaped with waterfalls and lakes, a glaciated volcano, and a viewpoint of the Mazama and Klickitat Glaciers on Mount Adams's southeast flank. Your small access

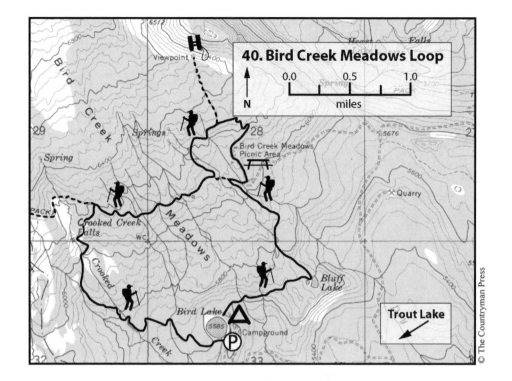

fee goes a long way on the Bird Creek Meadows Loop.

The hike begins at the Bird Lake Campground and follows Bluff Lake Trail 105 toward Bluff Lake. At 0.1 mile a creek crossing leads to a wide-open slope decorated with lupine. At 0.3 mile the trail passes through a thick patch of bear grass, aster, paintbrush, and other wildflowers before stepping up a blocky rock section, which in early summer can be wet with runoff. The attractions continue at 0.4 mile, where the trail enters a small, open, grassy area colored with mountain buttercup and phlox.

You reach Bluff Lake at about 0.6 mile. The shoreline of this small lake is mostly ringed by trees. Follow the sign for Bird Creek Meadows, continuing through a pocket meadow, again decorated with wild-flowers. You are afforded a brief view of the high slopes of Mount Adams. Metal signs tagged to trees at various points assure you that this is the right trail.

Next, you climb for a short stretch along a rock outcropping and then arrive at a large meadow with a quaint waterfall set in the shadows (1 mile). The trail climbs again, ever so briefly, passing through heather and bear grass to a large, sandy stretch dotted with smooth, black volcanic rock.

At 1.3 miles, just before the junction with the Around the Mountain Trail 9, there is a 15-foot waterfall blanketed at its feet with vibrant green grass, monkeyflower, shooting star, and paintbrush. Head right at the junction, or east-northeast. You soon reach a set of picnic tables, with access to a short loop called the Trail of the Flowers and views of Mount Adams.

Bird Creek Meadows beneath Mount Adams

Hike past the picnic tables and over a small bridge (0.1 mile) to another trail junction. Go left for the loop around Bird Creek Meadows and the Hellroaring viewpoint. There are pit toilets just beyond this junction.

At 1.5 miles you have some nice views east-southeast to the open, mountainless expanse of the western edge of the Columbia Basin. The parade of flowers continues unabated up to the junction for the spur trail to Hellroaring viewpoint at 1.9 miles, and you have views of Mount Hood (11,239 feet). The trail to the viewpoint passes through an open area dotted here and there with stunted subalpine trees. This side trail is just under 0.6 mile round trip.

From the viewpoint you have a closer take on Mount Adams, especially the dark piles of gravel (till) in the moraine below a tall waterfall streaming from the Mazama Glacier. Hellroaring Meadows is in the valley below, and out of view and down valley are Heart Lake and Hellroaring Falls. The reddish rock peak across the way is Little Mount Adams (6,821 feet). If you were to remove Mount Adams (no problem, right?), the valley below would look like something out of a western film.

Retreat from the viewpoint and continue the loop, moving above Bird Creek Meadows to meet back up with Trail 9 at 2.9 miles (this mileage includes the round trip to the viewpoint). Ahead are bridge crossings over more ice-cold tiny creeks, colorful meadows, and views of Mount Hood rising just beyond the Columbia River Gorge to the south.

At 3.6 miles you come to the junction for Bird Lake Trail 100. Less than 0.3 mile from here is Crooked Creek Falls, which drops some 25 feet before splitting into little rivulets and sliding around spongy islands of green grass, yellow monkeyflower, and stunted subalpine trees. Below the falls, Crooked Creek re-forms into a single stream to finish its twisting run to Bird Creek.

The trail loses elevation all the way back to Bird Lake. At 4.5 miles, after paralleling the creek at various points, the trail crosses over a footbridge. From here, you mainly stay in the trees on the way to the parking area at 5 miles.

Climb a Volcano

With very little danger and an easy-to-follow route, the summit of Mount Adams is accessible to beginning mountaineers along the South Spur. The route runs from the Cold Springs Campground up to base camp at Lunch Counter (9,000 feet). It's a steep glacial hike (with no technical climbing) to the 12,276-foot summit. The false summit (South Summit) is at 11,657 feet. From there you drop down into a crater and up to the true summit. Mount Adams is the second-tallest peak in Washington and the third tallest of the Cascade volcanoes stretching from southern British Columbia into northern California. After the triumph of reaching the top, the next best part is glissading (French for sliding on your rear) nearly the entire way back to base camp.

41

Mount Aix

Type: Day hike or overnight

Season: Late June to mid-October

Total distance: 11 miles

Rating: Strenuous

Elevation gain: 4,100 feet

Location: William O. Douglas Wilderness, 50 miles west of Yakima

Maps: Green Trails Bumping Lake No. 271, Old Scab Mt. No. 272

Getting There

From the Naches RD, travel west on WA 12. At 4.1 miles WA 12 splits left and WA 410 right; follow WA 410. At approximately 32.5 miles, turn left on Bumping Lake Road. The road splits again slightly over 12 miles up. Follow the packed gravel road straight ahead. (The right branch takes you to the Bumping Lake Recreation Area.) At mile 46, or 2.3 miles up from the split, the road forks yet again; follow FR 1808 toward Deep Creek. In less than 2 miles you reach the Mount Aix Trailhead (48 miles). The trailhead is on the left and parking to the right.

The Trail

At 7,766 feet, Mount Aix is the highest peak in the William O. Douglas Wilderness, and there are wonderful panoramas from the barren, windswept summit. You will have private meetings with all the southern Cascade volcanoes: Adams, St. Helens, and Rainier. The lowland forest of the Bumping River valley contrasts with the open ridgelines and talus slopes of the Nelson Ridge and Mount Aix to the east. The difference between the two areas symbolizes both the wilderness and the legacy of the man it was named for, Supreme Court Justice William Douglas.

From the trailhead at 3,667 feet, the hike follows Trail 982 to the summit of Mount Aix—with an elevation gain of roughly 4,100 feet over 6 miles. Make sure to pack lots of water and energizing snacks; you're going to need them.

Approximately 0.2 mile up there are a couple of small creek crossings, which may

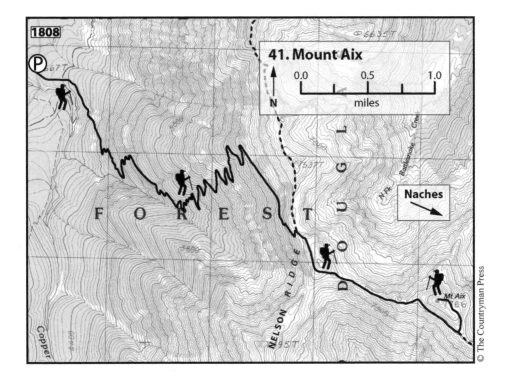

be dry later in the season. The trail makes a steady, moderate climb through a predominantly fir forest. Down low—usually below 5,000 feet—keep an eye out for fairy slippers, a member of the orchid family. These somewhat rare 4- to 6-inch-tall purple flowers have three sepals and two petals that form a bloom resembling a delicate slipper.

The trail passes through two or three rock slides covered here and there by kinnikinnick and wildflowers like white trillium and vanilla leaf. If you're into mushroom hunting there are numerous varieties to identify during early summer and the rainy days of autumn.

At 0.7 mile you start up a series of three-dozen or so switchbacks just above one of the many feeder streams for Copper Creek. Higher up along the trail you may find cinquefoil in bloom, complemented by red paintbrush. At 2.4 miles you come to cedar trees mixed with white pine. You've gained about 1,500 feet so far and are rewarded with views of Miners Ridge to the west and Bumping Lake to the north.

The rich fragrance of the subalpine zone diminishes where the trees begin to shorten and the forest thins. If you make this hike early in the season you'll see yellow glacier lily springing forth as the snow retreats. Wildflowers like bear grass and lupine eventually follow, and you will find an abundance of huckleberry and heather.

At 3.1 miles the slope opens up even more, with only small patches of trees left among the rocks. These subalpine fir and mountain hemlock trees can be quite stunted due to the severe effects of wind and snowpack, that can reach 20 feet deep. Still another 500 feet above you is 7,100-

Mount St. Helens

foot Nelson Ridge. The trail ceases its spiraling switchbacks and makes a 0.5-mile cut across the slope to the ridge at 3.7 miles.

Millions of years of volcanic activity and erosion by glaciers have produced the sharp ridgelines and peaks seen in Mount Aix to the east, Bismark Peak (7,585 feet) to the south, and Nelson Butte (7,072 feet) to the east-northeast.

Continue east at the trail junction on Nelson Ridge. The route slinks over the ridgeline to a short spur trail that moves up to the summit of Mount Aix at 5.5 miles. On a clear, warm day Mount Aix is a quiet sanctuary, but when the weather is rough you'll be ready to retreat in a matter of seconds. Still, the views are spectacular. The bluish hump of threatening Mount St. Helens is visible, as is bell-shaped Mount Adams a few miles to the east of St. Helens. You can also see Mount Rainier to

the west-northwest, all the high points in the William O. Douglas Wilderness, the dinosaurlike formation of Fifes Peaks to the north, and the western edge of the Columbia Basin.

Go East, Young Hiker!

Mount Aix also can be reached via the eastside trailhead for 982. This trail leads through a more typical east-of-the-divide landscape of ponderosa pine, whitebark pine, balsamroot, and rugged, dry, rocky basins. The hike passes by Buck Lake and over Dog Creek and climbs to open slopes with great views all around. It reaches the summit in 7.1 miles. Access to the trailhead is off Bethel Ridge Road (FR 1500) from WA 410 about 12.5 miles from Naches. Contact the Naches RD (see Resources) for trail specifics. The map reference is Green Trails Old Scab Mt. No. 272.

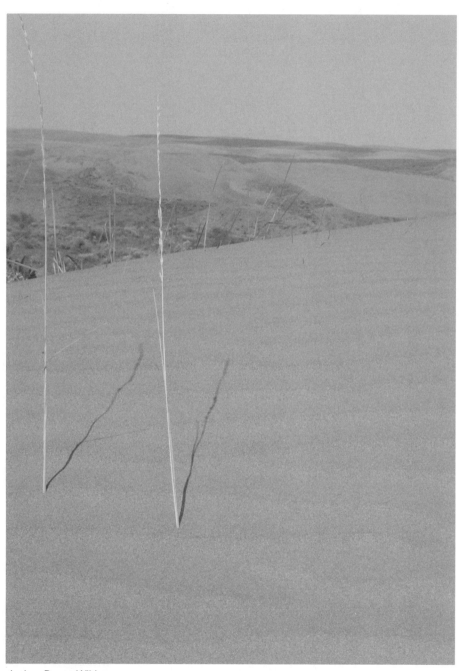

Juniper Dunes Wilderness

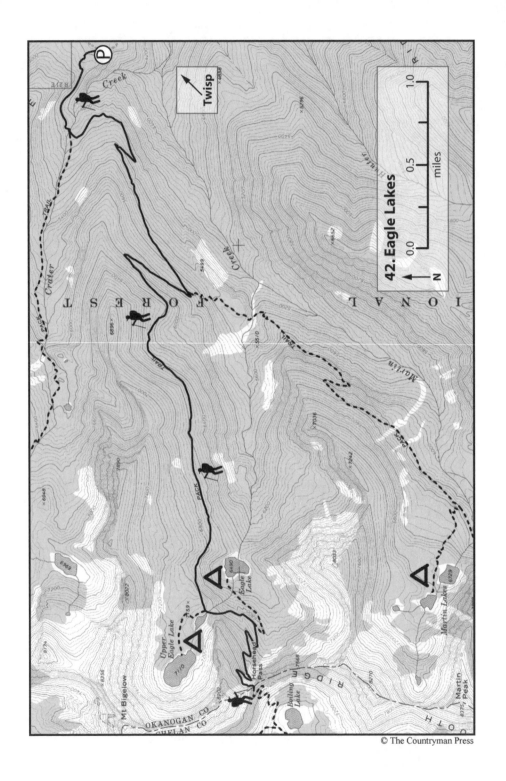

42

Eagle Lakes

Type: Overnight

Season: Mid-June to October

Total distance: 14.6 miles

Rating: Moderate

Elevation gain: 3,000 feet

*Location: Sawtooth Roadless Area,
15 miles southwest of Twisp*

Map: Green Trails Prince Creek No. 115

Getting There

The nearest local information center for this hike is in Winthrop, 8 miles north of Twisp. From Twisp, follow WA 20 east 2.4 miles until it splits. Bear right (south) onto WA 153, which is signed for Chelan and Wenatchee. At 14.3 miles turn right onto the Gold Creek Loop Road, which is signed for Gold Creek. Drive 1.5 miles (15.8 miles) to the intersection for Foggy Dew Creek Campground and turn right on FR 4340. The road forks slightly over 1 mile up; stay to the right on FR 4340.

At 18.8 miles the road forks again, the left fork crossing over North Fork Gold Creek in the direction of Foggy Dew Creek. Follow the right fork toward Libby Creek. The pavement ends here. One last fork in the road comes at 20.4 miles, but you want the left fork this time (FR 300). At 24.7 miles you arrive at a small parking area and the trailhead. There is more parking through the trees to the right, but typically this area is used by horsemen.

The Trail

Sawtooth Ridge has a grand collection of high-mountain lakes running its entire length, starting with Surprise Lake to the south and ending with Lake Juanita to the north, a few miles east and 6,500 feet above the town of Stehekin. Many of these lakes—like the Oval Lakes, Martin Lakes, and the Eagle Lakes—are tucked away in beautiful alpine cirques. Lower Eagle Lake sits in a basin surrounded by trees, while Upper Eagle Lake is inside a steep-walled

Horsehead Pass

talus basin beneath Mount Bigelow (8,135 feet). The hike to Eagle Lakes is full of wildflowers and includes high vistas of the Sawtooth Ridge region from tiny Horsehead Pass (7,600 feet).

The hike begins through a forest with a grassy understory, then moves down a shale slope to Crater Creek. You must walk through the creek to reach the junction with Crater Lake in approximately 3 miles. This is just one of the dozens of beautiful lakes that cling to Sawtooth Ridge. Stay to the left to continue on toward Eagle Lakes.

Slightly over 0.2 mile up you come to a second, unmarked junction. Stay right for the continuous climb to the junctions for both Eagle Lakes and on to Horsehead Pass. The trail moves along the north side of the Martin Creek drainage, fed in part by the lakes above. The trail mostly contours along with a few switchbacks thrown in, and it's nicely lined with wildflowers like lupine and aster and edibles like thimbleberry.

At 2.5 miles you come to the Martin Lakes/Eagle Lakes trail junction; stay to the right for Eagle Lakes. By now you will have realized that this hike is popular with horsemen, but other potential users—ones you hopefully won't come across—are motorcyclists. This area is classified as semiprimitive motorized, which means that motorcycles are allowed despite the name Sawtooth Ridge Roadless Area. Even though the trail is partially maintained with the help of a regional motorcycle trail-riding association, no hiker really wants to hear the whine of a two-stroke motor in such beautiful country.

Past the junction, the trail begins a string of switchbacks that last for approximately 0.8 mile. At 4.5 miles the trail opens up to a grassy slope decorated with an array of wildflowers like mountain daisy, fireweed, and paintbrush. You also have a few vistas across the drainage to the rocky and treed Sawtooth.

Another faint trail, this one signed NOT MAINTAINED, comes in at 4.9 miles. Stay to the right and continue burning calories and gaining elevation. You cross through a granite boulder field at 5.2 miles, with the first glimpse of Lower Eagle Lake 400 feet below. However, before reaching the trail for Lower Eagle you come to the junction for Upper Eagle Lake at 5.7 miles.

The trail to Upper Eagle passes by a shallow pond and then curves up to the right through lush grass and wildflowers. You reach the east-northeast shoreline of Upper Eagle in 0.5 mile, and there are plenty of campsites. The lake is pressed against the loose talus and scree slopes of the basin, with the upper ridgeline rock tinged a sooty color. Larch trees grow up between the rocks closer to the lake, glowing like golden torches in autumn.

The trail to Lower Eagle and Horsehead Pass leaves the cover of the trees and edges along a rocky slope above the lake to reach the junction for Lower Eagle at 6.1 miles. The trail makes a hard switchback to the left, winding down an open grassy slope and passing a horse camp before taking a straighter run down through the trees to the head of the lake in approximately 0.8 mile. There are campsites on this end of the lake.

The main trail continues on through and above the basin, climbing six switchbacks to reach Horsehead Pass. This part of the basin shows off flowers like hellebore, aster, anemone, buttercup, lupine, subalpine daisy, Oregon sunshine, and arnica, along with a tree mix of Englemann spruce and whitebark pine.

At 6.8 miles you reach the two-steps-and-you're-over-it Horsehead Pass. This is one of the highest points of any hike in this book. Each direction reveals outstanding vistas. Looking back, you have a full view of the entire basin, Lower Eagle Lake, and the mountains beyond. Spin to the west and the round lake you see below is Boiling Lake, which sits in a broad, gentle glacial valley backed by a stunning collection of peaks and ridgelines.

A scramble up to the high point to your right (north) brings you to 8,200 feet and to views down on Upper Eagle Lake and west across Lake Chelan into the mountains of the Glacier Peak Wilderness.

It is possible to follow a number of different loops from here that continue to explore the mountains and lakes of this area. The best idea would be to buy Green Trails Prince Creek No. 115 and let your adventurous spirit guide you.

Larch Trees and High-Mountain Lakes

If you enjoy larch trees and high-mountain lakes, then a hike to the Oval Lakes is in order. This hike follows Eagle Creek and then Oval Creek over an easy to moderate trail. The only strenuous climbing comes in the final stage before West Oval Lake and then up through the talus basin beneath Gray Peak to Sawtooth Ridge. From there you look down on Middle and East Oval Lakes set against the Buttermilk Ridge, with 8,392-foot Courtney Peak on the southwest end and 8,795-foot Oval Peak on the north end. These lakes 600 feet below Sawtooth Ridge are surrounded by a wonderful collection of larch trees. Like the Eagle Lakes hike, there are options for creating different loops or just setting out on day hikes. The Eagle Creek/Oval Creek Trailhead is accessed off the Twisp River Road. Maps for the area include Green Trails Stehekin No. 82, Buttermilk Butte No. 83, and Prince Creek No. 115.

43

Columbia Mountain

Type: Day hike

Season: June to October

Total distance: 5.6 miles

Rating: Moderate

Elevation gain: 1,200 feet

Location: Colville National Forest, 20 miles west of Kettle Falls

Map: USGS Sherman Peak

Getting There

Head west from Kettle Falls on US 395/WA 20. Cross over the Columbia River at 3 miles, and then turn left onto WA 20, continuing west toward Republic. At 26 miles you arrive at Sherman Pass (5,575 feet) and a recreation sign for the Kettle Crest. Turn right to reach the outhouses and parking area in 0.1 mile.

The Trail

The 40-plus-mile-long Kettle Crest is the main attraction of the Kettle River Range, another of Washington's wildlands that's ideal for federal wilderness status. The Kettle River Range is a chain of big, rounded mountains linked together by open ridgelines of wildflowers, grasses, and healthy forests of Douglas fir, western larch, and quaking aspen. The hike to Columbia Mountain (6,782 feet) is a short sampler of this environment but adds its own elements in a grand collection of flora and Washington's oldest lookout.

From the parking area, the trailhead is back toward the highway about 50 yards. The high point you can see to the north is Columbia Mountain. The trail climbs pleasantly in the beginning, alternating between winding stretches and switchbacks. You pass through a fir and pine forest and grassy, open sections decorated with lupine, paintbrush, yarrow, buttercup, bluebell, huckleberry, and raspberry.

At 0.7 mile you begin a long contour with views to the south of Sherman Peak (6,998 feet) and Mount Washington (5,793 feet).

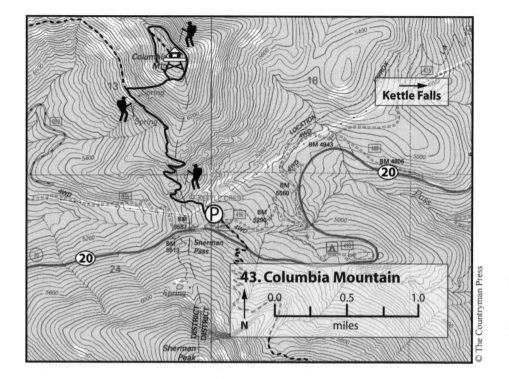

Kettle Falls

43. Columbia Mountain

0.0 0.5 1.0

N miles

The dead stand you see along Mount Washington is from a wildfire in 1988 that burned over 20,000 acres. It was called the White Mountain Fire, for another high point along the southern Kettle Crest. Although these mountains are on what is considered the dry side of the state, they're actually a weather barrier, catching upward of 35 inches of precipitation annually. This moisture feeds an abundance of plant life, including wildflowers and a range of shrubs like huckleberry.

Three other edible berries found along this hike are wild strawberry, thimbleberry, and kinnikinnick. Also known as bearberry, kinnikinnick berries are best if cooked, but even then they aren't very flavorful. Their leaves were dried and smoked as tobacco or used as a tea by various Indian tribes. Across the slope you can see alder and aspen trees growing among the conifers.

Just before the junction with the Columbia Mountain Trail at 1.5 miles, a trail cuts downslope to a spring tapped with white PVC pipe. This, along with one other catch system set along the Columbia Mountain Trail, is the only place to top off your water supply. The trail is a bit steeper from the junction, climbing up to the start of the Columbia Mountain Loop in 0.5 mile (2 miles). The entire Kettle Crest Trail has been designated a National Recreation Trail, marked by the red, white, and blue sign at the junction.

Follow the loop to the right, wrapping around the south, east, and then north side of Columbia Mountain before reaching the spur trail to the summit. The trail takes an easy path along the natural contour of the thick, grassy slope, with more wildflowers like wooly butterweed and fireweed, as well as views over the Columbia River drainage to the east and Kettle Crest high points

The Columbia Mountain Lookout

Wapaloosie Mountain (7,078 feet) and Scar Mountain (7,046 feet) marching off to the north. Thick stands of western larch (tamarack) can be seen on the north side of Columbia Mountain.

At around 2.6 miles you pass under a small boulder field that hosts huckleberry, raspberry, currants, and black elderberry. Just after you pass farther into the trees and over to the west/south side of the mountain, you reach the spur trail to the old lookout (2.8 miles).

The spur trail is steep but only lasts for about 0.3 mile. The 1914 lookout sits right on the ground, and three big windows and a door let the surrounding scenery into the single 10-square-foot room. A 15-foot platform once stood above the small cabin, allowing a broader view of the area. The lookout appears to be sinking, as if after 90 years it's ready to return to the earth.

This lookout was used until 1928, when a pole-style tower was constructed. That second lookout burned in the 1960s. Over the last 50 years the trees have grown tall enough to obstruct the views somewhat. The Columbia Mountain Lookout is one of the most unusual lookouts you'll ever come across.

Once back down on the main path, continue the loop for another 0.2 mile to return via the same trail you came in on.

This Kettle's Steamin' Ready

In 2000 a lengthy report advocating for the creation of the Columbia Mountains National

Monument was released by the Pacific Biodiversity Institute in concert with the Kettle Range Conservation Group. The bulk of the 400,000-plus acres is made up of the Kettle Range (older than the Continental Divide) and contains incredible stands of late-successional and old-growth forests. Wildlife like marten and the northern flying squirrel depend on the forests, and there is room for threatened and endangered species like the lynx and gray wolf and the endemic Okanogan fameflower (beautiful fuchsia blooms). Historic sites like the Columbia Mountain Lookout are also worthy of archaeological preservation. The land for the proposed monument is currently owned by multiple entities, and some of it, including old-growth forests, is open to road building and logging operations. For more information on how things are progressing in the attempt to preserve this unique setting, visit www.kettlerange.org.

44

Crowell Ridge

Type: Day hike or overnight

Season: Mid-June to mid-October

Total distance: 15.8 miles

Rating: Moderate

Elevation gain: 800 feet

Location: Salmo-Priest Wilderness, 6 miles east of Metaline Falls

Map: USGS Gypsy Peak

Getting There

From WA 20 east of Kettle Falls, take WA 31 north to Metaline. From the Sullivan Lake RD east of Metaline Falls, drive 0.8 mile on FR 33, crossing a bridge to reach Highland Road (FR 2212), where you turn right. At 4.3 miles, turn left onto FR 245 at the sign for Sullivan Mountain Lookout. The road is extremely rough and narrow at points for the 7.3-mile climb to its gated end beneath the Sullivan Mountain Lookout at 11.6 miles.

The Trail

This hike makes a glorious run along the rocky backbone of Crowell Ridge, part of the 200-mile-long Selkirk Mountains. There are two north-to-south ridgeline trails in the Salmo-Priest Wilderness: Crowell Ridge and the Shedroof Divide to the east across the Sullivan Creek drainage. Over 600 million years old, the Shedroof Divide can be hiked via a 21-mile trail running through forests and over a rounded ridgeline of mountains. Crowell Ridge, decorated with a phenomenal collection of bear grass, has a sharper profile, mainly due to the action of alpine glaciers. The best views across the wilderness and into Idaho and Canada are found along this ridgeline.

The trail begins beneath the Sullivan Mountain Lookout, put into operation in 1926 and used today only when needed. You're already at 6,300 feet, so you, and the lookout, tower nearly 4,000 feet over the valleys and creek drainages, giving this hike a top-of-the-world feel. The first 2 miles of trail are a roller-coaster ride of steep drops

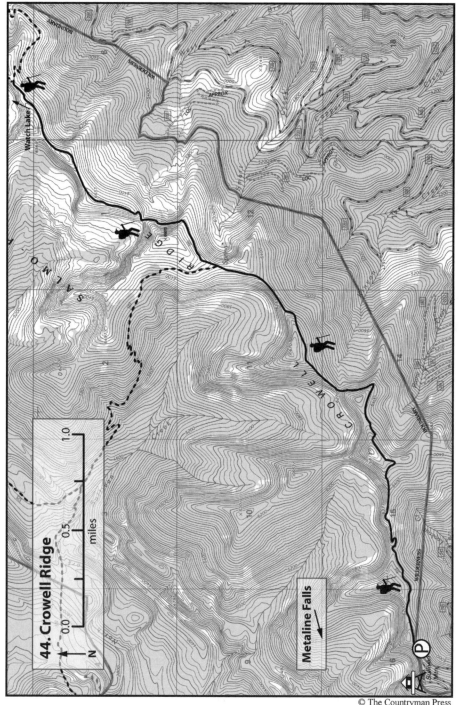

44. Crowell Ridge

N

miles

0.0   0.5   1.0

Watch Lake

SALMO

RIDGE

CROWELL

Crook

Metaline Falls

P

Sullivan Mtn.

© The Countryman Press

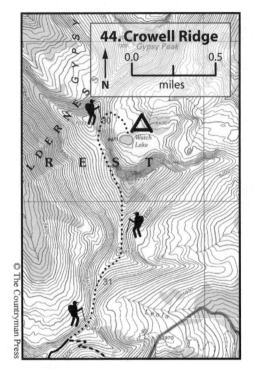

44. Crowell Ridge

subalpine spruce, huckleberry, and whortle-berry are just a small sampling of the plant life that joins the bear grass in a show of color during that brief snow-free window called summer. (Ten-foot snowpacks are not un-common along Crowell Ridge.)

At 1.9 miles the trail makes a steep drop for 0.2 mile onto the ridge. You then climb again, and at 2.3 miles you finally reach eas-ier hiking. The trail glides below the ridge-line to the east, dropping again onto a forested stretch of ridgetop and then mak-ing a steep but brief push up in less than a mile. At 3 miles you drop onto the west side of the ridge, with views over the North Fork Sullivan Creek drainage. You lose some ele-vation before climbing back onto the ridge and up to the North Fork Sullivan Creek Trail junction at 3.4 miles.

The ridge is quite broad and open in this area, providing an excellent viewpoint to study peaks along the Shedroof Divide like Round Top (6,466 feet), Thunder (6,560 feet), and Shedroof Mountain (6,764 feet).

In the height of summer this hike can be quite hot because of its nearly continuous exposure and lack of easily reachable water. There is a spring roughly 400 feet below the junction in the small basin off the east side. The only other accessible water source be-fore Watch Lake is at least 1 mile up the trail and about 275 feet below the east side of the ridge. It's another spring set in a small, shallow basin.

The junction marks the beginning of an easier stretch of open slopes and ridgeline. The trail rolls off the ridgetop and contours around and above the Smart Creek basin, rounding a point at 3.8 miles and making a downhill run for approximately 0.3 mile. It moves through a rock slide and then drops to a small saddle with a view down into a steep-sided basin to the west that holds a small lake nestled in the trees.

and ascents over open slopes, through stands of whitebark pine, and across the rocky ridgeback.

The entire stretch from the trailhead to the overlook of Watch Lake (a perfect overnight destination under 7,309-foot Gypsy Peak, the tallest in the wilderness) is a blanket of mop-top bear grass. In fact, this hike probably has the most prolific commu-nity of bear grass in the entire state. Peak bloom lasts from late May to July. Each mound of grass shoots a single stem up to 4 feet high, with an immense group of deli-cate white blooms clustered together in the shape of a light bulb. The rich, shaggy green bear grass seems to glow from the inside out, providing a stunning contrast to the surrounding landscape.

Wooly butterweed, lupine, paintbrush, penstemon, yarrow, white-flowered rhodo-dendron (July blooms), ground juniper,

Gypsy Ridge

The trail then slides over to the east side before climbing up the ridge for another wonderful 0.5-mile run through an open setting. The mix of subalpine trees, huckleberry, white-flowered rhododendron bushes, and the endless carpet of bear grass continue through this stretch.

At 4.7 miles, the trail droops briefly to the east before coming back on top for a stretch. After another dip to the east, you regain the ridge at the 5.6-mile mark—a point of decision since the next section is off-trail. This location isn't marked, but you'll know when you're there because this is the high point on the trail prior to the switchback. The route to Watch Lake is quite easy to follow, as described below. Just be aware that you should have a map and compass to help with route-finding.

To reach Gypsy Ridge, Watch Lake, and Gypsy Peak, continue along the spine of Crowell Ridge for a stretch and then move onto the more north-to-south ridgeline of Gypsy. Step off the trail and climb along the ridge 0.2 mile to the near high point (6,617 feet) and descend to the saddle via a faint path. Cross the saddle in the direction of the next near high point (6,853 feet) and ascend toward its summit, rounding it to the right (east) below the top. Next, you again drop down to a saddle.

You should see one high point (7,177 feet) nearly due north and another (7,033 feet) more to the north-northwest, approximately 0.7 mile straight away. Cross the saddle and climb toward the first high point. When the grade begins to noticeably steepen, start moving cross-slope to the left (west) of the high point. Be sure to keep a straight line across the 0.5-mile slope, aiming to the right of the second high point.

This brings you to a forested saddle between the previous two high points, set above Watch Lake (6,471 feet). It's approximately 2.3 miles from the point where you left the maintained trail to the lake, making the one-way distance from the trailhead 7.9 miles.

Small, round Watch Lake sits in a partially forested basin with tent sites. Hike a short distance along Gypsy Ridge to a gentler slope that leads down to the lake.

The Salmo-Priest Wilderness provides habitat for endangered species like grizzly bear and woodland caribou. A grizzly, which typically has a home range of approximately 50 square miles, can utilize the natural corridors found within this wilderness to move between the United States and Canada. Caribou in the area also split their time between the two countries. The caribou in the Salmo-Priest number a paltry 48 head, the grizzlies just five to eight.

Two Lookouts, Two Countries, Three States, One Hike

The Salmo Mountain Lookout is located at the head of the valley that separates Crowell Ridge from the Shedroof Divide. A wonderful 14-mile loop hike leaves from FR 270 southeast of the lookout and travels through a forest down to the banks of the South Salmo River. Across the river, the trail regains lost elevation and then some to reach glorious high grounds of huckleberry. Mountain vistas carry your eyes across the northeast corner of Washington, northern Idaho, the edge of northwest Montana, and beyond the Canadian border into the Selkirks and Purcell Mountains. You actually travel in Idaho for half of this hike, including a side trip up to the Little Snowy Top Mountain Lookout. Open meadows, panoramic viewpoints, creek and river crossings, and quaint forest settings are all part of the Salmo Basin to Little Snowy Top Loop. Maps for this hike are USGS Salmo Mountain, Washington, and Continental Mountain, Idaho.

45

Little Spokane River

Type: Day hike

Season: Early March to early November

Total distance: 3.4 miles

Rating: Easy

Elevation gain: 50 feet

Location: Little Spokane River Natural Area, 12 miles north of downtown Spokane

Maps: USGS Nine Mile Falls and Dartford

Getting There

From downtown Spokane, take Division Street (US 395) north for a little over 4 miles to Francis Avenue (WA 291) and turn left (west). Travel 10 miles to the Rutter Parkway and then turn right (14 miles). At 17 miles you reach a three-way intersection; turn left to continue on the parkway. In approximately 0.5 mile, after you've crossed the Little Spokane River, you arrive at the parking area and trailhead (17.5 miles). Pets and bicycles aren't allowed, and there is a $5 day-use parking fee unless you have an annual Washington State Parks pass ($50).

The Trail

A stroll along the Little Spokane River offers an easy hike, a scientific field trip, and a history lesson all compressed into a trail less than 2 miles in length one way. You pass through five different ecosystems yet gain only about as much elevation as you would climbing a tall ladder.

An impressive 1,700 species live along the river, the abundant wetlands, stately cottonwoods and rose-hip hedges, patches of prairie, and granite boulder hillsides of ponderosa pine. You might see a river otter collecting freshwater mussels, red-winged blackbirds singing from the tips of the iris gardens, deer feeding in the early dawn among the grasses of a meadow, or even a cougar on the hunt. Foldout brochures available on both ends of the trail contain information for self-guided tours matched to numbered white (1–10) posts set along the trail.

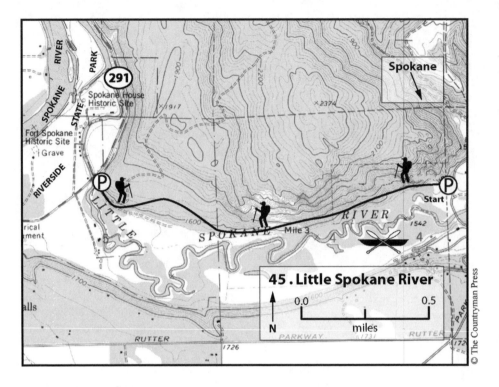

45. Little Spokane River

© The Countryman Press

You also follow human history, from the ancient Indian tribes to the work of explorer, fur trader, and naturalist David Thompson. In fact, the lesson begins at a miniature art museum right by the trailhead. A rock outcropping known as the Indian Painted Rocks contains a handful of pictographs created hundreds of years ago. Like many pictographs found across the Pacific Northwest, their meaning is unclear, but they were incorporated into the state park system—the natural area is managed by Riverside State Park—in the 1950s.

Sharp turns, oxbow bends, dead-end paths, and broad, straight stretches all characterize the river's course to its confluence with the Spokane River near the trail's end. Approximately seven of the Little Spokane's 30 miles are contained within the natural area. The trail doesn't mirror the twists and turns of the river, but it does glide through the lush and vibrant wetland and riparian environments that line it. The five ecological zones you encounter are the river, the marshy wetland, the streambank tree and shrub zone (riparian), the sections of dry grass meadows and prairie, and the granite and ponderosa forest on the slope north of the river.

Beyond the Indian Painted Rocks the trail edges along the river, passing the iris-clogged wetland and streamside aspen, cottonwood, elderberry, poison ivy, and wild rose. More than likely, bird chatter will reach you from the trees, marshland, and water.

At 0.5 mile the trail passes over a large, semismooth granite slab, a close-up example of glacial shaping. Snowberry bush separates the riparian and ponderosa zones. The colorful early spring blooms of buttercup and glacier lily are followed by arrowleaf balsamroot and then scarlet gilia, yarrow, and aster.

The Little Spokane River

At 0.9 mile the trail opens out onto a dry meadow of fescue and cheatgrass. The area through here, including the river and the cottonwood trees that line its southern bank, is a known heron rookery (heronry). A breeding pair will continue to use this area season after season as long as they find it safe and food-rich. The heron's fishing technique is to take up a position in shallow water, waiting for an unsuspecting fish to swim within reach of its long beak, which then slices through the water at lightning speed. Be aware that the area may be closed in the nesting season from March to mid-May.

This point also marks the trail's brief transition into the ponderosa pine zone.

Next you turn uphill for a slight overview of the area. Large predators like coyote, bobcat, and cougar roam this area and the territory above the cliff bands. These secretive animals make every effort to stay clear of humans, and sightings are more likely at dusk and dawn than midday.

Rolling back down along the west end of the meadow/rookery (1.3 miles) you transition back to the wetland zone of iris and water lily. The meadow is also great for spotting white-tailed deer. If they stand still in the brown and golden grass they are nearly impossible to sight. However, when they're spooked their snow-white tails are clearly visible.

The trail finishes in an open environment, with cottonwoods along the river and ponderosa pine on the slope (1.7 miles). If you follow the paved road toward WA 291, you cross the Little Spokane River 0.1 mile from the western trailhead. There is an easily identifiable osprey nest on top of a power pole across the highway on the south side of the river.

Another worthwhile trip within walking distance (0.7 mile) of this area is the Spokane House Interpretive Center. The center recalls the history of David Thompson and the fur-trading industry that thrived in the Northwest for a few decades before over-harvesting and market decline brought it to an end. The center is open Thursday through Monday from 10 AM to 6 PM.

Walk on Water

To gain the full effect of the Little Spokane River Natural Area, hop in a canoe or kayak and paddle the same stretch this hike follows or add a few more miles by putting in near St. Georges School. You can reach this put-in by continuing on the Rutter Parkway, which turns into Waikiki Road. Across the Little Spokane there is a sign for the school and a small boat launch on the right. Deer, moose, bass, otter, beaver, heron, red-winged black-bird, mallard, turtle, and a wealth of flora all congregate along the river's course. Except for the dark, cold days of winter, nearly any day offers good paddling.

46

Trees of Stone Trail

Type: Day hike

Season: Year-round

Total distance: 1 mile

Rating: Easy

Elevation gain: 200 feet

Location: Ginkgo Petrified Forest State Park, 25 miles east of Ellensburg

Maps: USGS Ginkgo. Vantage

Getting There

Take I-90 to Exit 136 for Vantage. Whether coming from the west or east, turn left at the intersection past the off ramp, following the signs for the Ginkgo Petrified Forest Interpretive Center and trails. At 0.6 mile turn right onto Ginkgo Road to reach the interpretive center (1.2 miles); or continue straight for another 2 miles on what is now the Vantage Highway to reach the trailhead at 2.6 miles.

The Trail

The Trees of Stone Trail is as much about what you would've seen millions of years ago as it is about what you can see today. During the Miocene epoch (5 to 25 million years ago) this place was akin to the cypress swamps of the southeastern United States. However, growing alongside tropical trees and plants like teak, cinnamon, magnolia, and witch hazel were temperate- and cold-climate species like redwood and spruce. In all, there were as many as two hundred species of flora that today you could see only by traveling to a variety of life zones spread over several continents.

The ginkgo tree also lived in this area prior to, and in part during, the Miocene, managing to survive the world ice ages (12,000 to 2 million years ago) only in remote ice-free zones of China. Today, only one of the original 15 species remains (*Ginkgo biloba*). It has been extinct in the wild for hundreds of years now but was cultivated in gardens in China and eventually reached Europe and the United States. The

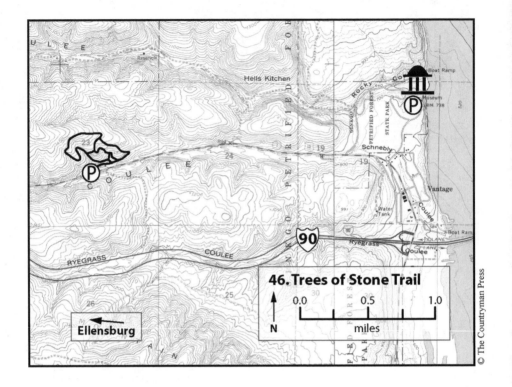

46. Trees of Stone Trail

N   0.0   0.5   1.0
miles

Ellensburg

tree is one of the world's oldest, having first appeared 150 million years ago. It has delicate fan-shaped leaves, and its soft electric-green coloration in spring and summer turns to bright yellow in the fall.

The ginkgo and other former species in this area were eradicated by two major geologic and geographic transformations. The growth of the Cascade Range some 40 million years ago built a weather barrier that blocked the precipitation needed to sustain many species. More devastating, but also key in the preservation of the petrified examples you see today, were the layers upon layers of lava that flowed over this region, at points up to 6,000 feet thick, during violent periods of volcanic activity 7 to 17 million years ago. Speculation as to why the trees didn't disintegrate in the intense heat of the lava centers on the fact that they

were submerged in what was once a lake—the very area that the Trees of Stone Trail circumscribes.

Today's landscape is open sagebrush and prickly pear, dotted in the spring with showy phlox, bitterroot, balsamroot, and a variety of other wildflowers and blooming shrubs. The Trees of Stone Trail is a marvelous treat, taking you through millions of years of geologic activity in less than one hour.

Ginkgo Petrified Forest State Park is one of only six known petrified forests in the United States. The interpretive center has an incredible collection of petrified sections and cross-sections of trees. Specimens include birch, sycamore, cypress, elm, oak, Douglas fir, spruce, maple, hickory, redwood, and ginkgo, by far the rarest, which makes this area so unique. The center also

Gingko tree

has a map of the trail and other information about the park. There are two live ginkgo trees outside the south end of the building, as well as Indian petroglyphs salvaged before the damming of the Columbia submerged their former location in 1963. A tall ginkgo tree stands next to the ranger residence, although it's not as tall and old as a ginkgo in China that stands 200 feet and is estimated to be 1,000 years old.

The Trees of Stone Trail, set along Rocky, Schnebly, and Ryegrass Coulees, takes you around a few different loops with excavated petrified trees. Each specimen is labeled and numbered to match the map available at the visitor center. They are encased in stone walls covered by open grates to prevent their being touched. These sites are memorials to a past life, set against hillsides of sagebrush.

One of the most interesting things you can do while strolling along the trail—with the help of the short video shown at the visitor center—is to imagine what this area once looked like compared to how it looks today. Trees have been replaced by sagebrush and overviews of the Columbia River, and much smaller creatures like pocket mice, rattlesnakes, and falcons now live where the three-toed horse and sabertooth tiger once walked.

In the warmer months, make sure to hydrate and carry sun protection. Even short exposure to such dry and hot conditions can be a problem.

Many projects of the CCC in the 1930s were about controlling nature, but the Ginkgo Petrified Forest State Park, created in 1935, protected nature so that we could better understand the world of the past.

Don't Forget Your Climbing Shoes

Just across the Columbia River from Vantage is an exceptional climbing area with routes ranging in difficulty from 5.1 to 5.14. The columnar basalt rock is typical of the area. The climbing area is known as either Vantage or Frenchman Coulee, and the key walls include the Feathers, Sunshine Wall, M&M Wall, and River Point. There is a camp area near the Feathers. Take Exit 143 for Silica Road off I-90 to access the area. The most comprehensive guide available is the second edition of *Frenchman Coulee: A Rock Climber's Guide*, by Marlene Ford and Jim Yoder.

47

Frog Lake/Marsh Loop

Type: Day hike

Season: Year-round

Total distance: 3.8 miles

Rating: Easy

Elevation gain: 200 feet

Location: Columbia National Wildlife Refuge, 8 miles north of Othello

Map: USGS Soda Lake

Getting There

From I-90 at Moses Lake, take WA 17 south to Othello. From the office of the Columbia National Wildlife Refuge in Othello, take Seventh Avenue north, or right, out of the back parking lot. At just under 1 mile turn left on Lee Road. In another 0.5 mile turn right onto unsigned McManamon Road. Approximately 5 miles down the road, turn right onto Morgan Lake Road (6.5 miles), which is paved for the first 1.5 miles. The trailhead is on your right and the parking area on your left 3.7 miles up Morgan Lake Road (10.2 miles).

The Trail

The greater Columbia Basin encompasses 140 million acres, an area the size of France, stretching from the Canadian border to northern Nevada and from the Cascades to the Rockies. This tremendous natural indentation ultimately funnels the region's numerous waterways into the Columbia River, which empties into the Pacific Ocean. The Columbia National Wildlife Refuge, situated within the interior Columbia Basin, and more specifically the Drumheller Channels, was formed because of water. But before there was water, there was fire, ice, floods, and wind.

Eruptions over 20 million years sent lava flow after lava flow across this area, building a basalt rock foundation upward of 10,000 feet thick. A retreating ice sheet then displaced billons of tons of soil and rock as recently as 100,000 years ago. Next, the action of a succession of ancient floods

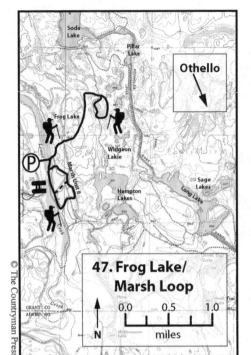

Othello

© The Countryman Press

47. Frog Lake/ Marsh Loop

0.0   0.5   1.0

N   miles

Coulee Dam in the 1930s. Further irrigation projects to supply the farms of this area began in the early 1950s, which directly or indirectly filled the nooks and crannies that then spawned a whole new ecosystem in the sagebrush desert environment.

The Columbia National Wildlife Refuge, established in 1955, hosts tens of thousands of waterfowl, mostly mallard, but also redhead, gadwall, Canada goose, and tundra swan. Falcon, kestrel, swallow, sandhill crane, blue heron, and on occasion the white pelican all call this place home at times. Be aware that November through January is hunting season for waterfowl and upland game birds like pheasant. The Frog Lake Trail and Marsh Loop are fully ensconced in the environments described above, making this hike a field trip full of discoveries no matter what time of year you visit.

The hike begins in a channeled bottom dominated by sagebrush and surrounded by blocky columnar basalt. You pass through a marsh section of tall reed grasses and cattails, with long, natural hedges of wild rose bushes that produce soft pink blooms in May.

After following a wide cobblestone path for 0.1 mile, you come to a sign indicating Frog Lake Trail to the left and Marsh Loop Trail to the right. Start off by taking the trail to Frog Lake, which includes a variety of interpretive signs. Besides birds, there isn't a large number of animals in the area. Smaller creatures such as the pocket mouse and muskrat live in dry and wet areas around this hike, while large mammals including mule deer, coyote, and less common bobcat and badger also find sustenance in the marshland and sagebrush zones. Phlox, lupine, balsamroot, sagebrush, rabbitbrush, and cactus show their colors in spring.

At 0.6 mile you pass Frog Lake, which later in the summer is almost completely

dating back 16,000 years or more ripped through to create the coulees, steptoes (isolated hills or mountains in a land of basalt), pothole lakes, and gorges that now define the Columbia Basin.

The floodwater was replaced by winds that blew what is referred to as loess (nutrient-rich volcanic soil) from the Cascade Range, depositing it on the newly transformed landscape. This made it possible for plants and a small number of trees, mainly cottonwood, to grow. But with an annual precipitation of just 8 inches, not much besides sagebrush, prickly pear, balsamroot, and bluebunch wheatgrass could survive.

The water you see today in Frog Lake and the dozens of pothole lakes scattered about the refuge is the result of an irrigation project begun in the early 20th century, culminating with the completion of the Grand

Wild rose bushes on the Marsh Loop

empty. Another 0.1 mile up you reach a short cliff wall. If you time it right—April through mid-June—there will be plenty of other wildflowers and blooming shrubs to enjoy, such as buckwheat, desert yellow daisy, and bitterbrush.

Follow the trail another 0.1 mile to the top of a small butte for an even grander view of the area. The lakes to the east are Pillar, Snipe, Cattail, Sago, Widgeon, Hourglass, Lemna, Shoveler, and Gadwall. To the north there is Migraine, Elbow, and the southern end of Soda Lake. A 0.5-mile loop rings the butte, hugging the edge of the cliffs and providing you an exposed but safe journey filled with great vistas.

The Marsh Loop begins at the same in-tersection as the Frog Lake Trail (0.1 mile from the trailhead). The trail stays low in a wetland zone of tall reed grasses, cattails, and other aquatic plants. The packed gravel walkway is as wide as a road. The loop makes its way around two man-made marshes, and bird species include yellow-headed and red-winged blackbird, sandhill crane, blue heron, mallard, yellow-breasted meadowlark, common snipe, and Caspian tern.

The loop begins about 0.2 mile past the junction. You can follow it either way. Just make sure to keep your eyes and ears open for the incredible amount of bird activity. Cliffs line both sides of the marsh.

At 0.5 mile you can take a shortcut that loops around only the first marsh. If you continue on, a sign at the end of the second marsh guides you around to the end of the loop. Take your time on this stroll, and don't forget your binoculars.

At 0.9 mile the trail cuts into the sage zone, a bit above the marsh. This gives you a slight overview of the marsh, which again should make bird-watching interesting. The loop covers approximately 1.3 miles.

Rattlesnakes like to sun themselves in the more exposed and rocky areas, but they also can be found near the marsh. This area also has a large population of ticks, so make sure to check yourself (and especially dogs) after your hike and over the next few days.

The Refuge System

This country's national wildlife refuge system was established by Theodore Roosevelt in 1903. The first refuge was Pelican Island in Florida, and the most recent addition, in 2002, was Cahaba River in Alabama. There are over 540 refuges nationwide covering 95 million acres. Species like the brown pelican, wood stork, least tern, and Florida panther owe their continued existence in part to the refuges—even though humans created these species' hardships in the first place. Washington has 20 national wildlife refuges with approximately 150,000 total acres.

48

Juniper Dunes

Type: Day hike

Season: Year-round (north access open to the public from March through May)

Distance: Variable

Rating: Easy to moderate

Elevation Gain: Variable

Location: Juniper Dunes Wilderness, 15 miles north of Pasco

Map: USGS Levey NE

Getting There

From Pasco, drive approximately 15 miles north on US 395 to Blanton Road near the town of Eltopia. Follow Blanton north for 6 miles to Overturf Road and turn right (21 miles). In 2.7 miles, turn right (south) on Gertler Road (23.7 miles). In 3.3 miles the road makes a hard bend to the left (east) and becomes Blackman Ridge Road.

From the bend, it's another 2 miles to Joy Road (29 miles). Turn right on Joy and follow it to the end (31 miles). At the circular parking area you head south-southwest through two stock gates and pass through about 150 yards of pasture to reach the start of the Juniper Dunes Wilderness. The road, parking area, and pasture are all on private property, and public access is allowed only from March 1 to May 31.

The Trail

Juniper Dunes is a 7,000-acre sandbox with an ecosystem just as dynamic as the state's forested zones. At the end of the last ice age (70,000 to 12,000 years ago) apocalyptic floods blasted the landscape with an incredible display of devastation. The size and force of these floods would've pulverized today's towns and cities and sent them rushing southward to the Columbia River.

The Wallua Gap, the natural funnel that led water to the Snake River, became so overrun by the tsunami waves of water from the north that it was impossible for the water to flow, causing a tremendous backup. The slack water that was finally released left behind fine silt that covered the landscape. Southwest winds eventually

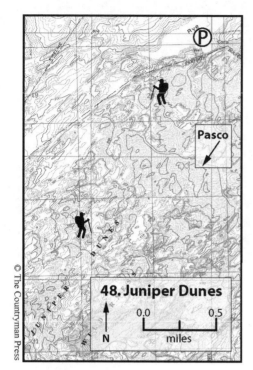

48. Juniper Dunes

0.0   0.5

N   miles

prevalent throughout the year in the northern section of the dunes. In between you find wildflowers like yellow bells, phlox, larkspur, and prairie star from late April through May.

The shape of the dunes is in constant flux. The wind today moves predominantly from west to east and you can clearly see the gentler west-facing slopes and the steeper east-facing drops of the dunes.

Look closely at the dunes to pick out the numerous serpentine paths of the beetle, horned toad, and lizard. The smooth bellies of bull snakes and rattlesnakes leave a more pronounced curved pattern in the sand. There are also tracks from smaller creatures like red ant, cricket, and pocket mouse, as well as larger ones from deer, elk, and coyote. You may also see magpie, oriole, goshawk, burrowing owl, pheasant, bunting, hummingbird, and sharp-shinned hawk, to name a few of the permanent, seasonal, and migratory birds that inhabit this dry land.

The only obstructions to the open views come when you pass between dunes. There is no tree line, but there are trees. The western juniper tree is found in the center of the wilderness, although the largest stands are in the southwest corner. These trees can grow over 35 feet tall. They aren't present in any other wilderness area in Washington except on desert like islands in the San Juans, caught in the rain shadow of the Olympics.

From Kidney Troubles to Perfume

The western juniper has an incredible number of uses. Native Americans utilized leaves as a natural laxative, berries for treating joint trouble, and young twigs for stomach aches. The berries can be eaten raw or cooked and can even be distilled to make gin. The wood is used for carvings and fenceposts, and burning branches make an aromatic incense. More recently, western juniper oils have been incorporated in fragrances and wood polishes.

added more fine sand and silt, and the dunes were the result.

From the Joy Road entrance you quickly climb onto the first dune, edging along a noticeable trail to eventually wander among the sand hills. You will see a number of trails shaped by human feet and the hooves and paws of animals like deer and coyote. There is a natural tendency to follow these trails. However, a good sense of direction and a compass will serve you much better than trusting a game trail to lead you back through the sand to your starting point, particularly on windy days or when visibility is low. Juniper Dunes certainly isn't a vast desert without distinctive points, but it always pays to be prepared.

Quite a variety of plant life grows in the area, despite the scant 8 inches of rainfall each year. Grasses like blue flax, wild rye, wheatgrass, and slender fescue, as well as shrubs like sagebrush and bitterbrush are

Wandering among Juniper Dunes

49

Kamiak Butte Loop

Type: Day hike

Season: March to November

Total distance: 3.3 miles

Rating: Moderate

Elevation gain: 700 feet

Location: Kamiak Butte County Park, 8 miles north of Pullman

Map: USGS Albion

Getting There

From Pullman, take WA 27 north for 12 miles to Clear Creek Road and turn left. There is a sign for Kamiak Butte County Park. In approximately 0.3 mile the road splits; stay to the left on Fugate Road. The signed left turn for the park comes in 0.8 mile (13.5 miles). You arrive at the lower parking area in 14.2 miles and the upper parking area (and start of this hike) at 14.5 miles.

The Trail

The Palouse Country is famous for its rolling fields of wheat, barley, bluegrass, lentil, and intermittent patches of yellow canola blooms. The heavily forested—and heavily logged—Clearwater Mountains rise to the east of the Palouse in Idaho, drawing a sharp line between the two zones.

Prior to the farming boom in the 1880s, the Palouse was rolling grassland as far as the eye could see. Today, less than 1 percent still exists. You can view the Palouse of today, and imagine the Palouse of the past, by way of the Pine Ridge Loop on Kamiak Butte, a natural island in a man-made sea.

Kamiak Butte (3,641 feet) is long and squatty, especially in comparison to the area's other butte, Steptoe (3,612 feet), 10 miles to the north-northwest. Pointy Steptoe Butte is known more for historical reasons than for its natural attributes, even though it is made from pink granite, unusual since the foundation for the Palouse is thousands of feet of basalt.

In 1858 a small regiment from Fort Walla Walla led by Colonel Steptoe found

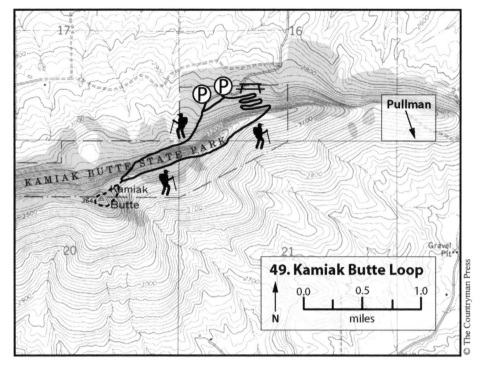

themselves pinned down and then in a running gun battle with a thousand Native American warriors, the fighting largely taking place near Steptoe Butte. Kamiak Butte, named for the revered Palouse chief Kamiakan, is also unusual geologically in that it was formed of quartzite some 500 million years ago.

The north side of Kamiak is forested and the south side is covered in grass. You experience both these zones, as well as the ridge environment, on this short loop hike. The trail begins to the north, moving through Douglas fir, ponderosa pine, western larch, and a healthy understory of ninebark, ocean spray, and serviceberry. Less than 0.1 mile up you reach a junction. Stay to the right and continue upslope along a roadlike swath through the trees.

At 0.3 mile the trail narrows to more of a hiker's path a short way past a small clearing. The climb to the ridge is somewhat strenuous, but with the effort you quickly gain a broad overview of the landscape to the north. In moist, shady areas you might find brittle bladder fern, white trillium, and the delicate fairy slipper.

Since 1980, the Pine Ridge Trail has been part of the National Recreation Trails program, qualifying it for federal dollars for trail and facilities maintenance. Kamiak Butte is also a National Natural Landmark. Kamiak and Steptoe Buttes are both "steptoe" formations: isolated hills or mountains in a land of basalt.

You take one switchback to the left before reaching the ridge at 1.1 miles. The loop continues to the left. However, if you take one of the two trails to the right you will reach—by way of authorized access over private property—the summit of Kamiak in under 0.2 mile round trip. From the summit you can see the towns of Moscow and Pullman as well as

Kamiak Butte

Paradise Ridge, Moscow Mountain, and thousands of square acres of farmland.

The ridge run is wonderful. You slowly drop some of the 700 feet of elevation gain as you edge along the open grass slopes of Kamiak's south side. The trees run up to the ridge and then, like a wave crashing into a rock barrier, they splash across the Idaho fescue and downy cheatgrass slope. In the early days of spring a wide smattering of sagebrush buttercup and glacier lily appears on the south slope. You also find showy aster, yarrow, and bluebell. The most impressive collection of wildflower blooms—and a defining one for many regions in eastern Washington—is balsamroot in May and June. For a comprehensive list of all the vascular plants and their primary location on Kamiak Butte, visit www.wsu.edu:8080 /~wsherb/kamiak_family.html.

By 2.5 miles you reach two wide unmarked junctions. Descend the north slope via the second junction. The pathway widens as it slowly drops through the trees to reach a picnic area, the lower parking lot, and interpretive signs at 3 miles. Just before the parking area you'll see a trail off to your left. Follow it through a corridor of shrubs to reach the upper parking lot (3.3 miles).

Invisible Giant

National Recreation Trails (NRT)—you can find one in every state in the Union. There are over 900 trails totaling 9,000 miles and passing through millions of acres of rural, urban, and wilderness landscapes. They are available to bicyclists, walkers, paddlers, motorcyclists, horseback riders, backpackers, runners, snowmobilers, and in-line skaters. The federal program began in 1968 with the National Trails System Act, which also included National Historic and Scenic Trails (23 trails). The NRT program is managed by the National Park Service, which qualifies trails for acceptance based mainly on their unique and natural features in relation to the surrounding area and their proximity to population zones. Washington currently has 42 National Recreation Trails.

50

Oregon Butte

Type: Day hike

Season: Mid-May to late October

Total distance: 5.6 miles

Rating: Moderate

Elevation gain: 900 feet

Location: Wenaha-Tucannon Wilderness, 20 miles southeast of Dayton

Map: USGS Oregon Butte

Getting There

From Dayton on US 12, follow the sign for Bluewood Ski Resort (Fourth Street). The road changes to the North Fork Touchet River Road (FR 64) around 1.5 miles. You leave the pavement at 19.5 miles. Turn left at the junction for FR 46. Travel 9.6 miles to FR 4608, 0.2 mile beyond Godman Campground (31.9 miles). You arrive at a three-way split in the road 3.5 miles up FR 4608 (35.6 miles); take the road on the right. You reach the Teepee Trailhead and the parking area at 38.2 miles.

The Trail

The Wenaha–Tucannon Wilderness in the Umatilla National Forest is a crazy canyon-land of ridgelines and creek drainages, with over 4,000 vertical feet between the low point at the Wenaha River and the high point at Oregon Butte (6,387 feet). From Oregon Butte you have sweeping vistas of countless ridgelines topped by peaks like Round Butte (5,904 feet), Weller Butte (5,540 feet), and Diamond Peak (6,379 feet). The ridges are bisected by dozens of creek drainages, bounded by the calm Tucannon River to the north and the wild Wenaha River to the south.

In the near distance, the Seven Devils Range is perched above the Snake River to the southeast, the stout formation of the Wallowas to the south, and the Oregon Blue Mountains to the southwest. The Wenaha-Tucannon is like an inverted mountain range— you start high and descend to the waterways, the opposite of the Cascades.

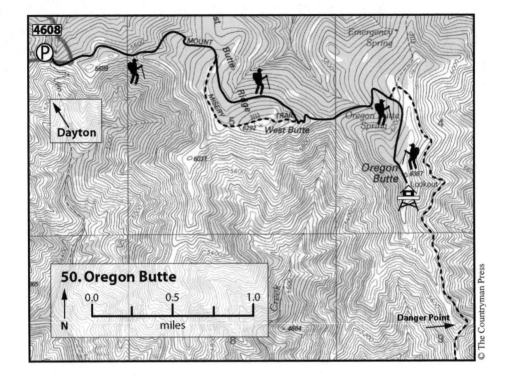

Luckily, the hike to Oregon Butte stays along a canyonlike rim trail before venturing out on the Oregon Butte Ridge, gaining only 900 feet over 2.8 miles.

From the Teepee Trailhead you leave behind the wonderful view across the southwest portion of the wilderness to enter a brief but steep run through the trees. The trail is lined here and there with huckleberry and mountain ash, and the forest is a dense mix of fir and larch.

At 1.1 miles, after a decent elevation gain, the trail breaks from the trees into a clearing of grass and wildflowers. The trail splits, the right staying high and the left moving back into the trees. You can take either. The upper remains out along the rim of the drainage, and the lower winds through the trees. The distance for each is 0.7 mile.

Where the trails rejoin you have a view of the Oregon Butte Lookout, which is still a few hundred feet above you and about 1 mile away. The trail takes a slight dip before climbing up and around a spring-fed water trough and on to a trail junction (2 miles).

Take the trail to the right as it climbs to a noticeable campsite. If you miss this first junction, don't worry, there is a second junction with signs mounted to a tree about 10 yards off the trail. The faded signs say nothing about Oregon Butte, but they do list Weller Butte, which is in the direction you want. The campsite (0.1 mile from either junction) marks the continuation of the trail south to Danger Point (1.5 miles), Weller Butte (6.5 miles), and the Wenaha River (15 miles), a total loss of 4,200 feet in elevation if you were to go that far.

Oregon Butte

In spring and early summer the ridge-lines are ablaze with penstemon (in shadier, wet areas), forget-me-not, lupine, arnica, paintbrush, and scarlet gilia. It is a beautiful final approach. The trees retreat behind you like green glaciers, and the marvelous "inward mountains" grow before you. A lone fir tree stands by the Oregon Butte Lookout (2.8 miles).

Constructed in 1931 and one of only a dozen of its kind still standing, the lookout is staffed by volunteers during the fire season from June to September. The vast and amazing views include the Seven Devils Range (9,000-foot peaks), the Wallowa Mountains (9,000-foot peaks), and the more rounded Oregon Blue Mountains (8,000-foot peaks). Sixty miles to the northeast you can spot Steptoe and Kamiak Buttes, and over 150 miles to the west—when the sky is really clear and the setting sun creates natural backlighting—Mount Adams (12,276 feet) and Mount Rainier (14,410 feet) are visible.

The geography of the Wenaha–Tucannon can be thought of as a layered cake. An uplifting of rock occurred 20 million years ago, followed closely by a succession of 90- to 120-foot-thick lava flows that built up this area by 5,000 feet. The rock you see today is millions of years old and consists of black to dark-gray basalt. Ancient winds carried fine glacially ground material and deposited it across this area, at points up to 300 feet thick.

Umatilla means "water rippling over sand," and that water came with the great floods 16,000 years ago. It tore away the loose top layer, exposing the basalt and deepening the numerous creek drainages, which were cut primarily by the creeks themselves.

To continue the day hike or to reach a different overnight destination like Lodgepole Spring or Weller Butte, keep sliding down the Smooth Ridge Trail. It's a wonderful combination of open ridge, pockets of trees, and private meadows. Large loop hikes of 30 to 40 miles are possible by combining high-line trails and creek/river side trails in a serious game of elevation fluctuations. Mule deer and Rocky Mountain elk (transplanted in the early 20th century) roam the Wenaha–Tucannon in healthy numbers.

The Columbia Plateau's Niagara

Palouse Falls State Park is not a place you arrive at easily, at least figuratively. It just doesn't seem possible that the dry, open, flat landscape that surrounds the park could hide a 200-foot waterfall shooting from thick, dark layers of basalt into a beautiful round pool. It's especially dramatic in spring. From Dayton, take US 12 north for about 12 miles to WA 261 toward Starbuck (that's without a final "s" or a double-tall latte). You pass Lyons Ferry State Park before reaching the turn for Palouse Falls State Park (35 miles). A trail leads down from the parking area along spectacularly bizarre rock formations and ends directly above the falls, close enough to change any plans you may have had that included a barrel. For a completely different take on this natural wonder, drive to Lyons Ferry State Park and paddle 8 miles upriver.

Resources

OLYMPIC PENINSULA
Dungeness National Wildlife Refuge
33 South Barr Road
Port Angeles, Washington 98362
360-457-8451; http://pacific.fws.gov/
refuges/field/wa_dungeness.htm
Dungeness Spit

Hoh River Visitor Center
360-374-6925
Hoh River to Hoh Lake

Hood Canal District, South
150 North Lake Cushman Road
P.O. Box 68
Hoodsport, WA 98548
360-877-5254; www.fs.fed.us/r6/olympic
Mount Ellinor

Hood Canal District, North
P.O. Box 280
295142 US 101 South
Quilcene, WA 98376
360-765-2200; www.fs.fed.us/r6/olympic
Marmot Pass

Makah Tribe
P.O. Box 115
Neah Bay, WA 98357
360-645-2201; www.makah.com
Shi Shi Beach to Point of the Arches

Moran State Park
3572 Olga Road
Eastsound, WA 98245
360-376-2326; www.parks.wa.gov
Mount Constitution

Olympic National Park Wilderness
Information Center
600 East Park Avenue
Port Angeles, WA 98362
360-565-3130; www.nps.gov/olym
*Shi Shi Beach to Point of the Arches;
Cape Alava to Sand Point; Hoh River to
Hoh Lake; Klahhane Ridge Loop; Royal
Lake/Royal Basin*

Ozette RD (seasonal)
360-963-2725
Cape Alava to Sand Point

NORTH CASCADES
Glacier Public Service Center
542 Mount Baker Highway
Glacier, WA 98244
360-599-2714 ; www.fs.fed.us/r6/mbs
Heather Park/Galena Chain Lakes Loop

Methow Valley Visitor Center
Building 49, State Route 20
24 West Chewack Road
Winthrop, WA 98862
509-996-4000; www.fs.fed.us/r6/oka
*Cutthroat Pass; Rainy Pass to Maple
Pass Loop*

Mount Baker RD/North Cascades National
Park Service Complex
810 State Route 20
Sedro-Woolley, WA 98284
360-856-5700; www.fs.fed.us/r6/mbs, or
www.nps.gov/noca
*Heather Park/Galena Chain Lakes Loop;
Mazama Park and Park Butte Lookout;
Thornton Lake; Cascade Pass; Diablo Lake*

North Cascades Visitor Center
502 Newhalem Street
Newhalem, WA 98283-9725
206-386-4495; www.nps.gov/noca
Thornton Lakes; Cascade Pass;
Diablo Lake

Tonasket RD
1 West Winesap
Tonasket, WA 98855
509-486-2186; www.fs.fed.us/r6/oka
Horseshoe Basin to Windy Peak Loop

CENTRAL CASCADES
Cle Elum RD
803 West Second Street
Cle Elum, WA 98922
509-852-1100; www.fs.fed.us/r6
/wenatchee
Waptus Lake to Spade Lake; Bean
Creek Basin

Darrington RD
1405 Emmons Road
Darrington, WA 98241
360-436-1155; www.fs.fed.us/r6/mbs
Green Mountain; Boulder River; Pilot
Ridge to Blue Lakes

Department of Natural Resources
919 North Township Street
Sedro-Woolley, WA 98284-9395
360-856-3500; www.dnr.wa.gov
Greider Lakes

Leavenworth RD
600 Sherbourne Street
Leavenworth, WA 98826
509-548-6977;
www.fs.fed.us/r6/wenatchee
Alpine Lookout via Merritt Lake; Estes
Butte; The Enchantments

North Bend RD
42404 SE North Bend Way
North Bend, WA 98045
425-888-1421; www.fs.fed.us/r6/mbs
Bandera Mountain

Skykomish RD
74920 NE US 2
Skykomish, WA 98288
360-677-2414; www.fs.fed.us/r6/mbs
Lake Serene; Necklace Valley

SOUTH CASCADES
Beacon Rock State Park
34841 State Route 14
Skamania, WA 98648
509-427-8265; www.parks.wa.gov
Beacon Rock

Cowlitz Valley RD
P.O. Box 670
10024 US 12
Randle, WA 98377
360-497-1100; www.fs.fed.us/gpnf
McCoy Peak; Lily Basin to Heart Lake

Mount Adams RD
2455 State Route 141
Trout Lake, WA 98650
509-395-3400; www.fs.fed.us/gpnf
Bird Creek Meadows Loop

Mount Rainier National Park
Longmire Wilderness Information Center
(seasonal)
360-569-4453; www.nps.gov/mora
Pinnacle Peak; Van Trump Park

Mount Rainier National Park
Tahoma Woods, Star Route
Ashford, WA 98304-9751
360-569-2211; www.nps.gov/mora
Spray Park; Palisades Lake; Summer
Land Meadows; Pinnacle Peak; Van
Trump Park

Mount Rainier National Park
White River Wilderness Information Center
360-663-2273, ext. 222; www.nps.gov
/mora
Summer Land Meadows; Palisades Lake

Mount Rainer National Park
Wilkeson Wilderness Information Center
360-829-5127; www.nps.gov/mora
Spray Park

Mount St. Helens National Volcanic
Monument
42218 NE Yale Bridge Road
Amboy, WA 98601
360-449-7800; www.fs.fed.us/gpnf
/mshnvm
*Mount Margaret Backcountry Loop; Lava
Canyon*

Naches RD
10061 US 12
Naches, WA 98937
509-653-2205;
www.fs.fed.us/r6/wenatchee
Mount Aix

EASTERN WASHINGTON
BLM Spokane Office
1103 North Fancher Road
Spokane, WA 99212
509-536-1200; www.or.blm.gov/spokane
Juniper Dunes

Columbia National Wildlife Refuge
735 East Main Street
P.O. Drawer F
Othello, WA 99344
509-488-2668; http://pacific.fws.gov
/refuges/field
wa_columbia.htm
Frog Lake/Marsh Loop

Ginkgo Petrified Forest State Park
P.O. Box 1203
Vantage, WA 98950
509-856-2700; www.parks.wa.gov
Trees of Stone Trail

Methow Valley Visitor Center
Building 49, State Route 20
24 West Chewack Road
Winthrop, WA 98862
509-996-4000; www.fs.fed.us/r6/oka
Eagle Lakes

Pomeroy RD
Route 1, Box 53 F
Pomeroy, WA 99437
509-843-1891; www.fs.fed.us/r6/uma
Oregon Butte

Riverside State Park
9711 West Charles
Nine Mile Falls, WA 99026
509-465-5537; www.riversidestatepark.org
Little Spokane River

Sullivan Lake District
12641 Sullivan Lake Road
Metaline Falls, WA 99153
509-446-7500; www.fs.fed.us/r6/colville
Crowell Ridge

Three Rivers District Kettle Falls Office
255 West 11th
Kettle Falls, WA 99141
509-738-7700; www.fs.fed.us/r6/colville
Columbia Mountain

Whitman County Parks and Recreation
310 North Main Street
Colfax, WA 99111
509-397-6238; www.whitmancounty
.org/Parks
Kamiak Butte Loop

WEB SITES

Green Trails Maps,
www.greentrailsmaps.com

Leave No Trace, www.LNT.org

National Park Service,
www.nps.gov/parks.html

National Weather Service,
www.nws.noaa.gov

Tide Information,
www.tidesonline.nos.noaa.gov

USGS Maps, www.usgs.gov

Wild Washington Campaign,
www.wildwashington.org

References

Arora, David. *All That the Rain Promises, and More . . . : A Hip Pocket Guide to Western Mushrooms.* Berkeley, Calif.: Ten Speed Press, 1991.

Huschke, Kai. *Washington's Wilderness Areas: The Complete Guide.* Englewood, Colo.: Westcliffe Publishers, 2003.

Mueller, Marge, and Ted Mueller. *Exploring Washington's Wild Areas: A Guide for Hikers, Backpackers, Climbers, X-C Skiers & Paddlers,* Second Edition. Seattle: The Mountaineers Books, 2002.

Pojar, Jim, and Andy MacKinnon. *Plants of the Pacific Northwest Coast: Washington, Oregon, British Columbia & Alaska.* Vancouver, British Columbia: Lone Pine Publishing, 1994.

Spring, Ira, Vicky Spring, and Harvey Manning. *100 Hikes in Washington's Alpine Lakes,* 3rd edition. Seattle: The Mountaineers Books, 2001.

Wood, Robert L. *Olympic Mountains Trail Guide: National Park & National Forest,* 3rd edition. Seattle: The Mountaineers Books, 2000.

Index

Index

Y